PENGUIN BOOKS

The Mottled Lizard

Elspeth Huxley was born in 1907 and spent most of her childhood in Kenya. She was educated at the European School in Nairobi, at Reading University, where she took a diploma in agriculture, and at Cornell University, U.S.A. In 1929 she joined the Empire Marketing Board as a press officer. She was married to Gervas Huxley in 1931 and travelled widely with him in America, Africa and elsewhere. She was on the B.B.C. General Advisory Council from 1952 to 1959, when she joined the Monckton Advisory Commission on Central Africa. She has written novels, detective fiction, biography and such well-known travel titles as *Four Guineas*. Her other books include *The Challenge of Africa* (1971), *Livingstone and his African Journeys* (1974), *Florence Nightingale* (1975), *Scott of the Antarctic* (1977), *Nellie: Letters from Africa* (1980), *Whipsnade: captive breeding for survival* (1981) and *The Prince Buys the Manor* (1982). Penguin also publish her famous *The Flame Trees of Thika*, an evocative description of her early childhood in Kenya.

Elspeth Huxley

THE
MOTTLED LIZARD

PENGUIN BOOKS

Penguin Books Ltd, Harmondsworth, Middlesex, England
Viking Penguin Inc., 40 West 23rd Street, New York, New York 10010, U.S.A.
Penguin Books Australia Ltd, Ringwood, Victoria, Australia
Penguin Books Canada Limited, 2801 John Street, Markham, Ontario, Canada L3R 1B4
Penguin Books (N.Z.) Ltd, 182–190 Wairau Road, Auckland 10, New Zealand

—

First published by Chatto and Windus 1962
Published in Penguin Books 1981
Reprinted 1981, 1982 (three times), 1983 (twice), 1985, 1986

—

—

Made and printed in Great Britain by
Richard Clay (The Chaucer Press) Ltd, Bungay, Suffolk
Set in Linotype Plantin

FOR V.G.
WHO REMEMBERS ROBIN

Put forth to watch, unschooled, alone,
'Twixt hostile earth and sky –
The mottled lizard 'neath the stone
Is wiser here than I.

RUDYARD KIPLING

Chapter 1

JUST before she sailed, Tilly got a telegram from Robin saying: 'Please bring shaving brush and windmill.' With everyone being demobilized, even the shaving brush was difficult, a windmill impossible; it was hard enough to get passages for the wife and daughter of a repatriated soldier, let alone for a large metal construction. Tilly had only managed to squeeze us both into a ship by a combination, as she said, of sucking up to shipping clerks and bullying managers. So she left the windmill and took instead a cigar-box full of silkworm cocoons. These were to pioneer a new industry in East Africa; now that the First World War had ended everyone would be crying out for luxuries, the market would expand.

In the Red Sea the sticky heat was appalling. At night we took our mattresses on deck and tried to sleep, impeded by lascar sailors and even more by rats, which abounded. After Aden, we noticed that, about five o'clock every morning, and with a great deal of clanking and creaking, the ship swung her bows round to face backwards. The engine stopped for a few minutes and then started up again, and the vessel swung back to resume her course.

Tilly was puzzled by this and so was Randall Swift, a fellow farmer also returning from the wars. Three days out of Aden he came to Tilly with as grave a look as any countenance so merry could assume to say that, despite the heat, we had better sleep in our cabins.

'We couldn't sleep,' Tilly pointed out.

'We can spend the night there, for if we don't, we'll be spending it in kingdom come, from what I hear. There's bubonic plague on board.'

The purpose of turning the ship round, it appeared, was to allow the bodies of those committed to the deep to avoid entanglement in the screw. Randall had found this out by sleuth-work; the bubonic plague was a secret, for if the health authorities at Mombasa heard of it, we should be kept in quarantine for weeks, at a heavy cost to the owners, and no one would be allowed to land. So those of the passengers who suspected anything were just as anxious to keep the matter quiet as the Captain and crew, and there was no ship's doctor.

We went about drenched in Keatinge's Powder, of which Tilly had brought a liberal supply, our eyes alert for dead rats. Luckily we were due at Kilindini in less than a week.

'It's touch and go with the cocoons,' Tilly observed, two days before our hoped-for arrival.

'Don't tell me they're starting to hatch,' Randall said.

'I think, if the ship's punctual, they may just hold out. I don't know what the Customs would say to a lot of grubs crawling about the baggage.'

Each morning Tilly examined the cigar-box with mounting anxiety. Whether she had miscalculated, or whether the ship had taken longer than was expected, or whether the Red Sea's heat had disarranged the hatching schedule, I do not know. The day before we were due at Kilindini, she observed unmistakable signs of activity among the cocoons.

'They can't possibly hatch *now*,' she exclaimed, frowning at them with entreaty and dismay.

But they had made up their collective mind. Not only that, in their new-found freedom no cigar-box was going to keep them confined. On our next visit to the cabin, which Tilly said was hot enough to cook a rice pudding or a meringue, we found little black grubs crawling about all over the drawers.

'We must catch them, that's all,' Tilly said firmly. She was not going to let a lot of silkworm grubs defeat her on the threshold of their new career. So she and I, Randall and the bride he was taking back with him, chased grubs among handkerchiefs and underclothes, on the floor and in the bunks, and put them into a tin in whose lid Randall punched tiny holes.

'They'll die of starvation,' Tilly said in distress. 'I wonder if I can find any mulberry leaves in Mombasa? Or if they would accept a substitute?'

On the morning we were due to dock the entire cabin appeared to be a mass of little grubs. Assisted by Randall, Tilly hauled our luggage into the passage and stood guard to prevent any member of the crew from penetrating into the insect-

8

ory she had established. Our feelings of relief as we at last walked down the gangway, our heavy double-felt hats (called *terais*) clamped firmly down on our heads, were immense. Both the bubonic plague and the silkworms were still concealed from the authorities, and once we were ashore we were safe.

The up-country train left about four o'clock. The smell of dust, the crowds of jostling, sweaty Africans in tattered shirts or red blankets, the beaded women thrusting bananas, oranges, scrawny live fowls and gourds of gruel up at the passengers from a gravel platform, the clean bright air, the hard bright sunshine, the brilliant creepers, the monstrous glistening baobabs – all these had not changed. Soon coconuts and cultivation gave way to nondescript and spiky bush, harsh as old iron, reduced by extremities of climate to a vegetable equality where no bush rose above its fellow, no proud tree threw its shade, all was level, featureless and sterile; there was no water, and patches of red gritty soil, leached of all enriching humus, gaped from the bush like raw wounds.

At Voi the train stopped for about an hour while its passengers were fed, or fed themselves. It was dark by now, the soft velvet darkness of the tropics we had not felt for four years. You walked as through a warm conservatory whose great dome was encrusted with all the diamonds in the world, and all the scents in the world were there too, changing like currents in the sea, from the overwrought sweetness of frangipani to the crisp pungency of dried cattle-dung, from smoke of brushwood fires to heat-baked sand and stones, from the rich oiliness of fat-smeared bodies to the alien twang of the oxtail soup which awaited us in the *dak* bungalow with our evening meal.

On level ground serving as a platform, and behind the goods shed, a lot of little fires sprang up, as native passengers concocted their meals of maize-flour, rice and bananas. Firelight flickered like a snake's tongue over bronze or coppery limbs and caught the gleam of white teeth bared in laughter. Our fires, our lamp-lit bungalow, our little knot of sound and movement, must have seemed from above like a tiny prick of light in a great encircling darkness, a firefly flashing out and then vanishing. Close by, we could hear two hyenas calling to each

9

other and, farther off, the throaty grunt of a lion. The slave and ivory route to the Great Lakes that had crossed this waste of thorns long before railways were invented did not seem far distant in time, you could sense a ghostly trudge of feet bound for exile; indeed, less than thirty years earlier you might have come upon an Arab caravan camped near the site of our station. Bleached skulls and thigh-bones, overlooked by hyenas, might still be found to mark this long and bitter road.

'A lot of things have changed in the last four years,' Randall Swift remarked, 'but not the Uganda Railway.'

'No, it's just the same, only more so,' Tilly agreed. And indeed the little wood-burning locomotives, brought out to pull the first trains less than twenty years ago, were still manfully puffing their way up to the highlands, considerably exhausted after four years of war. They were very thirsty engines, needing constant long drinks at tanks fed by pipelines from distant springs, and proceeded under a great arc of wood sparks, which always started grass fires in the dry weather. They quite often broke down. On a pre-war journey, Randall told us, the train had stopped for several hours near Tsavo while an important official had disembarked to hunt a lion spotted out of the window. The trophy was skinned amid the rejoicings of a posse of native passengers who had followed at a safe distance, and in due course the official, the skin and the passengers had resumed their journey, to arrive about half a day late in Nairobi.

'Perhaps we shall see a lion tomorrow morning,' suggested Tilly, who was always ready for some stirring event. 'Then we can stop the train, and go after it.'

'We're hardly important enough,' Randall objected.

'We can always pretend to be. No one knows that you're not a new Colonial Secretary, or I'm not a cousin of the Governor's.'

'They might make a shrewd guess at it,' Randall said, glancing at our clothes. After nearly four weeks in the crowded little vessel, these appeared serviceable rather than elegant. 'That's what we should have to look like, to be believed,' he added, indicating a young man at a nearby table dressed in the official uniform, a khaki suit with shiny brass buttons and a collar and tie. His clean new suit was perfectly pressed; a big cork helmet, with a long sweeping stern shaped like an otter's tail and with a flashing badge in front, lay by his side next to a *debe* – a four-gallon paraffin tin – of water. The conversation he was holding with one of the waiters did not appear to be going well.

The young official was giving an instruction in flawless Swahili, the kind that everybody knew they ought to speak, but no one did. After a while the waiter, still looking baffled, said '*ndio*, bwana,' went away and returned with a bottle of Worcester sauce.

The young man was patient and verbose. At last the waiter, grasping at least part of the order, removed the *debe* in which some oysters awaited their doom.

'It must be difficult for him to understand that oysters must be eaten raw,' Randall observed, 'when we're always insisting that everything else must be cooked or boiled, even water.'

'What an odious young man,' concluded Tilly, who did not like displays of privilege. Meanwhile the waiter was in difficulties with another passenger, a red-faced North-countryman who could speak nothing but English. He explained slowly, loudly and repeatedly that he did not like steamed sponge, but wanted cheese instead. The waiter brought a bottle of Worcester sauce. It was perhaps a relief to the waiter to encounter our clumsy, basic version of the language, which at least he understood. The words were Swahili, but by ignoring all the grammar everything was greatly simplified, provided that no profound, complex or subtle thoughts had to be conveyed. Our gastronomic needs were not profound, subtle or complex and we avoided the Worcester sauce.

At last the engine-driver, who had a table to himself, rose to his feet, fastened a belt loosened for the meal, nodded to the oyster-eating official and remarked that we had better be on our way. There was a general gathering together of hats and bags and equipment, a scraping of chairs and settling of bills, and we strolled across to mount the train, while the guard shouted at the native passengers, whistles blew and people scurried about getting either in or out of carriages. With a great deal of chugging and huffing the locomotive pulled itself together, digested a mawful of logs, emitted a cascade of sparks and heaved the crowded carriages away from the friendly little station into the encircling blackness of the Taru desert.

When we awoke next morning, we felt that we had really come home. During the night the red dust had drifted in through open windows and settled over everything. Our faces had become a milk-chocolate colour, with white circles round the eyes, like coons, and the peculiar, tingling, feathery smell of the dust, as native to this high country as the whistling thorn, the twisted olive, the flat-topped acacia or the lolloping giraffe, was never out of our nostrils. And with it through open windows came the smell of early morning, the essence of the fresh and young: of dew on biscuit-shaded wiry grasses, of wind off distant grape-blue hills, of innumerable acacias, of lees of century-accumulated sunshine, of hidden moisture in silent sand-rivers, and simply of freedom and space, the smell of the highveld of Africa that one can never forget.

Away across a rolling and ravine-creased plain speckled by twisted thorn-trees more numerous than the stars, there floated in the soft early-morning sky, and in a most unlikely manner, a mighty mound or hump the colour of mother-of-pearl above a great ruff of pale lavender cloud. This cloud masked the base of a mountain which did not seem attached to the ground, but rather to have been created out of light and space and fancy where it floated, like the sail of some great celestial ship. The sun's early beams now lanced the plain in shafts that seemed a thousand miles in length, giving rise to shadows longer than the spires of the tallest cathedrals; and as for our train, we could see a moving replica of it, in silhouette, gliding across the golden grasses on our left-hand side. We gazed in silence at the majesty of Kilimanjaro, pink and delicate as a flamingo's breast-feather, and might have imagined it to be a trick of light and cloud that would dissolve in full daylight had we not known of its reality.

I think that if one lived to be a hundred, and watched the dawn break and the sun rise over the highveld of Africa every morning, one would never tire of it, just as a sailor will always find delight in watching the sea. And indeed there is the same play of light, the same endless changing, forming and reforming of cloud and shadow, the same sense of the creation of the world before one's eyes. The rolling up of long shadows thrown by rocks and trees never fails to enthrall; their tips race in utter silence across the plain; behind them, trees and grass and bush and ant-hills spring into a new golden life of their own. It is like watching the rolling up of a gigantic carpet at an incredible speed. The fascination of beginnings – of the daisy that opens its petals to the sun, the yellow chick drying from the egg, the spring that trickles from the rock, the clenched bud just parting on a twig – all this wonder is packed every morning into the birth of an African day. Heat and sweat and weariness come later, but all that is forgotten at the start; it was four years since we had seen this miracle and we gloried in it again.

And, of course, the animals were a major part of it. These great herds of moving, unhurried, innocent creatures, at home in their element, numerous as buttercups in an English May meadow and as beautiful, were like the heart that gives life to a body; without them, the features of the landscape would still be there and still be shapely, but they would be lifeless as the contours of the dead.

The wonders of this journey to Nairobi have been described many times, the tens of thousands of animals to be seen from the train, the sense of travelling through some tremendous park full of tame beasts, almost as if one had journeyed through the Garden of Eden, before the fall. It would be tedious, therefore, to repeat all this and to dwell upon the great shining herds of zebra and wildebeeste, the close-packed, gracefully-horned gazelles with tails always a-wag, the patchwork giraffe arching their necks to nibble a tree-top, the red, lyre-horned impala, the cow-like eland with their dewlaps swaying, the lithe hunting cheetahs and ungainly hyenas and silver-backed jackals.

I searched with hopeful eyes for a lion, or even a pride of lions sloping off into a thick-bushed gully, or sunning themselves on a cluster of rocks. It was always an event if one saw a lion, a small triumph scored. It was not a rare event, but on this occasion lions eluded us; we saw, however, a procession of three rhinos, a father and mother and half-grown child, walking in single file, their insect-like heads weighed down by their long curved horns, like a prehistoric frieze. When the leader heard or smelt the train he halted and swung a lowered head round to face it, pawing with one big foot on the ground, searching for something on which to vent his irritation, like a Victorian father whose privacy is invaded not by an individual but by an untoward event. Rhinos had been known to charge the train itself in sheer outraged fury, and I hoped this family party would not decide to do so, for they could only stub their noses and get themselves shot. They did not realize that all their heavy armour, which for centuries had protected them from every hazard Africa could offer, had become a mere encumbrance in their last and hopeless battle agains a species infinitely more ruthless, ferocious and clever than their own.

We made another stop for breakfast and stretched our legs along the red gravel platform, and sniffed the smells of morning mingled with those of bacon and coffee and of native bodies smeared with rancid fat. Randall had found a one-armed acquaintance to whom he introduced us: this was Mr Eastwood, a former general manager of the railway who was returning to Nairobi to retire. The arm had been lost as a result of a charging rhino, which had knocked him out; he had regained his wits just in time to drive away the vultures about to peck out his eyes.

'I 'eard 'em buzzing like bloody great bluebottles in a meat-safe,' he sometimes remarked, when telling the story. Then he had shouted for his retinue, who had cautiously returned, and carried him on a stretcher for four days to the nearest doctor, while gangrene rotted away a crushed arm. Within six weeks he was back at his desk, writing with his left hand. Mr Eastwood was one of the old school. He had started as a builder's apprentice, taken to ledgers and worked his way up to become chief accountant to the railway. In this capacity, he had once demonstrated his system of accounts to a visiting Under-Secretary of State for the Colonies, Mr Winston Churchill. 'On this side 'ere we 'ave the money coming in and on that side there we 'ave the money going out, and they 'as to agree,' he began. 'Yes, yes, I know all about that,' Mr Churchill impatiently remarked. 'Yes, but you see, they don't,' Mr East-wood had responded.

I grew more and more excited as we approached Nairobi and so did Tilly, since four years is a long time to be away from home. During those four years I had scarcely seen my father, and now I even wondered, in a panic, if I should remember what he looked like; I had a photograph, but he was in uniform, apparently on a dark afternoon, and people did not look the same in farm clothes, and in the bright sun of Africa.

Nairobi in those days was self-effacing; you were on it before you realized anything was happening, and it appeared to consist of little more than a cluster of bungalows and sheds, whose tin roofs winked like heliographs, and a few dusty blue-gum trees. Trains reached it from Mombasa three times a week, and practically everyone in the town came to meet them. The native coaches with their wooden benches exploded with people; one could scarcely believe that quite so many had been packed inside; for every traveller there were perhaps a dozen greeters, and the excitement and commotion were intense.

Beside the European coaches things were more sedate, especially if a white-uniformed civil servant, with a large white pith topee, was there officially to welcome an official guest. When the head of a department returned from leave one might even see belted swords and be-medalled chests. Humbler travellers wore shabbier khaki and broad-brimmed felt hats, and sometimes spine-pads made of quilted cloth interwoven with a red material, and buttoned to the outside of the shirt. The sun was still regarded as a kind of dangerous wild animal that would strike you down if you did not watch it every minute of the day between nine and four o'clock.

I had no difficulty, after all, in recognizing Robin. He was thinner than I remembered him, but still wide-shouldered and strongly built, his sandy hair cut very short, a small moustache, a wide-boned, good-humoured face crinkled by a huge grin, and blue eyes twinkling with pleasure.

'I've got a surprise for you,' he said, when all our luggage had been extricated from the train and Tilly had broken the

15

news that she had no windmill. 'I hope you'll like it, also that it will behave itself; I haven't had it long enough to be quite sure of its temperament.'

'I hope it's not a kind of pet,' Tilly said. She was devoted to pets, but we generally had far too many of them.

Robin led us to the station yard where rickshaw boys crowded round us, battered motor-cars with high-roofed box-bodies awaited their owners, and a character called Ali Khan, in riding breeches, beard and turban, waved a greeting with his whip as he stood beside a mule-drawn buggy suspended on four enormous, spidery wheels. Before we could reach Robin's surprise Njombo was upon us, seizing our hands, crying out and jumping up and down in the sunshine in a joyous ecstasy.

My own delight, if more restrained, was no less genuine. Of all the people on the Thika farm, he was the one I most clearly remembered: Njombo the smiling, the robust, the gay, with his dashing air, his laughter, his lively and intelligent expression and his gift of rhetoric. He was a sort of Irishman among Kikuyu, an actor to his fingertips with all the world for his stage.

'Eeee-eee, but you have been away a long time!' he cried, shaking my hand again and again. 'Eight times the maize has been sown and harvested, eight times the rain has fallen, the coffee berries have been picked! Twice the youths have been circumcised! Now you have grown like a tree, like the trees your mother planted, and all the Germans have been killed, destroyed like bird's-nests, or like grass burnt by hunters on the plain! The soldiers of King George have slaughtered all their enemies and returned to their wives, although we have not yet seen the cattle, the sheep and the goats they have taken – and what is the profit in war if the warriors do not bring back the cattle of the enemy?'

'And your news, Njombo? You have been well? Your wife and children –'

'All, all are well, they are healthy and strong, my wife has given birth twice while you have been away and now once more her belly is as large as a gourd full of beer! As for the shamba, I, Njombo, I have looked after it as if it had been my

16

own, as a hen looks after her chicks, as God looked after bwana while he was among the bullets of the Germans! It was as if bwana had left his eyes on a tree and his tongue in the office to see and instruct us. Although I had many affairs of my own to attend to, I left them as a young man leaves the dancing when lions smell his father's cattle; he takes his spear to drive away the wild animals. I thought only of bwana's affairs, of his house and crops and cattle. I left my own, and kept everything of his safe from thieves and wild beasts and plundering askaris, and all the dangers that threatened his property when he was away.'

'That is splendid,' Tilly said warmly, moved by this recital. 'Indeed, you have looked after things well ... Though as Njombo's job was to look after the ponies, and there weren't any, and Sammy was the headman,' she added as an afterthought to Robin, 'I wonder what he actually did do?'

Although Njombo knew no English he understood the gist of her remarks, and renewed the recital of his labours. 'I, Njombo, I was everywhere; I guarded the cattle, I pruned the coffee, I swept the house, I mended the roof when the rain came in, I saw to the garden by the river and kept out the buck, when strangers came I watched them in case they were robbers. I was like the right hand of bwana, and his eyes, and his tongue, and his feet; so long as I was there, no harm could come to his property. Eeeeeee! but it has been a long time and I have grown weary; now you are back, the dangers are over, you will see for yourself the mighty work of Njombo; bwana will bring wealth to the farm and we shall all grow rich.'

'Thank you very much,' Tilly said, conscious of the remark's inadequacy. 'I am very happy to be home, and to hear your good news.' To Robin she added: 'And now, how are we going to get to Thika?'

'That's where the surprise comes in,' Robin said. He led us proudly to a small, open two-seater with a short round snout, a good deal of shining brasswork, an elevated dickey and a generally rakish air. 'I was lucky to get her; you can't get cars for love or money in Nairobi now.'

'Then how *did* you get her?'

'Her owner went down to South Africa; he's going to bring back a couple more ... Isn't she a beauty? Goes like the wind, plenty of clearance, good strong springs – there's a big future for these cars, and with lots of soldier-settlers coming out and the country developing ...'

'You mean it was love rather than money,' Tilly suggested, after she had admired the car.

'I had to offer him something, of course. I haven't had a chance to tell you yet, but I put in for a farm under the soldier-settlement scheme and drew one that seems to be almost on top of Mount Kenya – and that was what the windmill was for, but I think we can manage without it. Anyway, I got him to accept a half share in the land to pay for the car. Not a bad bargain, I thought.'

'Yes, I see,' Tilly said, determined not to let her doubts about another partnership – Robin's ventures had been unlucky – gain the upper hand. A stream of porters now arrived, each bearing one piece of baggage – no porter ever carried two – some of it ours, some of it other people's. Njombo took them in hand like an excitable shepherd with a flock of unusually stupid sheep. Tilly's habit was to travel light, which meant a great many small packages instead of a few large ones.

'Perhaps it's just as well I wasn't able to bring the windmill,' she remarked.

'But you have got the shaving brush?'

'Yes; aren't there any here?'

'I'm told that all the shaving brushes in the country have got anthrax,' Robin said.

Our heavy luggage was to go by rail to Thika, but even our light equipment filled to overflowing every nook and cranny of the two-seater; Njombo, in the dickey, was wedged in so tightly among the parcels, suitcases, hold-alls, baskets and things sewn up in sacking that it seemed impossible he would ever be able to emerge.

'I hope we don't have a puncture,' Tilly said.

'Not much danger of that, all the tyres are in good condition, except perhaps for one of the front ones which is a little worn; but the road's not too bad at present ...'

'It's down to the canvas,' Tilly remarked after a brief inspection. 'And this back one doesn't look too healthy.'

'Well, we'll see if she'll start.'

Motor-cars were spoilt in this respect; if they showed reluctance they were not coaxed or tinkered with, but simply pushed, since willing muscles were always available. Pushing was popular: it called for rhythm, stamping and song. We left the station in a crescendo of triumphant cries, a chuttering of cylinders and a shower of largesse, and bowled off down the hot and dusty main street, flanked by open-fronted Indian shops and by tin-roofed wooden bungalows, through the packed and noisy Indian bazaar, smelling of open drains and nameless spices, and out into the country, where dust lay even thicker, ruts went deeper and potholes of alarming aspect pitmarked the road.

It was all just as I remembered it: a film of dust over pale grass and twisted trees and yellow sodom-apples by the roadside, four-wheeled wagons with their eight pairs of humped oxen creaking along, little naked boys with balloon-like tummies herding shiny-coated scurrying goats, women plodding under heavy loads suspended by leather straps that bit into their foreheads, and a baby's head, black and shiny as a croquet-ball, peering out from its sling; high, piled, whipped-cream clouds in an immense blue heaven, blinding sunshine, shrilling crickets, a tinkle of bells, a smell of earth and heat-baked cow-dung, wide-sweeping views towards distant plains. In twenty minutes we were as thick with dust as a working bee with pollen.

'It's nice to be back,' Tilly said.

'I forgot to ask, did you have a good voyage?'

'Well, yes and no; it was very hot in the Red Sea, we both got prickly heat, the ship ran out of soda water and plague broke out on board. Still, there was quite a cheerful crowd.'

'The farm may give you one or two surprises,' Robin said. 'It's rather like that bit in *Henry V* about docks, thistles, keckies and burrs in the fields of Burgundy, although in this case mainly blackjacks and thorns and just the bush coming back. I'm afraid the garden has more or less disappeared. However, we shall soon get things put straight again.'

'I've brought some lovely roses, the latest varieties. I only hope they haven't sprouted in the Red Sea.'

Now and again we came to a causeway laid across a papyrus swamp, into which streams that started in the mountain forests degenerated when they neared the plains. We stopped at one to fill the radiator, for by now the car was wheezing and panting.

'The engine sounds a bit rough,' Tilly suggested.

'Yes, there's something knocking; I'll have a look when we get to Thika.'

The car proceeded like a man gasping for breath, quivering with the effort, but Tilly's mind was on other things.

'Surely badgers don't get anthrax?' she inquired. 'I'm thinking of the shaving brush.'

'It was only a rumour. They're hideously expensive in Nairobi anyway.'

'Badgers are indigenous,' Tilly reflected. 'I'm sure I've seen them about.'

'I'm afraid it may be the piston rings ...'

'If they have the right kind of hair for shaving brushes, we might start a local industry. You could get an awful lot of brushes out of one badger, I should think.'

'The fellow *swore* the engine was all right,' Robin grumbled, 'and up to now it's gone like a bird. Something must have worked its way loose.'

With Robin's mind on pistons, and Tilly's on badgers, we proceeded erratically for several miles, until we reached a fairly steep hill. This was too much for the car and, about half-way up, the engine stalled.

'Quick, a stone,' Robin called. 'I'm not *absolutely* certain of the brakes.' An upheaval in the dickey expelled Njombo from the parcels, and Tilly and I jumped out too as the car started to roll backwards. Luckily, plenty of boulders were at hand to stem the retreat.

Robin unearthed some tools and went to work on the engine, while Njombo kept up a flow of advice and a dramatic commentary on the mysteries laid bare by the spanners. In no time at all a large audience had gathered, men in red blankets and boys in nothing at all. They fixed bright, unwinking, fas-

20

cinated eyes upon Robin, murmuring softly to each other as he made some move, and poised for flight at the first sign of danger. Tilly and I sat on a boulder with a thermos and sandwiches. The sun shone, crickets chirruped, weaver-birds in a nearby thorn-tree squabbled and flapped, little red-eyed doves with lustred plumage cooed contentedly, a hawk plunged down faster than my eye could follow into dry, rustling grass beside a shamba where women weeded among the waist-high maize. It was all peaceful, familiar and serene.

As a mechanic, Robin was dashing rather than thorough. Sometimes his methods worked and sometimes they failed completely, and when they worked he was never quite sure why. The various helpers who had pressed themselves into service under Njombo's directions handed him back bits of engine like theatre sisters supplying the surgeon with instruments. On this occasion the bits must have been put back in the right places, for when Robin got in and the stones were removed, the car burst into life as it ran backwards in reverse gear. While this started the engine, it did not get the car up the hill; the helpers practically carried it up, singing lustily, stamping and chanting, and proclaiming their triumph as they reached the summit. Tilly distributed cents and added the rest of the sandwiches, which they regarded with the suspicion people always accord to foreign food; they took them politely, but afterwards threw them into the bush.

'Now we should be all right,' Robin said proudly.

'That was very clever,' Tilly agreed.

They spoke too soon. Not even a hill was needed to bring the car to a halt a few miles farther on. Robin failed to repeat his performance, diagnosed the fracture of an essential part and made his way sadly to a coffee plantation we had passed a mile or two back. He returned with the owner and a team of oxen to which the vehicle was ignominiously lashed. It was not the home-coming Robin had hoped for. Several hours later, dust-immersed, sweaty, dry-throated, dispirited and cross, we arrived at the Blue Posts Hotel.

Chapter 2

WHEN we had left Thika, the flame-trees Tilly had planted before the war had been waist-high; now they rose above our shoulders as we rode by. But the rows were too close together, and Tilly remarked that she must have been thinking of prams. The flowers were scarlet and orange, and did indeed glow like fires among the dark-green foliage.

'Surely some of the coffee trees must be bearing,' Tilly said. 'What does it look like, now you've dug it out of the weeds?'

'It looks very well,' Robin said, with a note of caution. The first shamba he had cleared and planted lay on our right, stretching in what had once been orderly rows of erect, glossy-leaved bushes to the crest of a rise. Through the flame-trees' trunks we could see orderly rows, but of stumps, not bushes: stumps about six inches high.

'Did you say it looked *well*?' Tilly asked.

'Yes, healthy,' Robin replied defensively. 'Alec said that about a year ago it got badly hit by a disease. He got an expert over – said to be an expert, anyway – who advised cutting it right down to the roots. So that's what Alec did. Another expert came later and said that was wrong, he ought to have sprayed, but it was too late by then. Of course it'll grow again, but we shall lose four years.'

'I wonder what we'll live on,' Tilly remarked gloomily.

'The bank, I suppose.'

Alec Wilson was the only one among our neighbours who had not joined the army; the doctors had refused to let him, and so he had looked after our farm, together with three or four others, in addition to his own. He had worked from sunrise until sunset every day, and in the evening at the book-work, but had encountered difficulties nothing could overcome. The chief of these had not been so much a shortage as an almost complete lack of labour. Many of the able-bodied young Kikuyu were sucked into the war, those who were left had their own shambas to look after, and so the coffee plantations

22

grew more and more overgrown and shaggy; pruning was neglected, there was no one to spray against disease, and all the insects, fungi and bacteria that prey on coffee bushes went to work with a will. When Robin and his neighbours returned after the war they found, instead of healthy coffee bushes laden with berries, nothing but jungles of weeds and dead or dying trees.

So it was a question of starting again, more or less from the beginning, and in the meanwhile everyone had spent his capital. To balance this, the managers of the three main banks in Nairobi were in an expansive, benign and optimistic frame of mind. They conferred large overdrafts upon their customers, rather with the air of monarchs dispensing orders and stars, and details such as rates of interest and terms of repayment were considered by both parties to be almost too insignificant to be brought into the conversation at all. Happily for the banks, who in fact charged eight per cent, their liberality was rewarded by the stabilization of the rupee, which had been worth 1s. 4d., at the rate of 2s. This meant that one evening Tilly and Robin went to bed owing, I think, about £2,000, and woke up next morning owing £3,000; by a stroke of the pen, the banks had gained a bonus of fifty per cent at the expense of everyone who had borrowed from them, which meant almost every farmer in the country.

On the farm, everything was as I remembered it, only smaller and more shaggy; the garden had vanished under a tangle of undergrowth through which the rotting posts of a pergola protruded and, beyond, some close-foliaged grapefruit trees. Our grass hut was still standing, if only just; its walls rustled and crackled with colonies of termites, ants and other insects, chased continuously by small lizards. A little way off were the foundations of the stone house that Robin had been slowly building, whenever he could afford an Indian mason, before the war.

Beyond the store and office, which was roofed with badly rusted corrugated iron, was a straggle of round, windowless native huts. A thin film of blue wood-smoke rose through the thatch, and the ground was swept bare all round them. A woman with long, dangling bead ear-rings that rocked like

23

a pendulum was pounding millet with a heavy wooden mortar in a hollowed-out log; fly-encrusted children with bulging tummies peered from the doors of huts. None of this had changed, and I was thankful. Like all children, I did not want change, but wished that everything would stay as it had always been, and behave in a way that I was used to.

But, of course, there had been changes, more among people than things. Njombo was there but not Sammy, the Masai headman, nor his fellow tribesman Andrew the cook. When Alec Wilson came over that evening – a little heavier and quieter perhaps, not quite so fidgety and full of nervous energy, but still gay and well-informed – he told us that Sammy had left of his own accord.

'I think he'd made so much money out of perks, and out of cattle trading, and I daresay theft as well, that he had either to pay a manager, or leave to look after his affairs. But he promised to come to see you when you got back, so I must write and let him know.'

The place did not seem the same without Sammy, who had been Robin's prop and stay since the farm began.

'Andrew went soon after you did,' Alec added. 'He went back to his flocks and cattle, as all Masai do, and I expect forgot his cookery, there couldn't have been much call for jam pancakes or cheese straws in the *manyatta*. Then he met with a disaster, which perhaps you haven't heard about; I always meant to write, but never had time.'

Andrew the cook, it seemed – a tall, well-built, proud and handsome young man – had gone with his companions to hunt a lion in the old Masai fashion, each warrior with his tall spear and long, oval shield of buffalo hide, and his head-dress of ostrich plumes. They had ringed it round with spears and wounded it, and then it had charged out of the circle, striking down one of the warriors as it bounded past, only to fall with its hide as full of spears as the quills on a porcupine. The warrior who had been struck down had been Andrew. Although witch-doctors had applied all the known Masai remedies, three days later he had died. So now he would never more preside over our smoke-filled, crowded kitchen like a dhow-captain on his deck, with a quiet and commanding

24

dignity, nor should we eat the strong salty soups, the rather tough roasts, or the savouries made from sardines, cheese, olives and bacon all pounded together. He had not been a very good cook, but he had been a good character and a cheerful friend, and we were sad to know that we should never see him again.

In his place came a young Kikuyu supplied by Njombo, named Kigorro. Njombo said with pride that Kigorro's father was a *mundu mugo*, a good kind of witch-doctor, and therefore a respected member of society, and that Kigorro himself was a magnificent, a pre-eminent, cook. Tilly found that his experience had been confined to a few months in an Afrikaner household where he had learnt, it appeared, how to turn all forms of meat swiftly into biltong, and to brew coffee like a tincture of wormwood and gall. He seemed, however, willing and quick to learn, cheerful and fond of dogs, so Tilly kept him, and soon had him making soufflés, sponges and *baba au rhum*.

Although our household consisted only of my parents, myself, and a variable number of Kikuyu retainers, it often seemed as if an invisible presence shared the house and ruled our lives. I thought of this presence sometimes as a touchy, unpredictable old gentleman with a beard and craggy eyebrows, rather like Zeus clutching his thunderbolt and having to be propitiated by sacrifices but, unlike Zeus, the victim of a fluctuating fever. When Tilly, for instance, asked whether the foundations of our stone house would soon grow into walls, Robin answered: 'I'm afraid the overdraft seems a bit shaky just now, we shall have to wait till it improves.'

Or sometimes Tilly would remark: 'I wonder if the overdraft would stand us half a dozen peach trees? I do so want to try some down by the river.' They were not above cheating it, if they saw the chance. 'I bought a pipe-wrench in Nairobi,' Robin said. 'I was lucky to snap it up, and I expect we can slip it by the overdraft for once.'

Although it seemed to brood like a spirit over our lives at Thika it lived, as I knew, in Nairobi, cared for by a Mr Playfair. Although I had never seen him, I had a great regard for Mr Playfair, because it was he who had decided that I was to stay at home. 'Of course,' I had heard Tilly say, 'we ought to send her away to school but it's too expensive, Mr Playfair would never stand for it.' I therefore looked on him as an ally, but Robin and Tilly did not. Although he did his best to help them, his first concern was with the overdraft, and sometimes he demanded harsh sacrifices to keep it quiet. Ours, of course, was not the only one in his charge. A farmer whose overdraft had grown particularly troublesome was said to have driven a flock of sheep down to Nairobi, along Government Road and up the steps into the National Bank of India, in order to meet Mr Playfair's demands.

Sometimes Tilly talked about asking Mr Playfair to Thika for a week-end.

'The question is,' she said, 'whether to do him awfully well, really slap-up, in the hopes that he'll weaken after the second liqueur brandy, or whether to keep him strictly to *posho*, barley-water and earnest talk so as to convince him of our sober worth and grinding poverty.' (*Posho* was the native maize-flour.) The pros and cons of these two courses were so evenly balanced that Tilly and Robin never could decide which to adopt, and so Mr Playfair was never invited.

Because of the state everything had fallen into during the war we could not expect an income from the coffee for three or four years, and Robin doubted whether Mr Playfair and the overdraft would support us, unaided, for as long as that. So both he and Tilly cast about in all directions for ways of tiding things over. Robin was a seasoned inventor, and his mind now overflowed with new ideas represented by sketches, hieroglyphics and calculations on scraps of paper lying about all over the house, and especially in the garden privy, in various stages of creation. But either, like something called a fluid flywheel connected with the clutches of motor-cars, the invention needed complex machinery to make a prototype and tens of thousands to launch, or else, like a trouser press designed on a revolutionary principle, its value to humanity was dubious, especially in the colonies. And so, while full of promise, like unsown seeds the inventions never germinated, and offered no way out of our predicament.

Many other farmers were in the same boat. Some went off

to hunt elephants, others to work as transport contractors or as road-gang overseers for the Government, one man to collect the skeletons of hippos on the shores of Lake Victoria, pound them up and sell the resultant bone-meal as fertilizer. Another way to turn a modest penny was to recruit labour for the sisal companies, or for some other large employer. One of our neighbours, Jack Nimmo, had taken to this. Before the war he had spent his time poaching ivory, leaving his wife to run the farm and returning now and then, always unheralded, to reprimand her for extravagance, sack about half the labour force, repair his boots and disappear again in some unspecified direction.

One day he rode over to propose to Robin that the two of them should go together to a district he knew of, hitherto neglected by other recruiters, in search of stalwart young men willing to put their thumb-marks on a contract binding them to work for six months on some distant plantation. Then the young men would go off to see the world, or as much of it as could be seen on a sisal plantation, provided with a free cooking-pot and blanket. As for Robin and Mr Nimmo, they would get one shilling for each recruit delivered to a prospective employer. There was not much money in this, but there was some, and that was better than nothing, so Robin gladly accepted the offer and departed with Mr Nimmo and a sleeping-bag, a supply of quinine, a box of cheap cigars and a change of clothing, leaving Tilly in charge of everything at Thika.

Tilly had been searching just as anxiously as Robin for ways to help the overdraft. Before the war, they had planted and grafted several acres of oranges and lemons, whose fruit was to supply a citrus-juice factory to be erected near Nairobi. The war had put an end to the factory project, but the citrus trees had survived, and now flourished and fruited profusely amid a jungle of weeds. To see anything going to waste upset Tilly. All over the world were people longing for, and badly needing, just such succulent fruit as this, and here was the juicy harvest rotting in the bush. Only a link between the two was lacking. Her inquiries in Nairobi were abortive; the shops had more oranges and lemons than they needed. But across the border of the Kikuyu reserve were thousands of people who had never tasted fruit of any kind. Surely, she reasoned, they would be willing to pay a few cents for such a health-giving harvest: what was more, they would come and fetch it away. She consulted Mugu, the headman who had replaced Sammy.

Mugu was a Kikuyu, but from another district, so that he counted almost as a foreigner, and formed no part of the network of local family relationships whose members were no good as headman, because they could never deliver judgement against one of their own relatives, or give orders to anyone of an age-grade senior to their own. Mugu was a stocky, alert, light-skinned man of about thirty-five, who always wore a heavy army greatcoat, however hot the weather, and a battered felt hat rather like Robin's. He gave out that he had been a sergeant in the K.A.R., a fighter of valour and ferocity who had slain many Germans and marched many miles, but this no one really believed. Few Kikuyu had taken any active part in fighting, they had served rather as carriers and orderlies, as store-keepers and cooks. Robin thought that Mugu had performed some useful function of that nature at the base, but kept up the illusion that he had been a warrior of renown in the hope that it would impress the rest of the Kikuyu. This was most unlikely, as the bush-telegraph could be relied upon to have told them all about him long ago.

'No, the people of the reserve will not come to buy these oranges,' Mugu decided, after some reflection.

'They taste delicious,' Tilly suggested.

'Yes, they are good; people like them very much.'

'Then why don't they come and buy them, if they are cheap?'

'Because they will say: "Why should we pay for these fruits that grow on trees, when we can send a boy to steal them at night? They are cheap to buy, but cheaper still to steal."'

'They have not stolen oranges so far,' Tilly pointed out.

'No, because people have not eaten oranges yet. But if you sell them, people will say: "Now we can see that these oranges must be valuable, the memsabu is selling them, so we had better steal some for ourselves." As it is, they think the oranges are like wild fruit in the forest, and not worth anything.'

So Tilly was defeated by Kikuyu logic, and seemed condemned to watch the fruit rotting away. But on her next visit to Nairobi she discovered a scarcity of marmalade. It was all imported, and shipping was still so difficult that supplies were short and erratic.

'How ridiculous,' Tilly exclaimed, 'to bring marmalade five thousand miles in overcrowded ships, when both the fruit *and* sugar are to be had locally, dirt cheap. All we need is a small factory . . .' And even this could be whittled down to a quantity of *debes* and jam jars. She had labels printed with the name 'Jams and Jellies', bought some sacks of sugar from an Indian, gave Kigorro a marmalade lesson and set a number of small boys to work shredding orange peel.

When Mrs Nimmo heard about all this she came trotting over on a mule, wisps of hair flying under a large cork helmet and red in the face from timing her rises in the saddle to the mule's erratic gait. She had a recipe inherited from a grandmother known to be the best preserve-maker of her day in all Edinburgh. The grandmother had had it from her mother, who had been housekeeper at Abbotsford, and Sir Walter himself had praised the marmalade, which had soothed the cramp in his stomach. Mrs Nimmo was swept into the enterprise and in no time the veranda of the grass house, the bathroom and all other available space was full of shredded orange peel steeping in *debes* of water. What we should have done without these *debes* I cannot imagine; they were used for carrying water, for measuring coffee-berries in the picking season, for growing plants, for heating bath-water, for boiling ghee, for roofing houses, for making sheds, chimneys and pigsties, in fact for almost every purpose under the sun.

Difficulties soon appeared. The most serious was a shortage of jars. New ones were unobtainable and used ones, collected from neighbours, totally inadequate. Tilly had read somewhere, or been told, that an empty bottle could be turned into a tumbler by tying a piece of twine round its neck, setting the twine alight and plunging the bottle into cold water; the top could then be knocked off neatly, leaving a serviceable glass. This, she thought, sealed with greaseproof paper, would surely make an excellent marmalade jar. So empty bottles were gathered together and Tilly was everywhere among them, dipping twine in paraffin, tying it to bottles and setting fire to it. The Kikuyu entered into this with great enjoyment, and soon the lawn looked like a battlefield, with people setting themselves alight and gashing their hands and arms all over the place. For the process did not always work, by any means, as it was supposed to do; sometimes the top of the bottle came off and sometimes it refused, and it never came off cleanly. Tilly's jars were more like death traps, with jagged spikes, splintered edges and lurking cracks, and Mrs Nimmo, deeply upset, wanted to abandon the whole enterprise.

'People must learn to be careful, that's all,' Tilly replied. 'It's a valuable lesson, and they should be grateful for the opportunity.'

A few moments later she gashed her own finger, while smoothing down a greaseproof paper top.

'Look, look, you're bleeding into the marmalade!' Mrs Nimmo cried.

'You should add that to your grandmother's receipt,' Tilly remarked, binding up the wound with her handkerchief and continuing to seal the jars. 'It's very strengthening, and improves the flavour as well.'

Mrs Nimmo was shocked by this flippant approach to a matter so serious as a family recipe. A day or two later, she rode over on her mule to supervise the brew – Tilly was away for the morning – and saw a furry object dipping and revolving in the fast-boiling pulp. Her eyes widened, her comfortable bosom heaved and she clasped her neck as if short of breath.

'What is that?' she cried, pointing to the object as if the ghost of Banquo had materialized.

Kigorro approached, and gazed into the *debe* as if he had never seen the object before, although a few moments before he had been stirring vigorously with a broom handle.

'That?' he inquired, frowning at it. 'How did that get there?'

'It is I who am asking *you*.'

'Perhaps it fell from the ceiling,' Kigorro suggested, gazing

30

up as if to seek its companions among the smoke-blackened rafters.

'Is that the custom of this kitchen? Do rats fall every day from the ceiling, or jump up from the floor?'

'Not every day,' Kigorro protested. 'But do you not know that rats will come where there is sugar, like vultures to a kill, or relatives to a beer-drink, or brides to a rich man? This kitchen is old, I have told memsabu she must build a new one as big and fine as the stables for the horses, but she will not listen; how, then, can I keep out rats?'

'In any case you can remove this one,' Mrs Nimmo suggested, for the rat was still boiling merrily away. 'And then you must throw away the marmalade.'

'Throw it away?' Kigorro inquired incredulously. 'But it is good marmalade with a lot of sugar in it.'

'Do as I say,' Mrs Nimmo snapped. After a good deal of prodding and flicking, the rat was extricated and the *debe* taken off the fire. Kigorro carried this reluctantly outside and left it by the door, saying he would throw its contents in the bush so as not to attract ants to the kitchen. Something else claimed Mrs Nimmo's attention, and when she had gone Kigorro restored the *debe* to the fire.

Tilly, meanwhile, was collecting orders with great success, for the marmalade was indeed excellent. Her difficulty was to deliver it, because the jars could not be sent by rail. Output was high, stocks accumulated faster than deliveries could move them, and a reservoir of marmalade soon formed in the bathroom, the only room whose roof did not leak in the rains. The bathroom was divided from my bedroom by a thin reed partition and its only furniture was a tin tub, filled by *debe* when we wanted to use it. Soon the tub was removed and the bathroom wholly given over to marmalade, whose delicious smell permeated the house and attracted to it an infinite number of ants and other insects, with and without wings. These in turn attracted more lizards of the kind that looked, by lamplight, quite transparent, as if cut out of gelatine, as well as spiders and other predators, so the house became a battlefield and hunting ground, with dramas of life and death played out every moment, and Tilly remarked that we

31

should soon have to evacuate it and live in tents on the lawn.

It was our neighbour Alec Wilson who one day sniffed the air and said: 'What a delicious odour! There's something in it stronger than mere maramalade. Don't I detect alcoholic undertones?'

'It would be nice to think so,' Tilly replied, 'but I haven't distilled it.'

In a day or two the smell grew stronger, and several opened jars revealed signs of fermentation. Mrs Nimmo was dismayed, and kept on saying that she could not understand it, the recipe had been faithfully adhered to, and even when the smell became quite overpowering she could scarcely blame the marmalade.

'And think of all the sugar in it, bought at four cents the pound, and the care and the trouble, and the work and the jars! And now we shall have to throw it all away, and waste everything, and disappoint our customers.'

'Not at all,' replied Tilly; though at first downcast, she had a great talent for recovery. 'I can think of several customers who, far from being disappointed, would probably pay extra for alcoholic marmalade.'

'You have an answer for everything,' Mrs Nimmo said, half in exasperation and half in respect.

While the heavy, sickly yet not unpleasing odour of fermentation grew so strong as to permeate the house, the sequel took us all by surprise. I slept, as a rule, like a log, but was awakened one night by something unexpected which jerked my mind back three or four years to a Zeppelin raid. Zeppelins at Thika there could hardly be, yet without doubt I heard the crack of an explosion, the shattering of glass, an alarming thump on the reed partition between me and the bathroom. Anarchists with bombs? A gunpowder plot? A native rising? Yet everything fell back into silence after the thumps, until the dogs started up from my parents' room and rushed yelling into the night, but without the least response from lurking anarchists or plotters.

I groped for my bedroom slippers – essential to protect one from toe-burrowing jiggas – grasped my torch and emerged gingerly on to the veranda just as another muffled bang, followed by thuds and tinkles, shocked the night's tranquillity. The small black figures of the dogs were dodging like water-spiders among bush-shadows in a vain search for anarchists. Tilly's voice could be heard admonishing them and Robin, just back from his recruiting safari, emerged in his pyjamas with a lamp. The waxy petals of a frangipani on the lawn shone like ivory, but their intrusive scent, strong and sweet as a liqueur, was overwhelmed by the vapours of fermentation issuing from the bathroom. As Robin held up the lamp and peered through the open doorway another explosion made him jump back and then shake and slap himself as if he had been attacked by biting ants.

'Your blasted marmalade is blowing up,' he called angrily to Tilly. 'It's ruined my pyjamas.'

'But it can't be,' Tilly protested, arriving in a dressing-gown, attended by dogs.

'You'd better not stand in the doorway. I might as well be back in the trenches if this goes on.'

Bits of glass and gouts of marmalade, black as congealed blood, bespattered the little room and clung to the reed partitions, and the smell was overpowering. Tilly shut the door.

'It's not safe for the dogs.'

'It's far from safe for anyone. My pyjamas ...'

'At any rate that solves the storage problem. It's all blowing up.' By morning, armies of ants, beetles and bugs of all sorts had arrived to gorge themselves, and Tilly maintained that she could see insects reeling about as drunk as lords. The explosions had for the moment ceased, and all the remaining jars were packed, not without apprehension, into baskets and boxes, and loaded into the car, to be hurried to Nairobi.

'We must warn the customers it's dangerous,' Mrs Nimmo insisted.

'All the labels are marked "Store in a Cool Place",' Tilly replied. 'As there are no cool places in Nairobi in the hot weather, it'll obviously be the customers' own fault if it explodes before they eat it. But it's so good, they won't keep it long.'

Mrs Nimmo clucked at this, still unnerved by the disaster, and scarcely comforted by Tilly's remark that we must all be thankful the recipe had not blown up Sir Walter Scott. Tilly went off in the car, sitting very upright on the springless front seat with all the boxes and baskets piled at the back, and a shamba-boy on top to hold them down. As everyone considered this to be a dangerous mission, he was fitted out with an old sun-helmet and a discarded pair of goggles, and his friends and relatives came to see him off and wish him a safe return. One more jar blew up on the way. Tilly took the whole lot to the hospital and presented it to the matron, with the suggestion that alcoholic marmalade would be especially palatable to patients cut off from their usual tots. The matron frostily replied that she would have it all re-boiled. This, we later heard, disposed of the alcohol, but made the marmalade glutinous; however, it was used for puddings, and so served its purpose in the end.

Tilly was not discouraged. 'One has to learn by experience,' she said. And what she did, in fact, learn was that fluids, at the altitude of Thika, boiled at a lower temperature than the 212 degrees we had regarded as a law of nature in England. Some of the microbes, therefore, were not destroyed, and the marmalade had been imperfectly sterilized. Armed with this knowledge, Tilly and Mrs Nimmo took to making guava jelly and Cape gooseberry jam, both excellent and non-explosive. They built up a thriving little business which would have helped the overdraft, had not the shipping position so improved as to allow familiar English brands of jam to reappear in the shops at reasonable prices. And so Jams and Jellies, its purpose served, was closed down.

Chapter 3

'I GOT more malaria out of it than money,' Robin said of his recruiting trip; although he and Jock Nimmo had signed up quite a lot of stalwart youths, their expenses took most of the profit. In those days the people of the Lake Victoria region, which was very hot, sensibly wore no clothes, and did not feel bound to change their customs when they travelled to Nairobi. This so shocked prudish Europeans that the Government decreed that everyone coming to the capital must wear a blanket, or some other covering. At first the Kavirondo (as these people were then called) responded by wrapping the blankets round their heads, revealing to all that they were not circumcised: a fact which caused them to be held in profound contempt by the Kikuyu, and by other people who were.

After Robin had been at home for some time, and things were going as smoothly as they ever did on the farm, he and Tilly decided to look at the land whose leasehold he had drawn in a lottery under the soldier-settlement scheme. By visiting the land office in Nairobi he had found out all he could about it: that it was high up on the northern slopes of Mount Kenya, perhaps nearly nine thousand feet above sea-level, and fifteen or twenty miles from the nearest road or settlement. It appeared, on the map, to be covered with a network of small streams; and Robin was gratified to find that the terms of the lease forbade him to construct any waterways, docks, wharfs or jetties on the property.

No one had any idea as to what could be done with land so bleak, remote and inaccessible, but, as Robin said, there was no harm in looking; it might prove suitable for sheep of a breed that liked cold, exposed and craggy places. A journey to an unknown region always delighted Tilly, and preparations were made for a simple safari, to be made on ponies, taking only such kit as we could cram into saddle-bags, and staying the night with friends or acquaintances on the way. Tents, sleeping bags and the necessary porters we were to borrow from our last host. In due course we set out, Njombo bringing up the rear on a mule.

Soon after his return from the war, Robin had bought two ponies at a sale of remounts in Nairobi. They were cheap because they were in very poor condition after their treatment and experiences in the army. One of these remounts was a small, tough, battle-scarred, bony chestnut called M'zee, the Swahili word for old. When he came he was as thin as a kipper and walked in a crabbed, stiff manner that had suggested his name; Robin thought he had probably been infected by tsetse fly, a condition from which no animal could recover. But from the day of his arrival, M'zee started to pick up. His skin, which had been drawn as tight as a bandage over his bones, began to fill out and shine. Instead of drooping his head, he looked about him with interest, and instead of hobbling he walked carefully, but firmly, about the little paddock. At first he would not come near any of us, and he always remained suspicious of strangers, but gradually he grew used to being stroked and patted, though he retained a wily look, and sometimes put back his ears and snarled with lifted lip.

But M'zee did not kick in the stable; his previous rough treatment had cowed but not embittered him, and now that he was shown kindness, his natural sweetness of temper unfolded like a convolvulus. His intelligence was of a high order. Tilly called it low cunning, and that perhaps was true; there was nothing about him of the high-bred eagerness and quickness of the other pony Hafid, a little crossbred Arab, and he was always one to save himself trouble. Nothing would make him jump an object like a log, or a low thorn fence, that a high-spirited mount might leap for the fun of it; M'zee had no sense of fun, if it involved him in any extra activity. On the other hand he had a natural sense of politeness; if I fell off, which sometimes happened when he stumbled severely – he had a bad habit of stumbling – he would always wait for me to get on again. He did not in the least mind the crack of the rifle, and always knew the shortest way home. Altogether, although M'zee was ugly, and not at all a glamorous ride, as Hafid was, I grew very attached to him, and we understood one another pretty well. So it was on M'zee that I set off for north Kenya, a saddle-bag full of my possessions flapping on each side.

Our way lay at first through the Kikuyu reserve, along a red wagon track that writhed about in search of low gradients and crossing-places over the many swampy streams, mostly fringed with papyrus, on their way from the forests of the Aberdares to the bed of the Athi, which lay below us on our right hand. Most of them petered out on the tawny, hot, absorbent hollow plain and reached their destination only in the rains. Red dust carpeted the track, and our ponies' feet made little plopping sounds when they trotted. To each side lay deep ruts made by wagons embedding themselves in mud during the rains.

The finest sight we saw during this journey was a convoy of six wagons each travelling in the other's dust and each with a matched team: first came sixteen black oxen, then a brindled span, then some white as cotton bolls, then a red lot, and so on; the oxen were big and handsome and the wagons, too, good ones with fresh paint, all alike. Beside them walked lean, brown, dust-stained and slouch-hatted Afrikaners, with long whips, always to be found in charge of oxen, and with them also were big black askaris in blue jerseys and puttees and khaki shorts, strapping men with fierce looks; one, a sergeant, saluted us with a quivering hand as we rode by. These were the wagons of the King's African Rifles that carried supplies to Archer's Post in the Northern Frontier district and were coming back empty, at a great pace. Loaded wagons travelled fifteen miles a day and took a fortnight to reach Archer's Post, and of course much longer to the desert camps beyond.

We stayed the night at Punda Milia – Swahili for zebra – where the partners Randall Swift and Ernest Rutherfoord had a sisal plantation, and a factory to strip white fibres from grey-green, spiky leaves whose tips were sharp enough to use as gramophone needles. The fibre was hung up to dry on wires, like washing, and smelt unpleasant. All around were the long, straight ranks of the straight-leaved agave, beyond that coarse yellow-ochre grasses and flaring red erythrinas, the sealing-wax trees. A harsh crop in a harsh landscape, yet its owners loved Punda Milia, and spoke nostalgically of the game that thronged it when they first came: of the big black-maned lion they had shot where the decorticator now stood; of how they had broken, daily for three months, fifteen miles of furrow, one driving two pairs of untrained oxen and the other holding a single-furrow plough; and of how, on Sundays, they had sometimes walked twenty-five miles to see their nearest neighbour, an American weighing over three hundredweight called Sir Northrup Macmillan, who had lived up to his name for fabulous hospitality by greeting them with a bottle of champagne each. Now all the game had gone from Punda

Milia and they ploughed with a huge, wood-burning tractor.

The next night we stayed with the District Commissioner at Fort Hall in a bungalow with thick mud walls, whitewashed inside and out, that was cool and airy. On the veranda I noticed a native goatskin bag holding several long, thin gourds with stoppers made of cows' tails, and some calabashes containing objects hard to identify. I picked up one of these and started to examine it, but the District Commissioner told me sharply to put it down.

'It's paraphernalia taken from a witch-doctor,' he said. 'Don't meddle with it.'

Ordinary folk were not, I knew, supposed to touch objects charged with magic, but the Kikuyu did not apply these rules to Europeans.

'You never know who's watching,' the D.C. added. 'Suppose you fell off your pony tomorrow and broke your leg, it would be all round the reserve that you'd touched something with a curse on it. One can't be too careful.'

When a D.C. started to be nervous about witch-doctors, it was a sign that he needed leave. He did seem rather jumpy, and said that life was nothing but *shauris* – disputes, that is, or bothers, or palavers. The Kikuyu were always disputatious and difficult. No path ran straight, even for a yard, it twisted and turned not for an apparent reason, but because they felt safer walking in that weaving fashion, and their minds were much the same. They would never state a fact baldly, but would hint at it from many different angles, leaving it to you to piece things together. A hard, blunt fact they feared rather as they feared a straight open road, where you were vulnerable to poisoned arrows.

Next day we rode on to Nyeri, up and down steep green hills thick with bush and through patches of dark cool forest, and down into the valleys that glowed with so many greens: the May-meadow green of waist-high maize in patchwork shambas, the full deep green of drooping banana fronds, the yellowish green of sugar cane and the dark olive green of the bush. All the time we were climbing. No papyrus now fringed streams that were clear and flashing; ferns thrust out of crevices in boulders, mosses coated tree roots smelling secretive. There was a shrub with clusters of buttercup-yellow blooms, a *cassia*, and another with a big mauve flower a-buzz with bees. We could hear goat-bells in the hot sunshine, and sometimes the dry smell of goat mingled with the aromatic shrub-smell and the scent of leaf-mould, and a whiff of sweetness from a creeper in the bush. Our ponies jogged on lazily, and M'zee stumbled now and then, too idle to pick his feet up properly. Flies bothered us all, and it was very hot in the sun, but directly you passed into the shade of trees the air was cool again, like a dock-leaf on a nettle-sting.

One could always tell when a homestead was occupied by the blue smoke drifting up through the round thatched roof, from a central fire that must never go out while the hut's owner lived. We passed several smokeless homesteads, clearly deserted.

'The owners died in the big sickness,' Njombo explained. 'Many, many people died. They say the Germans sent a big black bird with one eye that shone like a lantern, and put this sickness into the rivers, because the askaris of the K.A.R. were stronger than theirs.'

Robin tried to explain that this was not just a Kikuyu sickness, but had killed many people everywhere, and was called flu.

'But who has sent this sickness?' Njombo inquired.

'No one has sent it. There is a very small thing in the air that Europeans call a germ ...'

'Like a little insect?'

'Smaller than that.'

'Smaller than a jigga?'

'Yes, it is something that gets inside ...' Robin was getting into his usual difficulty; no words existed for ideas so wholly new to the Kikuyu and, if they had, Robin's vocabulary would not have included them. Although he was an excellent linguist, with fluent French, German and Spanish, some curious barrier seemed to exist between him and our infinitely simpler up-country Swahili. I suppose he just did not take the language seriously and so did not bother to learn it, preferring to flounder, as he often did, in a bog of misunderstanding and chase will-o'-the-wisps of cross-purposes.

Njombo was silent for a little. I knew what he was thinking, or thought I did, for on the last occasion when he had dug a jigga out of my toe he had told me a story about these itchy, burrowing fleas. It was they, he said, who were responsible for the present dominance of white people over black. In spite of all their guns, white men could not defeat the Kikuyu warriors without resorting to guile: they sent for a supply of jiggas and scattered them round the countryside at night. These burrowed into the feet of the warriors and crippled them, so that they could not fight. I was old enough by now to disbelieve him, nor did he believe it as a fact himself, but he relished it as a good story.

'These small insects, smaller than jiggas, were sent by the Germans,' Njombo concluded. 'They were angry at the defeat of their askaris, and chose this way to kill many people, all over the country.' Like all Kikuyu, Njombo thought in terms of revenge. Hyenas, he said, had grown so bold and numerous that they had even entered homesteads and taken live children. But that was over now, and the country smiling again.

At Nyeri we stayed with the Provincial Commissioner, Mr Hope. He was busy at the time because the white farmers were thought to be about to rise against authority, kidnap the Governor and seize power, in order to prevent the Colonial Office from handing the country over to the Indians. The Governor, who was fond of fishing, was to be held captive in a camp beside a river, close to Nyeri, that had recently been stocked with trout. A flow of telegrams with directions for resisting this revolt was arriving from Nairobi but Mr Hope was taking it all calmly; in any case the post office shut at four o'clock and no rebellion could disturb his round of golf and subsequent leisure before about nine o'clock next morning.

'How's the rebellion getting on at Thika?' Mr Hope inquired.

'It can't have started,' Tilly said, 'because if it does, Alec's going to send a telegram saying "Bluebell ill", and then we must hurry back.' Bluebell was Tilly's favourite dachshund.

'What would happen,' Mr Hope asked, 'if something actually did go wrong with Bluebell?'

'Then Alec would send a telegram saying "Bluebell really ill".'

No summons came, and next day we rode on, leaving behind the juicy green ridges for a wilder terrain with thick, dark tongues of forest thrusting down to a plain dotted with thorn-bushes and creased by gullies. A wind blew off the mountain and the sky was full of huge, bold clouds like alpine ranges. The cattle-herds we passed leaned on spears and had greased pigtails tied into a queue, and wooden cylinders stuck into their ear-lobes like Masai; here on the fringes of their country the Kikuyu carried a good deal of Masai blood and tried to imitate their predatory neighbours, but there was no confusing the two; one could not avoid the feeling that these young Kikuyu were in fancy dress.

Our next hosts, the Orams, were people who never stayed long in one place. Harold Oram was a large, powerful South African condemned by Tilly as a swashbuckler, his wife a devoted naturalist always gathering plants, butterflies, fragments of rock, feathers and other objects; these lay about the house waiting for the time she never found to classify them. They had a brood of small children who, while strong and healthy, were not at all well-behaved. I greatly envied them their freedom and shagginess, and they seemed to have no lessons to do.

'They learn from nature's book,' said Mabel Oram. 'God's wonders are everywhere; they will learn truth and beauty from trees and streams.'

Soon afterwards Geraint – they had romantic Arthurian names – came in with a terrific gash down the side of his face, administered by Guinevere with a sharp flint. Mabel Oram looked considerably less benign, and later we heard distant yells suggesting that Guinevere's father was not quite so unconcerned with discipline as both parents would have had us believe. To me these children seemed like a pack of wild dogs, always on the move, unpredictable and full of menace, and one needed a rifle, or at any rate an adult, to feel at all secure.

The Orams inhabited a cluster of huts near an ice-cold river that hurried down from the glaciers of Mount Kenya to the brown plains below. You only had to walk a hundred yards to find yourself in a tangle of spiky undergrowth under sweet-smelling, fluted cedars, tall as cathedral columns, with grey moss hanging from twisted branches high overhead. Here it was dark, moist and at first silent, but after a while you became aware of a whole orchestration of muted sound, much of it just beyond the range of hearing, but some on the border-line: the rustlings and chewings of insects, the stirring of leaves, the burrowing of small creatures, the quiet flight of birds. Sometimes a turaco would screech in the distance, or you might catch a glimpse of its brilliant scarlet wings, and sometimes you heard a sound of agitated foliage, a sylvan splash, as invisible monkeys leapt from branch to branch. Here you felt crass and witless as a deaf mute: the tiny dikdik, the prowling Dorobo, knew the meaning of each rustle, saw the cocoon under the leaf, but I, with my supposedly superior intelligence, blundered dully forward, blind and dumb.

The exciting thing about all this country, after Thika, was its emptiness. Absolutely no one lived here. No one ever had; you came upon no relics of abandoned homesteads; since time began, no human hand had ever cleared the forest or dug shambas in the glades. This total emptiness of human content produced a feeling quite different from that of country where man has left his mark. It could be frightening, and yet to me it was not; there seemed to be a presence here, a spirit, an atmosphere, something almost sentient and actual, that had nothing to do with man, but was not hostile. I would not have been surprised to hear a voice coming out of the bush or forest, in fact I often half expected it: a message of some kind, something important, though what about I had no idea. Although I did not feel this spirit, or essence, or whatever it was, to be hostile, I did not expect it to be helpful either: for instance, I knew that if I lost myself, an exceedingly easy thing to do, it would not help me to find my way home. I was very careful not to go far without checking carefully the shapes of the trees and the direction of the sun. High above rose the great, silent, immemorial bulk of the mountain, and although it was invisible, in some mysterious way it dominated and pos-sessed the scene.

The other exciting thing about this country was that it was full of invisible animals. Although you could walk all day and see nothing, you would certainly pass within a few yards of many creatures. They would have heard and smelt you, and perhaps seen you, without your even suspecting their presence. Sometimes I wondered whether, in a like way, we moved among ghosts and spirits we could never see, but who watched us. In a mysterious way you felt yourself being watched all the time, and by anxious but not hating eyes. And you in turn watched the bush, peered down each glade, turned your head and flicked your eyes to catch the first sight of a pair of horns and pricked ears, the red flash of a retreating rump, the whisk of a tail, the silent vanishing of soft shapes into bush or forest with scarcely the stir of a leaf. The whole landscape was alert with life and you were part of it; curiously enough the absence of humans made the country more exciting and momentous, not less so, and you never felt lonely, although, of course, you might be frightened now and then.

Harold Oram had decided to come with us to see Robin's piece of land, so we had to wait until he was ready. One day was much like another at the Orams', and Tilly said they did not know the days of the week, as of course Africans had not previously known them, reckoning only in seasons and moons. The Orams had adopted this system. Instead of deciding to start next Monday, they would say that when the moon had entered its third quarter, or when it was three days old, they would be off. Nor had they any clocks or watches in the house; they claimed to be able to tell the time by the sun with less than ten minutes' margin of error. Tilly found this Oram vagueness rather suspect, and certainly irritating.

'It's no good pretending the calendar hasn't been invented,' she said. 'We're supposed to be advancing, not reversing; *I* don't want to go back to eating raw food and using stone-tipped arrows, whatever the Orams say.' Robin had discovered a waterfall in the forest and was busy making calculations about a small hydro-electric scheme to supply a township that would one day arise on the Nanyuki river, where the Government had set aside a site about as large as Birmingham, so he was quite content.

As a farmer, Harold had plenty of ideas but no one to sell his produce to. In order to reach a railway, it had either to traverse the whole length of the Kikuyu reserve to Thika, getting on for a hundred miles, or travel a rather shorter distance to Naivasha through forest, moorland and manless wilderness over the top of the Aberdare mountains. The only hope was to make the produce walk. Harold had sent some pigs to market that way, along a track made first by elephants and then by Masai warriors coming to raid Kikuyu cattle, and now fallen into disuse. The pigs had set off with several drovers carrying maize-meal to feed them on the journey. They had clambered through bamboos, over peaks ten thousand feet high and down again, across bogs, ravines and near-precipices to reach Naivasha in nine days, limping and emaciated but still alive.

'Nairobi's next batch of bacon must have been tough,' Tilly commented.

'They only lost twelve pounds apiece,' Harold replied. 'But the boys refused to do it again. They said they'd spent all one night fending off lions and another treed by buffalo.'

One of the legends of the district was a fight between a Shorthorn bull imported by a South African called Lex Smith, and a lioness. A careless herd had let the bull escape, and he was found next morning in a shocking state, his hide torn by deep gashes and his horns clotted with blood, but triumphant: several miles away the lioness, loser of this fearful and prolonged midnight combat, lay dead.

Harold Oram was building up a herd of cattle from which he could expect no return for four or five years. While nearly all the white farmers, at this time, were crossing tiny, humped, slow-growing native beasts with imported bulls in order to improve size, quality and speed of growth, Harold was using only native bulls, but of a superior stamp, bought from a wild, nomadic people in the north called the Boran. Most of his colleagues thought him idiotic; a native beast took six or seven years to reach maturity, and even then was not half the size of an English three-year-old. It was all part of the Oram cult of going back to nature, and African nature at that, and in the long run, ironically, it proved to be the soundest policy commercially. Boran cattle became famous and sought-after, but by that time the Orams, as so often happens to innovators, were no longer there to benefit.

One day Geraint, the eldest of the boys, offered to show me a very special secret, and would not rest until I had agreed to go. I was suspicious of his secrets; one had been a sloughed-off snake's skin which I had thought was alive, another a kind of large rat that had bitten my finger. However, once the Oram pack had made up its collective mind resistance was futile, so we set off up the banks of the river, which gurgled down over smooth stones and under ferny banks with a sucking, lapping sound that struck me as self-satisfied. The children followed a path, if you could call it that, quite invisible unless you knew it, made by animals, probably bushbuck.

As we scrambled forward I became more and more out of breath; we were over 8,000 feet up and climbing steeply. Only pinpoints of sunlight, bright shafts like spears, could penetrate the canopy to dapple the forest's floor. By the stream it was too thick even for that, and dank. Once I caught a waft of buffalo smell, and a little later heard a crashing across the stream – either buffalo or elephant.

'I don't want to go any farther,' I said.

'It's just here,' said Geraint.

We had halted on the brink of some immature rapids. On the other side a ghostly white object, larger than any man, appeared to be crouching in the gloom and staring at me with enormous hollow eyes, black with menace. My throat went dry, and horrible cold fingers tickled my spine. I would have run away if my legs had not felt heavy and if the Oram children had not been there, ready with their mocking laughter.

The ghost did not move. The eyes, I now saw, were black holes and I thought something moved inside them. Geraint jumped into the stream, leapt across the rapids, reached the ghost and then vanished. One moment he was there, then he was not. I called to him and, as I had feared, started a howl of laughter from the pack. They, too, raced towards the object and then, as I reluctantly advanced, I realized that it was a skull, high as a man, and bleached a yellow-white. Geraint's face suddenly appeared in an eye-socket and almost turned me

45

into jelly. I do not know why the skull should have looked so eerie, except that it was so large, and seemed to crouch. I tried to think of the dead elephant.

'Did you find its tusks?' I asked.

'One of them,' said Geraint. 'It's in the water. It's broken, but I bet it's worth a lot of money. We're going to get it out and cut it up and sell it. Then I shall buy a belt with beads on it and a camera. Only don't tell Dad, you promised.'

I could just see a bit of broken tusk jutting out from the rocks. There seemed to be nothing else left of the elephant, only its hollow skull. Probably it had been wounded and had dragged itself here, away from the herd, to slake its thirst; then it had lain down forever. The children had made a sort of cubby-hole inside the skull and had stored some food there in a tin box, ready for an expedition to the top of Mount Kenya. As a great favour they gave me a biscuit, which was mouldy.

'When I grow up I'm going to be a hunter,' Geraint said. 'I shall kill thousands of elephants and buffaloes, more than anyone has ever killed before. I've got a bow and arrow hidden in a tree. I got it from a Dorobo, he swapped it for my knife, only you mustn't tell, because I said I'd lost the knife and that was a lie.'

'If Mummy finds out she'll wash your mouth with carbolic,' said Guinevere.

'She won't find out.'

'God knows, he can see anything, and he'll punish you.'

'I'm not afraid of God. If he tries to hurt me I'll shoot him with an arrow. In the foot.'

'Then he'll turn you into a centipede,' Guinevere retorted, 'and you'll get eaten by a crane.'

'If I had a hundred legs I'd run away.'

'He'd send a thunderbolt to squash you flat. Or *siafu* to eat you alive.'

Soon we left the skull and scrambled back. I thought we must have gone miles into the forest, but our return only took a few minutes, and I was thankful to feel the sun, like an embrace, on my back, and hot on my bare limbs.

46

Chapter 4

WE started next morning on our search for Robin's land, travelling light. Even so, we needed eight or ten porters to carry our minimal needs: two small tents, sleeping-bags, camp-chairs, cooking-pots and food for three or four days. These porters belonged to the Meru tribe, related to the Kikuyu but more like Masai to look at. The young men were red and shiny all over, like billiard balls, and wore their hair either in two queues, fore and aft, like Masai, or in a mop of little pigtails that must have taken hours to twist and arrange. But then they had hours to spend on adornment, and were vain of their looks. Normally they wore short cloaks made of calico and stained with red ochre, which exposed most of their lean flanks and shapely buttocks and were sometimes caught in by a belt encrusted with blue, red and white beads, but for the safari they wore blankets, knotted over the right shoulder, into which they rolled themselves at night. These blankets were grey, and when they walked their red skins showed beneath like the bud of a red lily between two grey sepals.

We and the porters had to scramble and force our way through about ten miles of forest to reach a belt of moorland above, where the farm was thought to lie. Two men with pangas went ahead to cut a way through the worst of the thickets. After a while we found ourselves on a trail made by elephants. They had broken down a lot of branches and left large, puddled footprints and frequent piles of droppings on the forest floor. Although this made the way plainer. the surface was laced with fallen branches and the porters' bare feet slipped on damp, greasy mud from which our ponies extracted their hooves with sucking noises. We had to lead them through most of the forest, or branches and creepers would have dragged us off their backs. It was hard work scrambling upwards without a load, but with tent-poles, chop-boxes or fifty pounds of maize-meal on one's head it must have been appalling. However, the porters seemed quite cheerful, and concerned only about the elephants. Harold Oram assured them that the droppings were two days old at least; they walked round them dubiously, and continued on their way.

'It seems an odd place to find a farm,' Tilly remarked. But Harold was undismayed.

'We'll soon be out on to the open downland. You'll feel different there – magnificent country, unspoilt as God made it. Finest country in the world for sheep, I should say.'

'A job to get them there,' Robin said.

'Oh, it wouldn't be much to make a bit of a track through this patch of forest. Do it in a couple of days with a good gang.'

'The transport problem . . .' Robin began.

'My dear fellow, it's no good dwelling on the difficulties; if you want a market on your doorstep you'd better grow cabbages outside Nairobi. They're going to develop Nanyuki, there'll be a road, one day there'll be a railway, you'll see. If it's good sheep land, get hold of it, that's my advice – can't go wrong.'

We toiled on endlessly through the slippery and treacherous forest, expecting at any minute to meet a herd of elephants, for whatever Harold might say the droppings were quite fresh, and there was plenty of evidence that elephants had just passed that way: large bamboos uprooted and flung about, their foliage half-devoured.

'Untidy feeders,' Tilly remarked. In spite of the elephants, she enjoyed getting farther and farther into the wilds where everything was new and fresh. Tilly was far from being a total shunner of her fellow-beings, but she liked also to feel that she had plenty of space all around her, and was not at the mercy of her neighbours. Robin, on the other hand, became gloomier as we climbed higher; for one thing it hurt him, I think, to scramble about so much at this altitude. He had a piece of shrapnel still embedded in his chest, and dysentery contracted in the Boer War was liable to return if he got unduly chilled or exhausted. Also he was irritated by Harold Oram's proprietary attitude towards the mountain and everything within its orbit.

'I should think a herd of okapi would do better here than sheep,' he remarked crossly.

'You're too impatient, my dear chap. Wait till we get through this spit of woodland, then you'll see. Besides, the sport ...'

Njombo, who was leading the mule, shared my father's opinion.

'It is a very long way,' he remarked, during a halt to seek a passage across a ravine. 'A very long way indeed. And this forest, it is very, very bad.'

'Bad in what way?'

'It is cold, and full of evil spirits.'

The peak of Mount Kenya was believed by the Kikuyu to be the dwelling-place of God, so as we advanced towards it the evil spirits should have diminished in number, rather than thickened. But Harold told us that a race of dwarfs had once lived in holes in the ground in this forest, exercising magical powers, and had perhaps given rise to legends about spirits.

'A folk tale based on pygmies,' he said. 'You find it everywhere – a small, magic race of hunters that died out, or was exterminated.' But there was no one in the forest now, only a few wandering Dorobo honey-hunters who lived near the edges and bought grain from the Kikuyu, and traded in illicit ivory.

After this I struggled on with added uneasiness, expecting to see dim white shapes among the undergrowth, and queer creatures whose eyes would glow like embers, with many arms, and claws like crocodiles, and bushy tails. When a sudden whirring sound, like a low-pitched sneer of laughter, broke suddenly from, as it seemed, under my feet, I stood frozen like an icicle. Then I saw a flash of wings – a mountain francolin, Harold said, the most handsome of birds, its black wings banded with chestnut and a shiny black crest falling like a plume over its red beak.

At last the forest thinned and all at once sunshine warmed our shoulders with a bland, familiar welcome, and our spirits lifted like a cloud. Here was the downland Harold had spoken of, treeless, windswept, biscuit-coloured in the sun and creased by gorges, stubbled by rock. We halted on a crest and looked

49

down upon a view more magnificent and limitless than any we had seen before. The land below us vanished into a blue immensity beyond which, Harold said, lay the great lava deserts of Turkana and, beyond those, the Abyssinian hills. We stood in silence, feeling as dwarfed as perhaps one blade of grass might feel in the Sahara, or a single sparrow in the whole wide dome of the sky.

'Look any way you like,' Harold said with satisfaction, 'and you won't see a trace of a roof-top or a native hut for a hundred miles.'

'There's a view, certainly,' Robin guardedly agreed.

'A little difficult for the furniture removal, possibly,' Tilly suggested. 'But certainly one wouldn't be troubled by neighbours unexpectedly dropping in.'

'Nor by sheep buyers,' Robin added. 'The nearest market must be at least a hundred miles.'

'Oh, no,' Harold protested. 'It's not far to Meru, round that shoulder. Not more than thirty miles.'

'And what happens at Meru?'

'Well, there's a D.C., and some Indian *dukas*, and a depot for the K.A.R. – at least half a dozen Europeans.'

'They wouldn't absorb much mutton.'

'You're in too much of a hurry, old man. They'll push the railway through to Nyeri, you'll see – barely fifty miles.'

Harold evidently regarded that as quite suburban; and both Tilly and Robin, having demonstrated their hardheaded business acumen by talking of markets, surrendered to the enthusiasm that this blue-and-golden, lonely, bright-aired country naturally aroused. There is no feeling like being absolutely alone with creation, even perhaps the first man to stand upon this particular rock and set eye on this particular scene, with nothing spoilt or sullied or abused. Grass bends before the wind, a soaring buzzard seeks a nibbling shrew, crickets trill, the hyrax drowses in his hollow tree, the spider waits in a crevice of sun-blistered rock – a whole world revolves in balance with itself, more perfect than the finest symphony. Man alone plays no part here save as a destroyer, who must cut trees to warm himself, kill beasts to feed or to amuse himself, and trample the shining beetle, the fruiting moss, when he moves about. Only man is not content to leave things as they are but must always be changing them, and when he has done so, is seldom satisfied with the result.

It was now time to find a camping-place. Robin's map showed a network of streams, but they did not seem to be actually there. Our ponies stumbled along through tufty, treacherous grass that grew in hard, slippery clumps difficult for the loaded porters. We kept on crossing little rocky gullies, all quite dry.

'The surveyor must have had hallucinations,' Robin said crossly. 'Flowing water everywhere. Probably with skiffs and punts, like Maidenhead.'

Eventually we found a very small patch of swampy ground that must conceal, Harold said, an underground spring, to be revealed by digging. Here we camped, in an exposed position on a hillside, with no trees anywhere near. Our two small tents, and one for the porters, did not take long to pitch, and then everyone was busy collecting firewood and making a fire. It was cold enough to need one already, although the sun still stood some way above the horizon. Harold and Robin took their guns to look for francolin and I climbed with Tilly farther up the hill to admire the view. The land stretched it seemed forever into a setting sun that had inflamed the whole sky with purple, crimson and gold. And then the peak emerged from its sheath of cloud, incredibly sharp and delicate, its snow-covered glaciers stained a deep pink and little wisps of violet hovering about its icy pinnacles. The black rock-faces, tooth-edged crags, all the weight and massive solidity of those twin towering peaks, Batian and Nelion – named after the greatest of Masai magicians – all this was transmuted into something as light, as airy and ethereal as a phantom ship riding upon a fleecy ocean. Why such sights should sadden one I do not know, but I felt like bursting into tears, and the meaning of two hitherto obscure lines of verse became perfectly plain: 'Comrade, look not on the west – 'twill have the heart out of your breast.' But as soon as the sun had disappeared everything began suddenly to lose its sharpness, like an unfixed photograph. Tilly remarked that it was too much like living in the middle of a Wagnerian opera, and we returned to camp.

Already there was a sharp nip in the air. Harold had shot two francolin and Tilly fried them on the camp fire and served them on toast, and very excellent they were, eaten by the light of flames devouring dry timber which gave out a sharp, aromatic tang and spat showers of sparks. At home his family lived wholly off the country, Harold said; there was nothing on earth you couldn't shoot or grow, and yet a lot of donkeys lived out of tins.

Over the camp fire Harold told us tales of his experience in South Africa where he had been born, and in Rhodesia where he had gone as a boy, always seeking out wild and distant places that had escaped being civilized. When civilization caught him up he moved on – like, as Robin said, a Mad Hatter's tea-party with whole countries in the place of crockery. What would happen when he had moved right round the table? The supply of empty, uncivilized lands must give out some time, in fact quite soon: this was probably the last.

'I must admit I'll be sorry when the last fence is up,' Harold said, 'and the last native has his pair of trousers. But that won't be for a hundred years.'

'You're putting fences up yourself,' Robin pointed out, 'and improving the cattle.'

'One's got to civilize the country, and make a living for one's family.'

'But you don't like it when it's civilized.'

Harold laughed. 'I'm not against civilization really, it's got to come. The natives can't be left as savages, they've got to be brought on and raised up. And then, think what a magnificent district this will be when it's opened up! Perfect climate, well watered, all the game you can want, healthy, a white man's country ...'

'The game may not last. It hasn't in South Africa.'

'It'll last my time, all right. And I want to build up something here I can hand on to my sons. One day they'll have something to be proud of.'

'So you want *them* to be civilized.'

'Well, of course. Civilization's what we're here for – to tame the country, bring the natives up, build a new colony like they've done down south and in Australia. There's no finer thing.'

As Tilly afterwards remarked, Harold wanted civilization for everyone else, so long as he could get away from it himself; he wasn't logical, but then few people were. When Harold, and many others like him, obeyed an irresistible urge to move on to new and wilder places, they carried with them the seeds of the very things from which they were trying to escape. The Government, which could not bear to think of people evading its clutches, would stretch out a tentacle, and before long there would be a post office, a tax collector, a flag; it was only a matter of time before railway lines, produce inspectors and schools appeared, and one day factories and flats and tennis clubs. So the shunners became the spreaders, and people like Harold were hard at work destroying their own salvation. They always hoped that things would last their lifetime, and sometimes their hopes were realized, for their lives were often cut short. But those who survived the various hazards found they had not looked facts in the face.

Perhaps that was their characteristic: they were romantics, and thought of themselves as torch-bearers of civilization, while all the time in their hearts they loved the dark places, which they did not really think dark at all, and feared the torch. Although they hunted wild animals themselves, they hated to see these animals exterminated; and yet they wanted to breed better cattle, finer sheep, which could not be done among the wild beasts. In fact their whole lives, so simple on the surface, were a mass of complexities and contradictions. 'And each man kills the thing he loves,' Robin quoted, and said that this would one day be the epitaph on all pioneers.

The night was cold, our single fly-sheets scarcely broke a chilly wind, damp rose from the ground to penetrate our blankets. So clear was the sky that the Milky Way looked like a plume of spray thrown across it by the bursting of some colossal breaker and held there in a myriad frozen droplets. Above us the peak loomed silently in darkness. Rocks were black as tarn water, grass a misty grey, mysterious shapes waited on the fringe of vision, and we seemed to be afloat on some motionless

53

vessel high above all the oceans of the world. I was glad to huddle into my nest-like sleeping-bag.

'We should have brought more blankets,' Tilly remarked.

'You said we were to travel light,' said Robin.

'Blankets don't weigh much, and would be more useful than that dumpy level you insisted on bringing.'

'What's the good of looking at the land if we don't take proper levels?'

'It's a lovely bit of country,' Tilly said with a tinge of regret, suggesting that its beauty was greater than its value.

'For mountain goats ... I think we must be careful of Oram.'

'Careful?'

'He seems awfully keen on our taking up this land. Says it would be good for his wife to have another woman handy. Do you know, she makes their own candles out of eland fat? And cures snake-bite from an infusion of a wild shrub? And makes awfully good scones. With a skillet, she said. What is a skillet, exactly?'

'American for frying-pan.'

'They were awfully good scones.'

Next morning there was a film of ice over the jug water, and the air stung as you drew it into your lungs. From beneath the tent-fly I watched the world change from grey to silver as the strengthening light touched a film of cobwebs lying on the tufty grasses, each strand beaded with dew. Majestic and tender, the great peak stood up against a rose and saffron sky, its rocks and glaciers black and white like ostrich feathers. But lower down, a layer of mist obscured everything. After a while it enveloped us, and isolated our camp in a clammy island. Voices were muffled and strange. I slid reluctantly from my fleecy nest and shivered while I pulled on my clothes. Harold, who went out early to shoot for the pot, came back empty-handed, and reported that a herd of buffalo had been grazing a few hundred yards away, placidly as cattle, ignoring our camp.

We spent most of the day looking for beacons. I pictured a beacon as a large, unlit bonfire, like those ignited to celebrate the defeat of the Armada, but Tilly assured me that they were merely short lengths of angle-iron stuck in the ground to mark the extremities of the holding. Late in the afternoon

54

one was found, and this proved to be the case; a few stones were heaped round its feet. We never found the others, and no doubt elephants or buffaloes had demolished them.

'Something very odd has happened to the rivers,' Robin complained. 'The map shows at least a dozen. Have you seen even one?'

'It's the dry season,' Harold said. 'We've crossed a lot of gullies. They all flow in the rains.'

'What do the sheep do in the dry weather? Give up water for three months?'

'You could run it as a hill farm,' Harold suggested. 'Bring the sheep down in the dry season. You must admit the grazing's superb.'

Robin looked wily. 'And where would they go in the dry season?'

'Good heavens, man, look at the country! Empty as a pauper's larder from here to Nyeri. You could buy a bit of land for next to nothing down on the plains. I might even let you have a bit of mine if you liked.'

Robin shot Tilly a triumphant look, gave a knowing smile and lit up one of his small cheroots. 'Thank you very much,' he said, gazing intently at the end to see if it was burning.

We had a tiring day, stumbling about on horseback among tufts of coarse grass, up and down steep ravines and through an occasional tongue of forest. Njombo continued to deplore the whole expedition and harped on the number of spirits and devils that abounded in these chilly regions.

'What sort of devils?' I inquired.

'Bad devils, very bad indeed.'

'What do they look like?'

'People do not see devils. It would kill them if they did.'

'Then how do you know there are devils here?'

'Do you see any vultures?' Njombo asked.

'No, not now.'

'If bwana shot a buck, in half an hour there would be many vultures, thick as ants. So I know there are vultures here. Also devils.'

'There is no one here they can harm.'

'Devils do not stay in one place. Perhaps they come here

55

to rest, or to hold circumcision ceremonies. Who knows? They should be left alone. We shall fall sick if we stay any longer.'

To what extent Njombo really believed in the devils, I was not sure; he was cold and uncomfortable and wanted to go home. Certainly he believed in spirits, who shared his world and needed constant appeasement by sacrifices if they were to be kept in a benign frame of mind. They were the spirits of relatives recently dead. Devils were different: they were no one's relatives, and stories about them were told to children, and over the fire at night. As we rode Njombo told me one about a girl called Wanjiru, who ran away from home because her mother beat her when she broke a water-gourd. She had a small brother, and he ran away too. They wandered for a month through the forest until they came to a clearing and a hut, whose owner, a very tall man, offered them shelter and killed three goats for them to eat.

Whenever they wanted to leave, the tall man killed another goat and they stayed to eat it, and the girl grew extremely fat. One day a fly settled on Wanjiru's face and said: 'I have a message, but I shall deliver it only when you give me some blood.' Wanjiru drove the fly away, but her brother said: 'Let us hear what it has to say,' and pricked her finger. 'Your host is a man-eater,' said the fly, 'and you are to be killed tomorrow. Strip off all your ornaments and clothes, disguise yourself in grass and leaves, and hide in the forest.'

Wanjiru took the fly's advice and fled to the forest with her brother, dressed in leaves. They met the man-eater, who was on his way to invite his friends to the feast. This ogre looked at her and said: 'That's a poor girl, a beggar, not Wanjiru,' and passed on his way to tell his friends to come next day. But he got back to find his hut empty. However hard he searched, he could not find Wanjiru. 'Now my friends will be very angry,' he said. 'I must hide from them.' So he dug a hole in the floor, got into it, and covered its mouth with a big cooking pot.

Next day his friends arrived. They found the hut empty, except for skulls and bones left from previous feasts. 'He's cheated us!' they exclaimed. They searched the hut: a skull fell down and smashed the cooking-pot. They saw a man

56

inside. 'Here's our feast!' they cried, and ate him up. They were all man-eaters. 'In the forest there are many, many man-eaters,' Njombo ended, 'with heads as big as granaries and hair all over. They can make themselves invisible. The forest is a bad place, and we should go home.'

Robin shared Njombo's distaste, if for different reasons, for these bleak, windswept moorlands. However splendid the scenery, however bright the air and wide the sky, to make a living here seemed impossible. The native breed of brown, hairy little sheep came from the plains and would infallibly have died here to the last one, even if provided with permanent water. So we slithered down the forest path again, through bamboos and cedars, to the Orams', which seemed no longer at the back of beyond but in the hub of civilization, as no doubt it always seemed to Harold and Mabel.

The Oram family had enjoyed a quiet interlude: they had killed three puff-adders in the stable, acquired a baby serval cat, and lost a calf to a pack of hyenas. The two smaller boys had come out in veld sores and Geraint had shot Guinevere in the leg with an arrow, but the family had perfected its rendering of *Alouette* and started to learn their parts for a simplified version of *The Tempest* they proposed to act out of doors to celebrate the flax-harvest. It was a pity none of the audience would understand a word of English, since Prospero and Caliban were characters they would instantly have recognized, but Geraint was to give a résumé of the plot in the Meru tongue, in so far as the story lent itself to translation.

This perhaps was not very far. To begin with, the Meru people had never heard of the sea, and the best that could be done to describe a ship was 'a thing like a cart that travels on top of a great deal of water'. Even then, for cart you had to use the Indian word *ghari*. If you stuck strictly to Meru, for cart you would have to say 'a thing made of wood on top of things that are round like pots and roll like stones', or something of that sort, for as both boxes and wheels were unknown, the language had no words for them. The simple word shipwreck would then become something like: 'the thing that travels on top of the water like the thing made of wood on top of things that roll like stones broke, and the people inside it fell into the water', so it was probable that the Meru would gather only a hazy idea of the story. However, they would certainly enjoy the performance, especially if they could use it as an excuse to brew beer; and they would understand about the spirits, although Prospero did not visibly perform any of his magic.

The Orams urged us to stay for the performance, for which no exact date had been fixed, nor indeed would it be – they would put on the play when the spirit moved them, summoning an audience by a blast on an old Meru war-horn they had bought for a blanket and some tobacco. As we rode away in the early morning there was a fresh tang of dew and cedar in the keen air.

Chapter 5

ON our way home we stayed with the Beatties by the Amboni River, whose banks supported groves of Cape Chestnuts that came out all over in a froth of pale pink flowers, like apple blossom on a much larger scale. Colonel Beattie was an Anglo-Irishman who had left the Indian Cavalry to devote himself mainly to horses, sport and whisky, while his wife had taken up dogs. A pack of enormous wolf-hounds occupied the cluster of rondavels in which the Beatties lived when they could squeeze their way in. To make room for us, a litter of puppies and an ailing foal had been re-housed. Everything at the Beatties seemed to be breeding, and a crisis was nearly always going on.

The Beatties themselves had only two children. Alan, who was twenty-two, had been intended by his father for an army career, but this had been cut short by some nameless misdemeanour. He was now living at home and, we understood, kicking his heels. His sister Barbara should, like me, have been at school, although she was nearly three years older, and therefore to me an object of nervous suspicion, as to her I was an object of tolerant contempt. Attached to the household was a young ex-Naval Commander who was learning to farm, though whether from the best instructors was a matter for doubt. At any rate he was learning polo. Colonel Beattie kept a log mounted on four legs in a cage of wire-netting so shaped that the ball always ran back to rest beside the wooden horse, and spent a lot of time lashing about with a polo-stick. On our first morning I was awakened by what I took to be a fusillade of rifle shots, accompanied by furious bellows and shouts and by the hollow, hungry baying of wolf-hounds. I cowered under the bed clothes, expecting at the least an attack by Masai warriors, but it was only Colonel Beattie at his early morning devotions in the cage and Mrs Beattie feeding the wolf-hounds. Commander Strudwick had to spend part of his day in the cage, but was not so enthusiastic.

I had been told more than once, as we rode along, that Barbara Beattie would be a nice companion for me, and no doubt she had been told the same, with the result that we took an instant dislike to each other. She was not only older but a great deal prettier and better educated than I. In my opinion she gave herself airs, and I distrusted her jaunty Irish attitude of taking life as it came, which I thought affected; besides, she boasted. I heard a lot about the grandness of their life in India, the servants and ponies and banquets and obsequious subalterns, all wildly in love with her. I was still too young to take an interest in young men as such, whereas she was of an age to think of little else. She was hard at work on the Commander, but he was quite resolved to concentrate on learning how to breed sheep and grow vines.

The Beatties, like everyone else, were building their dwelling by stages. They had started with the stables and got half-way with a living-room made of cedar logs and planks, which smelt delicious, but they slept in mud-and-wattle rondavels with open apertures for windows and never shut doors, so as not to interfere with the wolf-hounds' impulses. It was muddled up together; to reach the dairy, for instance, you had to go through the bathroom, and there was a story that the Kikuyu who made the butter, a gentle, oldish man, once walked through the bathroom with a pail in his hand while Mrs Beattie was in the bath. She was then new to the country and her Swahili limited to a few words, so all she could think of to say was the greeting 'Jambo'. The Kikuyu, a polite man, halted and said, 'Jambo, memsabu,' in return. Either losing her head, or thinking that the word might mean 'go away', Mrs Beattie repeated 'Jambo', and the Kikuyu, not liking to proceed while his employer's wife wished to address him, repeated 'Jambo' too. This went on for some time and Mrs Beattie said they would have been there saying 'Jambo' to each other still had a wolf-hound not bounded in and tried to get at the milk, which obliged the Kikuyu to break off the exchange of courtesies and make a dive for the dairy.

The Beatties seemed always to be doing something strenuous like rounding up flocks of sheep, or breaking in ponies, or galloping across the tufted plains, which were full of pig-holes, to shoot buck from the saddle with carbines. On Sunday mornings, Colonel Beattie went pig-sticking with one or two of his more sporting neighbours – if neighbour is the right word; Europeans were thinly scattered and the nearest farmer, an Afrikaner, was four or five miles away and took no interest in pig-sticking.

Wart-hogs were the Colonel's prey, and he speared only males; but his sport broke up many unions, for the wart-hogs went about in families with the male in front, his tushes white and ferocious-looking, followed by the slightly smaller female and then by a string of four or five little pigs in single file, their tails erect as flagpoles with a little tuft, like the flag, on top. They trotted with an impudent air at astonishing speed, and could outpace a pony until they tired, which they did easily; but the plains were so full of holes they had a good chance of escaping down one of them – always backwards – when pursued. Pig-sticking was dangerous because of these holes, and the Colonel and his friends were always taking tosses and coming back with cuts and bruises, sometimes with concussion or a broken collarbone.

I was anxious to go pig-sticking, but even Barbara was not allowed to take part – although she and the *syce*, according to her own account, had speared many pigs, unbeknown to her parents, after the most hair-raising adventures. To console me, Mrs Beattie said I might go next morning with Alan to shoot buck for the wolf-hounds; Alan looked furious, and mumbled something about not being cluttered up with kids.

'What time will you start?' I inquired.

'Oh, pretty early, I expect.' From this I inferred that he hoped to get off before I was awake, so I asked Njombo to call me at five o'clock.

'Shall we take the ponies?'

'Hardly worth it. I shall go on foot.' What I did, he implied, was none of his business.

Alan Beattie was a great disappointment to his father, who came of an army family and believed in discipline, a smart appearance, tradition and drinking the King's health with the port. Alan dressed on all occasions in a pair of torn and dust-stained khaki trousers and a shirt that could have done with a wash, he wore no socks and his nails were seldom clean. His father said he was slovenly and his manners boorish, and I found myself unexpectedly on the Colonel's side. Alan either ignored or snubbed me, and spent most of his days out on the plains shooting buck, or in the forest in search of buffalo. He was a tall, thin young man with hollow temples and a black moustache, good-looking in a saturnine way, and his eye sometimes had a sparkle in it that suggested he would be good company, if he tried. Obviously he did not try because that would please his father, the last thing he wanted to do.

As I had suspected, he left when the darkness was only just beginning to fade and stars still showed, if faintly, in the sky. Thanks to Njombo I was ready, clutching a little ·22 rifle Robin had let me use at Thika to shoot at birds. I had insisted on bringing it with me, so far to no purpose, and now I hoped its chance would come.

'What do you want with that thing?' he asked.

'It's my rifle. I might get a shot.'

'You do talk nonsense. D'you think you could drop a kongoni at three hundred yards with that? Here, if you want to carry something you can take this.' He handed me a much larger, heavier gun; the darkness hid his expression, but I suspected a wolfish smile. We set off, with one attendant, at a brisk pace, and soon the wet grass soaked me to the waist and wrapped itself round my ankles. But the sky was lightening, and the sun would soon make us dry and warm.

The freshness of the smells on the Amboni was what most

61

struck me: quite different smells from those at Thika, more
cedary and sharp and clean. I think there is a smell of open
plain and wind and distance, although no one could describe
it: just as you could feel the presence of the mountain, even
though, soon after sunrise, it was hidden by cloud. The Amboni flowed in a ravine clothed in forest; around it, the country
rolled away in undulating plains spotted with clumps of bush.
When the light grew stronger, Alan slowed down and walked
cautiously, halting often to scan the landscape for the twitch
of a tail-tip or the glimpse of a 'frozen' head with ears erect,
half-screened by bush. If the buck saw you first, they would
vanish in an instant, simply melt away.

Just after sunrise, we reached the summit of a low ridge
whence we could see across a shallow, rocky ravine to a thorn-
speckled slope the other side whose higher reaches were
flooded by a honey-coloured light. There stood, quite motionless, a group of three large, sandy-coated antelope with long,
tapering horns curved back a little like a bow, and a streak of
black down their white-muzzled faces. They were looking
away from us, at a dark patch of bush. Alan very slowly began
to raise his rifle: it was a longish shot, but a fair one for a
good marksman. A spear of early sunlight made their pelts
glow like soft gold. I had been told that the legend of the
unicorn was derived from this shy, handsome oryx with its
slender horns, seen in profile.

Alan had almost got the rifle to his shoulder when our
attendant, a Kikuyu called Matu, gave a low hissing sound,
which he repeated more urgently when Alan paid no attention.
Then he pointed at the bush at which the oryx were looking.
Something moved in the dense undergrowth. We stood rigid,
scarcely daring to breathe, for what seemed like hours, while
the bush shook and appeared to get larger, and the sun on our
backs grew stronger, and the shadows in front of us slowly
crept in. We heard a snort, saw something tossing, and a
black rhino stepped out of the bush and advanced in a stately
manner, but with surprising speed, towards the oryx; and then
an exact replica, about a quarter of the size, emerged too, and
walked in single file behind its mother. They paid no attention
to the oryx, but passed them in a purposeful way, the mother

swaying her head with its heavy scimitar-shaped horn from side to side. Alan waved me back and we retreated step by step with the utmost caution, keeping a bush in between us and the rhinos. A rhino's eyesight is, in fact, very poor, and we were downwind but, as Alan said, one never knew, and probably the male rhino was close at hand.

'Spoilt my shot,' Alan complained. 'I suppose I should get into real hot water if I bagged a rhino with you here.'

'It was a female, anyway,' I said.

'It's all the same with rhino: they're vermin, more or less. Dangerous brutes.'

'But there was a *toto*.'

'You wouldn't get sentimental over little rhinos if you'd ever had a big one on your tail. I'd have had 'em both if you hadn't been here. Pity about those oryx, too. Well, let's move on.'

We went on, and for a long time. The rifle I was carrying grew heavier and the bush emptier and emptier of anything but rocks, tufts of grass, spiky bush, wind-bent acacias and grey gritty soil that got into my shoes. It grew exceedingly hot, and the sky began to fill up with those mountainous, fluffy, multi-coloured cumulus clouds that were a sure sign of a dry, blazing day. The supposedly abundant game had vanished. The country grew more and more open, and whistling thorns appeared. In the distance we saw herds of gazelle, but they stayed in the distance, and there was insufficient cover for us to stalk them.

'Are we going in the direction of home?' I asked.

'Getting tired?' Alan's voice had a half-hopeful, half-gloating ring that made me say: 'Of course not. I just wondered.' But Matu grinned at me and took the rifle. 'Nothing to shoot here,' he said. A secretary-bird, large as a turkey, with a long, tufted tail supposed to resemble a quill pen lumbered across the plain and took off heavily. A pair of speckled bustards ran ahead of us through the long grass. Alan, of course, was doing this deliberately to get his own back. My stomach complained loudly of its emptiness, but I felt sure he must be just as hungry as I.

From the top of an ant hill, Alan saw some eland before

they saw him. No doubt he thought the joke had gone far
enough; he told Matu and me to wait in the shade of a small
thorn-tree, tested the wind and disappeared into the long grass
in a crouching posture. Then he vanished, and I supposed
that he was wriggling his way on his stomach, getting scratched
and torn, and zigzagging from bush to bush, as invisible to the
eland as to me, running with sweat and tense with excitement.
My ears seemed stretched to catch the rifle's crack. When it
came, one of the eland reared up, leapt forward a few paces
and fell. It was a big, tawny bull, big as a native bullock, and
it lay stretched on its side.

'How are you going to get it home?' I asked.

'We'll have to cover it up, and send boys. It isn't far.'

'It's miles and miles!'

'Not more than four. We'll be back by ten.'

'You said we'd be back early.'

'Well, you didn't have to come.'

'You didn't have to walk so far to find something to shoot.'

'That's my business.'

'Well, I call it silly.'

'For God's sake stop kicking up a row and make yourself
useful. The sooner we get this covered up, the sooner you
can get shot of my company.'

While Matu hacked off thorn branches with his hunting
knife, Alan and I piled them on the dead eland to protect it
from vultures, which were already circling high overhead. As
soon as we left, they would gather all round it like a meeting
of obscene old men, with their blood-red beaks and bald
heads and air of evil, sullen and angry at their inability to
penetrate the thorny barricade.

We walked back crossly and in silence, and it was closer
than I thought: Alan must have led us in a circle. Quite near
the farmstead we simultaneously saw a long, yellow shape with
a flat head and small folded ears streaking like a snake through
the grass, the black tip of a tail stretched out behind it. Alan
saw, aimed and fired almost in a single action. He rolled it over
with a splendid shot as its head rose for a moment above the
grasses. I ran towards it, and then remembered that you should
never approach a slain beast of any dangerous species until

64

after the second shot. But Alan did not pause. I found him bending over an outstretched, supple yellow body spotted with black. The black rubbery pads were enormous for the size of the beast, the powerful haunches strong and low-slung, like those of a racehorse, it was lean and springy, and seemed to glow with power. Its face was round and whiskered, just like a cat's.

'I thought it was a lioness,' I said, disappointed.

'They look a bit the same when they're going. This is a good skin, so I won't take risks.' So the cheetah was eviscerated and skinned, the heap of purple entrails and bloody flesh it was reduced to left to feed vultures, and Matu rolled up the skin, tied it with strips of bark peeled from a tree, and carried it back on his shoulder. It was pliant as a suede glove and had a fine barbaric look, although to man the cheetah is not a savage beast at all, but can easily be tamed. The Governor of the day possessed a cheetah that had the freedom of the house and had sent a visiting grandee's lady into hysterics when it met her on the stairs; and it used to jump onto the table during meetings of his Executive Council, scattering documents of state with a tail lashing in affection.

Tilly was annoyed that we had been away so long, imagining some disaster, and cross with me when she should have blamed Alan, who was praised by his mother for meeting the wolf-hounds' needs.

'If he spent one-tenth of the time he spends fooling about with that rifle, in looking after the sheep, he'd be some use to someone,' Colonel Beattie grumbled.

'You wouldn't like it if he wasn't fond of sport,' his mother pointed out.

'Fond of it! You can be fond of a glass of whisky without drinking all day from dawn to bedtime. I had to work for my sport when I was his age, lucky if I got a fortnight a year. He just helps himself, idle young pup.'

'Young men must sow their wild oats.'

'If that's wild oats, I'm the Akond of Swat. Wild oats came up a different colour from that when I was a lad, and they took a bit more sowing, too, I can tell you!' The Colonel roared with laughter and slapped his leg.

'You wouldn't like it any better if he did *that*,' Mrs Beattie said.

The Beatties were always arguing, it gave them an interest in life and the Colonel an excuse to soothe his nerves with Irish whisky. Alan never drank. It seemed to be a characteristic of the Beatties that whatever any of them did, was done to excess, and with passion; in what they did not do, they took little interest. They were rather like high explosive set for blasting, and you never knew when a detonator might go off.

The cheetah skin was pegged out to dry just outside Alan's rondavel, which had a creeper with clusters of dangling golden flowers climbing up it, a pair of buffalo horns over the door and a gramophone inside, judging by the sounds that emanated from it. He shouted at me to come in and I found him sprawling on his bed with his knees bent and his hands clasped behind his head, smoking a cheroot, the gramophone beside him playing a military march.

'I shouldn't think you'd want to play those tunes,' I ventured. 'I thought you hated the army.'

'That's why I play this stuff lying on my back,' he replied. 'Where I don't have to stand to attention. Besides, they're not bad tunes if you can lie back and enjoy them.'

Photographs of boys and young men in groups, mainly dressed for games or sport, hung round the curved and limewashed walls, together with some fox-hunting prints by Lionel Edwards; skins of various animals completely covered the cement floor. Several rifles occupied a rack by the washstand, even the hair-brushes were ivory-backed, and the only nonsporting notes were struck by a little jade Buddha and two photographs of young women next to the brushes. Both were attractive, one especially so, with blonde hair and bare shoulders. I put her down as an actress. Alan saw me looking at the photographs and grinned. The smile altered his whole appearance, he looked gay and friendly instead of morose.

'My downfall,' he said.

'You mean she was why you got the sack from the army?'

'Indirectly, I suppose you might say so.'

'She looks rather ... well ...'

Alan laughed and kicked one of his legs in the air. 'Rather, well – I daresay she was. There's a lot to be said for rather, well. And, of course, it's expensive. I'll tell you what's wrong with life – whether you come into money or whether you make it, you don't get it till you're too old to do anything with it but sit on your backside and read *The Times* and totter up now and then to spray the roses. Everyone ought to start with money when they're young and have such lots of ways to spend it. When they get older they need less and it could be tapered off. Everything's the wrong way round.'

It was a surprise to find that Alan could be so talkative, even if his ideas sounded, like all the Beatties', peculiar. Anxious to keep the conversation going, I shouted above the climax of the march: 'My parents have an overdraft.'

'So have mine; but as soon as I want one of my own, I'm in trouble. It's damned unfair.'

'Is that why you got into trouble?'

'Well, indirectly. I loathed the army anyway.'

'I would have thought it must be rather fun.'

'It wasn't my idea of fun.' Alan was changing the record and winding up the machine; he nodded towards a pile of discs and said: 'There's the army for you – and you're the needle, stiff and shiny, going round and round for ever in the same groove.'

'A needle's only in the same groove when it gets stuck,' I pointed out.

'My God, you do argue.'

'I wasn't arguing, it's just a fact. When the needle goes round properly, it plays different tunes.'

'It's in the same groove, isn't it? One groove all round the record. And the same tune repeated half a dozen times. Tumpity-tump. Suppose the needle jumped clean out of the groove and started to hop about on its own, everyone would be disgusted.'

'It would scratch the record.'

'So it would. And did, but the army's an awfully impervious record. You've got a very literal mind, haven't you?'

'Well, I don't know.'

'I was going to offer you a present.'

'Oh, thank you. But it's not my birthday or anything.'

67

The music was now easier to compete with, the military marches having given way to a wailing kind of blues that reminded me of dark, thick native honey, and was very sad.

'You can have that cheetah skin if you like.'

'That's awfully kind of you.'

'It isn't a bit, because I've got one already, and if I wanted it myself I wouldn't give it away. Do you know how to cure it properly?'

'We just rub alum into ours.'

'It wants a bit more than that, or you get it as stiff as a board and the hair falls out. I suppose I'll have to do it for you.'

'If it's a lot of trouble ...'

'It's some trouble, but not a lot; anyway it's a pity to waste such a good skin. I'll send it down some time when it's ready.'

'Thanks awfully ...'

'Don't keep thanking me. Anyway, there's your mother calling you.'

I had heard her too, but had tried to pretend I had not. 'Parents are always calling one,' Alan added. 'Especially mothers. Sometimes it seems to be about all they can do. One should either stuff one's ears with cotton wool or go to Australia. But I suppose it's different for a girl.'

'I think it's worse.'

I looked at the cheetah skin with pleasure as I went out; it was indeed a fine one and, as Alan had shot it through the head, unmarked. He might have sold it in Nairobi, and as he seemed short of money I thought he was being generous, even if in a grumpy way. But I kept his promise to myself, in case Tilly said I oughtn't to take the skin; in any case I had not yet got it, and Alan might forget, or change his mind.

Mrs Beattie was bringing the dogs back from their evening exercise. When she had first arrived in the country, she had insisted on riding side-saddle, but the local ponies had not taken to it, and now she bestrode her mount in a heavy divided skirt of hunting green that fell to her ankles, a tight-fitting green corduroy jacket with silver buttons and a topee that had once been white. Seen amid a cloud of lean, grey wolf-hounds bounding all round her with their red tongues lolling she was an imposing sight, though Tilly said she was like a pantomime version of Robin Hood riding to the joustings at Nottingham. Sometimes Barbara exercised the pack and on these occasions, but never on any others, they chased a lioness up a tree or fought off a pack of wild dogs. After supper we played draughts. I admired a bead necklace she was wearing, and she told me that it was a present from a young man who had obtained it in Mecca, where he had penetrated the holy places disguised as an Arab; he had been caught and tortured, but had escaped, stowed away on a dhow and fetched up in Mombasa, where he was working for the secret service against the Japanese.

'But why the Japanese?'

'Don't you know? There are dozens of them at Mombasa working as pearl-fishers. But really they're making charts of the harbour, ready for the Japanese invasion.'

I did not know whether or not to believe her. After we had started home next morning I asked Robin, who roared with laughter, and said she ought to make her fortune writing adventure yarns or for the movies. Like all the Beatties, she did nothing by halves, and I envied her the ability to enjoy in her mind so many things that had never really happened.

As we rode away the wolf-hounds were baying for their food, a fusillade of shots and a stream of curses from the wire cage indicated that the Colonel was enjoying his morning polo, Alan had sloped off with a rifle and Barbara waved frantically from the veranda, as if warning us against footpads, savage beasts and natural disasters. It was a relief, in a way, to leave the Beatties; but the cool windy air of the sweeping plains, the bushy gullies with their hidden life, the frothy mountain ranges of cumulus cloud piled one upon the other, the groves of pink-blossomed Cape Chestnuts by the Amboni, and then high above them the ponderous, cloud-screened purple bulk of the mountain – all these things possessed a magic that had already rooted in the memory, and twisted its tendrils into the mind.

Chapter 6

THE farm next to us at Thika had been bought by a new-comer called Harry Clewes. The Palmers had started it before the war, but they had not come back. Hereward Palmer had risen to become a General in the war, but Lettice had left him, and even Tilly, who had been her friend, did not know what had become of her. Tilly had received a postcard from Cannes and then a small, antique statue of a dog attacking an antelope from Ragusa, accompanied by a card scrawled in large, impulsive writing: ' "The days that make us happy make us wise." With love always, Lettice.' Then she had dropped right out of our lives. Tilly heard a rumour that she had married a Frenchman and, some time later, that she had fallen out of a window and killed herself in Tangier, but never found out if either of these stories was true. Now the Clewes were coming to live in the Palmers' well-built stone house, much grander than any other in the district. Robin met the Clewes in Nairobi, and came back to tell us that the newly-arrived family was about to move to the farm.

'A youngish fellow,' Robin said. 'He was in the Flying Corps in the war. They must have money, hers I should think, he's got a ripping new Dodge, and Hereward Palmer wouldn't have sold for a song. Clewes talks about putting in electric light and taking out an irrigation furrow if there's enough fall.'

Tilly sighed. 'It would be a nice change if sometimes you noticed what people were *like*, not the make of their cars and their views on machinery.'

Robin looked downcast, and said lamely: 'He seemed quite friendly. Bit of a rough diamond, I daresay. Someone hinted he was rather a lady-killer, I forget who, but he won't find many ladies here to kill, unless they're dusky ones. He's bring-ing, so to speak, a spare; they have a kind of nursery governess for their brats.'

'That might be useful,' Tilly said. 'They might like to share her.'

'I think their brats are younger than ours, but I didn't see them. Mrs Clewes seemed a rather silly woman, the sort who'd stay in bed for breakfast, but I only saw her for a moment.'

'Not the sort to know how to adjust a carburettor or grind a cylinder. When I see a female mechanic on the horizon, I shall know the time's come to feel the pangs of jealousy.'

'It's my place to feel them, really,' Robin said.

'I've tried hard for years to arouse them, but I'm not a new kind of flywheel, or a scheme for harnessing the Victoria Falls, so I am afraid I might as well give it up as a bad job ... If the Clewes are rich, I expect he'll want to buy some properly-trained ponies. If we could buy two or three raw ones, cheap, and I gave them a bit of schooling, we might turn an honest penny. It's worth looking into.'

'Yes; but you know what Playfair said about the overdraft.'

'Perhaps we could sell the Somali pony, for a start; he goes lame sometimes for no apparent reason, and has a mouth like iron, and not a very nice temperament.'

'In that case we could hardly sell him to one of our friends.'

'No, but he's just right for one of our enemies. If you come to think of it, they're more useful than friends, because one always has more dud things to sell than good ones; we must set about making more enemies.'

News of the Clewes' impending arrival had gone round by bush-telegraph, and next day Njombo remarked: 'A bwana with enormous wealth has come; they say he is bringing many fat cattle, and several motor-cars, and he has two wives already, and perhaps others he has left behind in Europe.'

'He's not allowed more than one,' I objected.

'What is the use of wealth, if a man has only one wife? But you are wrong, this bwana has two, both coming to Thika; the senior one is plump, and has two children, but the other is thin and barren.'

I was curious to see the children, but afraid I should be told to play with them, which would be boring because they were much younger than I. As they were looked after by a nursery governess they would be clean and tidy, and wear

71

respectable clothes. Mine consisted of a pair of khaki shorts and a bush shirt with large pockets, and I had no wish to wear anything else.

When they appeared, they proved to be twins of four – a third of my age and, as companions, even more useless than I had feared. Their names were Vicky and Simon and they lived under the thumb of Miss Cooper, the nursery governess, a dark-haired, sallow woman with prominent teeth, long jade ear-rings and a necklace of hard, shiny stones. With the children she was strict and with the adults chatty, contributing her remarks to the conversation as if they had been large, heavy stones. By contrast Mrs Clewes' remarks were more like butterflies flitting from leaf to leaf and brushing you with their wings; no observation appeared to follow from its predecessor and before you had time to work out a connection, she had gone on to something else. She was small and, as Njombo had observed, inclined to plumpness, and made many little gestures with a fluttery pair of hands kept soft and white. In a doll-like way she was pretty, with a fresh complexion, neat little features and deepset eyes, and she dressed in flowery *crêpe-de-Chine* to create an effect of rather exaggerated femininity.

'I'm quite enchanted with everything,' she exclaimed. 'Although the house needs a little tidying up – there seem to be white ants everywhere, there are bees in the roof and nothing left of the garden – but, of course, dear Harry is so clever at everything, he will know how – I've been given some jacaranda seeds and told to boil them, do you think that can be right? They can't be boiled in nature, and I was brought up to believe that nature knows best, but of course that was in Yorkshire. Have you met the Braithwaites there? They are my cousins – like characters from Surtees I always think, the house is full of masks and brushes, there are always wet boots and breeches being dried and boiled eggs for tea. In the war it was a hospital of course, Harry took such a fancy to the maze but the peacocks got on his nerves, they were so frayed after his crash, his nerves I mean. He was going to Australia, until he met a friend who persuaded him – so instead of sheep and blue gums I suppose it will be lions and savages. A girl my brother

72

was engaged to once, so attractive, from Northumberland too, but it wouldn't have done, she thought of nothing but horses and he's very fond of gardening, especially topiary, such an odd taste, don't you think, for a man, and wouldn't go with horses, but she – now how did I get on to Cecily? It's snakes I'm afraid of, it all comes from reading *The Speckled Band* as a child, and at home we had bell-ropes in the bedrooms, I don't think they worked, and the housekeeper had an illegitimate baby, but I don't think he's going to grow up to be another H. G. Wells. What happens here if the twins are ill, is there a doctor anywhere, what does one do?'

'One goes to Nairobi,' Tilly said. 'There are plenty of doctors there, if you can persuade any of them to take an interest in you. Most of them work for the Government, and only take non-officials in their spare time. But there's always Dr Burkitt.'

'He sounds a little as if he was a doctor you fell back on. Do you think he would do for the twins?'

'That's always the danger. But I know several patients of his who are still alive.'

Miss Cooper, looking shocked, intervened to say: 'Of course, I wouldn't dream of letting the twins go to such a man. Luckily I know a lot myself about children's ailments. When the Armstrongs' little girl was so ill, and the doctors unable to find the cause of the trouble, I nursed her night and day for a week and Dr Kirby said to me: "Miss Cooper, there is nothing I can teach you about children's illnesses, I have complete confidence in you." So I hope that we shall not need a doctor, while I am here.'

Mrs Clewes and Tilly murmured something; Miss Cooper exerted an effect like that of South American arrow-poisons said to paralyse the nerve centres and numb the brain. Rallying, Mrs Clewes fluttered her hands and suggested that the twins would like to go and look at the animals.

'You're sure to have animals, I suppose, on a farm? I hope they're quiet. They're getting restless – the twins, I mean. Miss Cooper, do you suppose that you ... I think Simon is going to take after Harry, he loves pulling things to bits, although, of course, it's putting them together that Harry really

73

enjoys. Did you come across the Hunters in Yorkshire? He was connected with steel; they had a most attractive old place but it was haunted by a nun; he said he felt spied upon and ran off with the daughter of a carpet manufacturer, they went to South America. Lydia had a sister in South Africa, I wonder if you've come across her, she married a Colonel Greyson and they went to the Transvaal, or no, I think it was Natal; he had a glass eye, something to do with the Kurds I think, or it may have been the Ashanti; you would like her, she is fond of racing, and weaves her own tweeds . . .'

'We are some way from Natal,' Tilly pointed out. It was as I had feared; I was palmed off on the twins and Miss Cooper. I forgot my hat, and when I came back to retrieve it I heard Mrs Clewes saying in eager tones, leaning towards Tilly : 'My dear, she came out with a mountain of luggage, really a mountain, and do you know, one of the boxes was absolutely full of *double sheets*!'

I showed the twins the ponies and some hens, turkeys and tame guinea-fowl but, as I had expected, they were not much interested, and darted about like beetles on a pond. Miss Cooper asked a lot of questions, first of all about my parents and then about our neighbours, especially Alec.

'This Mr Wilson must have made a lot of money,' she remarked, 'if he stayed behind while everyone else went to the war.'

'It wasn't his fault, the doctors wouldn't pass him; besides, he worked much harder than lots of people who got on to the staff.'

'I wasn't saying anything against him; it was very sensible, I think. I suppose he got paid for all the farms he ran, and kept his own in good condition . . . What sort of house has he got?'

'Just an ordinary one, like ours.'

'Do you call yours ordinary? It seems quite peculiar to me. The walls rustle all the time, I suppose with insects, and you never know what's going to drop out of the roof; and all those lizards . . . It's a wonder he hasn't built himself something better, since he's comfortably off.'

'I expect he's been too busy. Besides . . .'

There was nothing wrong with Alec's house, I wanted to say; it had one big room whose well-tied thatch rose above a forest of wattle-poles, and reed-lined walls like ours, and a cement floor covered with skins, and a big stone fireplace, and it was cool, airy and light. Like nearly everyone else he slept in a rondavel with bougainvillea climbing up the walls; there was no bathroom, but a houseboy brought a tin bath to his hut; the separate kitchen was out at the back and in front was a small veranda where he sat for a drink before dinner. I could not see that Alec needed anything better, but Miss Cooper exuded disapproval, as an aphis exudes honeydew for ants to feed on, when she spoke of the way we all lived at Thika; in her eyes we were not much better than a lot of savages.

'Well, we mustn't be too hard on him,' Miss Cooper said with an air of tolerance. 'He hasn't got a wife to look after him, and keep him up to civilized standards. Perhaps now that he's done so well, he'll think of making changes.'

'Perhaps he will,' I agreed, since Miss Cooper plainly thought a change to be desirable; but I could not imagine Alec with a wife. He liked to organize everything himself, and did it very well; his house was always clean and tidy and his boys cheerful and his meals excellent, I did not see how a wife could improve upon any of these things. Besides, he was well-known to be close with his money; he would spend half an hour haggling with a Kikuyu as to whether he would pay seventy-five cents or one shilling for a basket of fifty eggs, and whether he would give fifty cents or forty-five for a small cockerel.

Seen through Miss Cooper's eyes, I suppose our establishment was, in that useful Swahili word, somewhat *shenzi*. Our temporary house was merely a rectangular shed with two or three rondavels near it, and the foundations of the permanent house, surrounded by half-cut blocks of stone and heaps of soil, looked more like the ruins of an abandoned homestead than the beginnings of a new one. Tilly was an excellent gardener, but her plans had been disorganized by the need to make a new garden round the future house, so that the old one round the existing house became neglected, and the herbaceous border, bright with delphiniums and daisies, poppies

75

and salvias and every vivid-flowered plant, had to be reached over a pile of rubble among waist-high khaki grasses. This brought the advantage that one could watch from concealment the actions of the sunbirds who hovered above the flowers, their wings vibrating like violin strings, their plumage shimmering in the sunlight in a myriad shades of blue and green and bronze, all burnished like a new coin. Their favourite flower was the red-hot poker, and when Tilly discovered this she kept clumps of them especially for the sunbirds, who thrust their long, thin, curved black beaks right through the red and orange florets, puncturing them at the base, to reach the globules of honey.

On the river bank, Robin was erecting a pulper to strip the soft, red outside coat from the coffee fruit, and free the two greyish beans within; and he was making a reservoir to hold water pumped from the river by a ram. Alec already had a reservoir, in which he encouraged us to bathe. It was only a concrete tank, and half a dozen strokes took one across it. Here Tilly gave me swimming lessons, which consisted of pushing me in and telling me to imitate a frog, whose motions were easy to observe, as many lived in the tank. Alec invited the twins to bathe whenever they liked, and Miss Cooper often brought them over in a mule-buggy with a native driver. She told Alec that she would not allow the twins into the water unless a man was present; as Harry Clewes never came, the man had to be Alec.

The twins had water-wings, and could safely be left to splash and kick about without drowning, like playful pink seals, while I practised my swimming and Miss Cooper sat on the bank and talked to Alec. She wore a black two-piece bathing dress with frills round the legs and sleeves, and preened herself like a bird, although she had taken off her necklaces and ear-rings. Apart from her protruding teeth she was not bad-looking; she had fine eyes, a broad forehead and soft wavy brown hair which she brushed a great deal.

'I am glad I have a good figure,' she remarked. 'My waist is only twenty-three inches, and everyone tells me what good ankles I have, which is so important in a woman, don't you think? Mrs Clewes is a dear, and knows how to make the most of herself, but it is a pity about her ankles, poor thing, and she really ought to eat less starchy things, she is getting quite plump.'

'That's fashionable in Africa,' Alec said. 'The natives like their women plump.'

'Well, we're not natives, thank goodness; surely *you* don't let yourself go downhill. I haven't been out here long but I can see at once where the danger lies – losing a grip on our standards. Some of the people who came out before the war seem to live in a very odd way. I shall never let it happen to me, or to any children I look after. As Mrs Clewes said the other day: "Miss Cooper, I know that you have standards; I can trust you with the children better than I can trust myself." Not that I've always looked after children, you know, or have any real need to do so; my father was very much against my taking it up, but I have too independent a nature to live at home and be beholden to anyone; besides, country life at home is boring and futile, and I wanted to see the world. I always wanted to come to Africa. I expect you came out for much the same reasons, Mr Wilson; I can see that you're independent and adventurous too. I think we have a lot in common, although, of course, we don't know each other very well.'

'I came because I was broke, and had no prospects,' Alec replied.

'Really, that was very enterprising; and now I suppose your prospects are excellent. In fact I've heard it said that you have made a great success, Mr Wilson, through hard work and shrewdness, which I admire. I don't at all admire the flighty type of man, the lady-killer you know, the sort of man most women find so attractive; I've no time for frills and graces. Rank and fashion mean nothing to me, I'm not in the least impressed by anything of that kind. But a man who starts with nothing but his own abilities and makes the most of them, that I do admire. It's what I've had to do myself, so I can understand it. I know at once whether a person is my kind or not, and I think we speak the same language. They say you've made yourself very comfortable in your bachelor establishment, Mr Wilson, and that's another thing I admire. I don't respect a man who can't do anything without a woman hanging round him. May I come and see your house one day?'

'I'm afraid it mayn't live up to your expectations; we bachelors, you know, live rough when we're on our own. My cook was a cannibal, and I'm never *quite* sure whether I've converted him, or he's converted me; we have some rather odd meals. But you must come to dinner and see for yourself.'

'Thank you, I should like to; and I can understand when my leg is being pulled as well as anyone; I've always been told my sense of humour is exceptionally keen. I like nothing better than a good laugh, and you'll find me a lively companion. When would you like me to come? Tomorrow, or the next day?'

'Possibly the day after that,' Alec suggested. 'You must give me time to make some preparations; it isn't every day I have such an honour.'

'That's very charming of you; I'm not taken in by what I call soft soap, you know, but all the same I do appreciate good manners and the little courtesies of life, which sometimes seem out here to be lacking. I can see that we agree on many things, Mr Wilson; it's a pleasure to meet someone with whom one feels so instantly in sympathy ... Vicky, stop trying to drown your brother and come out at once; it's time to go home.'

Obviously Vicky and Simon were going to be very well brought up, with a set of proper standards and principles rare in Africa. From the earliest moment the character of a well-brought-up European child is poured like a jelly into a mould of strict routine, and sets in it, whereas African children are permitted to escape this treatment. Since routine is simply a means of controlling time, Europeans are better at it, and therefore accomplish more in a day, a month, or a year. They pay in monotony. Africans control time less efficiently, but enjoy it more: they pay in stagnation. People like Miss Cooper, the jelly-pourers, were the true guardians and transmitters of European predominance; but they were seldom appreciated, and Miss Cooper certainly was not.

Robin had by now sold the two-seater he had been so proud

of and acquired instead a Chevrolet with a box-body much too heavy for it, open on all sides but caged in with wire netting to prevent dogs and native children from hurling themselves out in panic when the vehicle began to move. It did not move fast by our standards, but by theirs, no doubt, it whirled along at a terrifying speed. It had only the one seat, on which you sat bolt upright clutching the sides and feeling like a potato on a riddle, for it had no shock absorbers, and with every bump sat heavily on its springs.

Once a month, Tilly and Robin proceeded to Nairobi to draw the wages, which travelled back in a small sack under the seat, in company with spanners and jacks. Harry Clewes' first visit to our farm coincided with their return from one of these monthly expeditions, and they hurried in to give him tea. He was a muscular man of middle height and a ruddy complexion darkened by the sun, a narrow face, a cleft chin and a small black moustache; he looked tough, but also something of a dandy in a well-cut pair of jodhpurs, a white silk shirt with his initials worked on the pocket and a strip of leopard skin round the crown of his hat. His voice was rather loud and he smiled a lot, possibly less at amusement with the world than at satisfaction with his own qualities. During the war he had won several decorations for gallantry in the Royal Flying Corps and married Betty, whose parents, we understood, owned coal mines and land in Yorkshire.

'I'm making a lot of changes in my shamba,' he told Robin. 'Can't see that my predecessor did much, except for the house of course, and that's got a damned great crack in it. Don't think *he'd* have done much if he'd stayed on – putting up an expensive house before you've got an acre in bearing isn't the way to go about things, eh, Robin? You haven't made *that* mistake, anyway. Though you'll have to do something soon, by the look of it; the water fairly pours in during the rains from that place in the roof over there, I don't mind betting.'

'It saves labour,' Tilly said, a little shortly. 'We put the bath under it, and then the boys don't have to fill it.'

Harry Clewes laughed heartily. 'Always got the ready answer, haven't you, Mrs Robin? You must come over soon and have a meal, and give Betty a few wrinkles. She's keen enough to learn, but it's all a bit strange to her, you know, after York-shire, and I'm not too happy about the way she handles the Kukes. That's the key to everything, of course. I hear some folk are having a lot of trouble over labour, can't get it for love or money, or keep it if they do. Well, I haven't had any trouble so far. All depends how you treat 'em, I say; I'm having some good permanent huts built and I believe in good rations too. A man can't work on an empty stomach, I don't care who he is. But no pampering: you've got to be firm with 'em and fair. That's how I look at it. Right?'

'Oh, certainly,' Robin said with a surprising degree of en-thusiasm. From the abstracted way in which he was puffing at his cigar and gazing at a pair of wagtails on the lawn I knew his mind was not on Harry Clewes' problems, or lack of them, but on how he could lead the conversation round to crocodiles. One of the legacies of his labour-recruiting trip with Mr Nimmo was a belief that our fortunes could be quickly made by trapping crocodiles in Lake Victoria, tanning their skins and turning the rest of them into fertilizer. He and Mr Nimmo had worked out a scheme in detail, from the moment the crocodiles were inveigled up narrow trenches, where they could not turn round, into pits from which they could not escape, to the conclusion when fabulous crops were reaped from fields made fecund by the rich fertilizer they would give rise to; all that was lacking was a small factory and a sales organization; and all that was needed for these was a little capital. Mr Playfair had not been at all helpful, and Robin entertained great hopes that Harry Clewes might wish to have a flutter which could not fail to succeed. Taking the plunge abruptly, he inquired:

'Is your wife fond of crocodile leather shoes?' Harry Clewes looked startled, and answered in slightly less affable tones: 'How do I know, my dear fellow? I've never asked her. I can't remember her wearing any, but I daresay she does sometimes. Whatever put that idea into your head?'

'If she is,' Robin went on firmly, 'you'll know that they're expensive, very expensive indeed. The American demand is so big there's a world shortage of skins. Now, the whole of Lake Victoria is seething with crocodiles, simply alive with

them. And Europe and America full of women wanting crocodile shoes. If one could bring those two things together at a
very low cost ...'

He was interrupted by Mugu, our foreman, who appeared
on the veranda to ask whether Robin had taken the bag of
shillings from under the seat of the car. Normally, Tilly or
Robin removed it themselves and locked it immediately in the
office safe, but on this occasion Harry Clewes' arrival had
distracted them, and Robin had told Mugu to bring the bag
to the house. Mugu now said that he had found no bag of
shillings in the car, and supposed that Robin had taken it, but
that it had just occurred to him to make sure.

A great hue and cry followed. Robin ordered an immediate
search of all the huts, though with little hope of recovering the
cash; there were too many places of concealment – ant-bear
holes, forks of trees, thatched huts, boulders in the river. As
luck would have it, he had extracted an extra large sum from
Mr Playfair to pay the men working on the pulping factory.

'We must resort to threats,' Tilly said.

'Such hollow ones! We can't round them all up and send
them off to Fort Hall, and if we don't get the money back by
nightfall it will disappear for good into the reserve.'

'Everyone must be summoned, and you must read the riot
act.'

Mugu beat with an old iron shaft on the length of the angle-
iron dangling outside the store that summoned the men to
work every morning. This drew almost everyone from the
huts, women as well as men; they gathered in a large concourse
and squatted on their heels if they were men, or stretched
their legs out in front of them if they were women, near the
office where Robin or Mugu marked the tickets, every morning, of those who had reported for work.

Already the sun was dropping behind the horizon, and in
its last piercing rays everything was suddenly to be seen
sharply and in detail, as if magnified; a brown furry caterpillar writhed through a grass-root forest, a speckled fly-
catcher with his white-rimmed eyes preened himself on a
twig of thorn, an armoured beetle waved his antennae as he
scurried for safety on his bent, spurred legs across a bare

patch of earth. Somewhere among those silent, apparently in-different people the secret of the shillings lay hidden, like a bird in a thicket; it was hard to see how any words of Robin's could persuade them to reveal it.

Mugu translated Robin's pidgin Swahili into a much more eloquent peroration. 'According to past customs,' he con-cluded, 'witch-doctors would have smelt out this stealer of shillings and severed his hands or stoned him to death. Now the white men do not allow such things. But the bwana says, I will catch this man. But first, I will give him a chance to bring back the shillings. If he does so before nine o'clock tonight, I will forget this affair and he will not be punished. But if he does not . . .'

Robin paused for effect, and gazed about him. He had a nice dramatic sense, and was enjoying this opportunity to indulge it; his audience was silent but attentive. I hoped that he would not get carried away and threaten things that he could not possibly carry out – divine intervention perhaps, a flash of lightning, an earthquake even, or a sudden affliction of the thief by sores. On the other hand, if he stuck strictly to European rules he would notify the District Commissioner at Fort Hall, who might or might not send out a policeman, if he could spare one, a few days later, by which time the money would long ago have vanished; and the chances of catching the thief would be about as good as the chances of our mule at the Derby.

So Robin was caught between two stools, and had to invent a method of his own. Actually it was Tilly's idea, but he took it up with gusto, and delivered the ultimatum with as much force as he knew how to summon.

'If the thief does not confess before nine o'clock by my watch,' he announced, 'that is in three hours, I will take a burning brand and I will go to every hut on this farm and I will set it alight, and every hut will burn to ashes, and that will include the granaries, and everything you have will be destroyed. Then you will sleep on the ground in the cold night, and your maize and millet will be gone, and your wives will return to their fathers because you will not be able to provide them with a home. I swear that I will do this according to this oath I make to God, and I will do it within three hours if the thief has not returned the money.'

No one said anything when Mugu had finished the translation. Some of the old men hoiked and spat, got to their feet and walked away, and the assembly broke up silently; even the women's voices were stilled. It was the women Tilly was counting on. 'They won't let the men risk losing all the food in the granaries,' she said.

But it was a big risk. If Robin really burnt down all the huts he would not have a leg to stand on legally. The huts, it was true, were his property, but not their contents, and if their occupants took the matter to the D.C. they would certainly be entitled to redress. British law looked to the individual, African law to the group: that was the great difference. In African law, Robin's threat was fair and reasonable, however unpleasant; if one of the group had stolen, the whole group must pay for his crime. Fines were paid by families, not by individuals; and Robin hoped they would accept his judgement and not call his bluff. But a few of the Kikuyu had by now picked up a little knowledge of British customs, enough to know that British law was helpless unless a particular individual could be produced, and others found to swear that they had seen him breaking one of the rules.

They also knew how seldom this could be managed, especially as no one who had in fact seen a man commit a crime would risk retaliation, probably with magic, by publicly accusing him, certainly not if he belonged to the same clan, age-grade or family. So if any person with such modern knowledge had heard Robin's speech, and this was highly probable, he would know, or suspect, that Robin was bluffing, and tell the rest of the Kikuyu that, if Robin really did burn down the huts, he would get into trouble from the D.C. and have to pay compensation.

After a strained and apprehensive meal, we sat on the veranda waiting for zero hour. 'There's less than half an hour to go,' Tilly said.

'Perhaps we could give them until midnight,' Robin suggested. He had still not made up his mind what to do if no one came forward, and was bitterly regretting his threat.

83

'If they don't produce the money before nine, it'll mean they've managed to get it away into the reserve.'

'And that'll be the end of it. I don't know what I shall say to Playfair.'

'I suppose we could sell one of the ponies.'

'That wouldn't cover it. Now, if only I could interest Clewes in this crocodile scheme ...'

'I think Harry Clewes is only interested in one thing, and that's himself. Is that someone coming?'

But it was only a dog scratching itself and thumping a leg on the floor.

'It's almost time,' Robin said. 'How on earth am I to set about this conflagration? Go round with a flaming torch, as if I was starting the Olympic Games?'

'We'll have to go round first to see that everyone's removed themselves, not to mention all the chickens and goats. I make it nine.'

'Let's give them five more minutes.'

We sat in gloomy silence, and Tilly snapped at me for fidgeting. Beetles and flying bugs bumped themselves repeatedly against the lamp-glass, and the usual sad little ring of dead and dying moths surrounded its greasy base.

'Well, I suppose I'd better summon Mugu,' Robin said at last. At that moment a dark form approached the veranda and stood before us, on the fringe of light. A cough sounded, and Robin said: 'Come forward, who's that?'

'It is I, Mugu.'

'Very well. Is there news?'

'Bwana, I have good news. Look, the shillings have returned!'

He stepped forward and dropped a heavy bag on to the table. It clanked, and the bump made the lamp splutter and the flame jump up and down.

'Very good!' Robin's voice made his surprise and immense relief quite plain.

'You will never guess where they had gone.'

'Into the hut of someone who is not your friend.'

'No, no, not in a hut at all. It was Chegge who found them.

You know he looks after those very large hens, as large as vultures?'

These were the turkeys, who lacked a local name.

'Chegge went to fasten the door of their house. He looked in their nest for eggs. He found eggs.'

Mugu paused dramatically, waving an arm at the bag of shillings. '*Mayai ya pesa!*' Eggs of coins, this meant. 'The big hen was sitting on them. Do not ask me who put them there, I do not know. But Chegge found them and I, Mugu, give them to you, bwana. Now everyone will sleep tonight warm and dry in his dwelling, and the shillings will sleep safely in your iron box.'

Robin, his head cocked to one side and his eyes narrowed, gazed at the bag as if it had been some extraordinary natural phenomenon fallen from the skies.

'It is a pity the hen did not hatch them into many small shillings,' Tilly remarked. Mugu roared with laughter and, just beyond the lamplit circle, unseen spectators laughed too. Kigorro and his colleagues appeared silently on the veranda to join in. Suddenly everyone was happy, as if at a feast or a successful party; even the lamp's hiss became cheerful and no longer menacing.

'Little shillings!' gasped Mugu, rocking with laughter so that he could hardly stand.

'Shillings giving birth!' Kigorro cried, doubled up and holding for support to a post of the veranda. A grin split Robin's face and he was shaking like a jelly; he always laughed silently. Imagining a fat turkey-hen walking proudly ahead of a flock of tiny scampering coins, I joined in, and for some minutes the veranda was gusty with communal mirth. At last Robin recovered sufficiently to pick up the bag of coins and remark that it would now go into the safe; he thanked Mugu, who departed still chuckling. Later on we heard shouts of laughter coming from the huts that had so narrowly escaped immolation, and later still the drums began, and then singing: the plaintive chant, solo alternating with chorus, of Kikuyu dancers, as rhythmic as the thrust of pistons. No doubt the turkey story was told over and over again in song and dance, and everyone for miles knew who the thief was, and how he had managed to secrete the coins under the turkey. Next day Chegge, a boy not much older than myself, recounted with dramatic gestures how he had made the great discovery, but when I asked him who had put them there he looked at me with wide, innocent eyes and said:

'Who can tell? Perhaps a spirit.'

'Can spirits carry heavy weights?'

'Eeee-eee! Cannot spirits do what they wish, turn into a caterpillar, or go through the roof of a hut? In Europe are there not white spirits?'

'I have never seen one.'

'It is better not to see them. It is better not to hear them, when they strike against the roof of the hut.'

And that was the last word to be spoken on the mystery of the stolen shillings.

Chapter 7

ONE of the pleasures I most enjoyed was that of riding the five miles to Thika station to fetch the mail. This was collected three times a week, when a train came from Nairobi. Normally the local post was dull, but an English mail was an event. I do not know why we were all so excited, as it seldom brought us anything momentous. We subscribed to the weekly edition of an English newspaper, to the *Illustrated London News* and to the *Autocar* for Robin, and received a number of catalogues. Tilly maintained a lively correspondence with seedsmen, poultry breeders, herbalists, handicraft experts and others who possessed some skill, or purveyed some new or unusual product, that she thought might be introduced into Africa, and Robin with makers of gadgets or inventions for which he thought he might get an agency. Both kept up a rewarding hunt for advertisements for free samples, and mysterious little packages would sometimes arrive containing things which everyone had forgotten about, whose use and purpose were obscure.

The mail would have been dull indeed had it held nothing for me, and quite soon after my return to Thika I started to throw upon the waters bread which returned in the shape at first of catalogues, and then of more ambitious packages. My interests at this time, other than local ones, centred round modern poetry and conjuring tricks. Poets such as Rupert Brooke, Siegfried Sassoon, Wilfrid Owen, Robert Nichols, William Davies and others more obscure, whose names are now forgotten by everyone but scholars, were then in fashion, a fashion firmly set by Mr Edward Marsh's anthologies of *Georgian Poetry*.

I liked war poems best, the more savage the better, and knew by heart most of Siegfried Sassoon's and many of Wilfrid Owen's and Robert Nichols'; and the gentle magic of Walter de la Mare worked as powerfully in the glare of the African bush as among the haunted shadows, moonlit orchards and crepuscular churchyards that inspired his muse. Riding M'zee through the coffee plantation my sun-warmed spine would chill to a vision of a host of phantom listeners thronging the faint moonbeams on the dark stair; I would see, among spiky, yellow sodom-apples beside a winding path through the reserve, a bank of ancient briars so old that no man knows through what wild century roves back the rose; and the two worlds joined when a red-eyed dove puffing its iridescent breast in song would recall the smooth-plumed bird in its emerald shade, the seed of grass, the speck of stone that the warfaring ant stirs, and hastes on. And although the poet's twilit northern land of yew-trees and goblins, and our scorched and dappled plains and heat-stunned ridges, were as far apart in character as in distance, there lay between them a bond of magic, of the feel of things just out of sight, of the blundering owl, the four-clawed mole and the hooded bat, and their enigmatic reminder that blind as are these three to me, so blind to someone I must be.

A parcel from the Poetry Bookshop was therefore the most exciting argosy to be looked for from an English mail. Next to that came a parcel from a purveyor of conjuring tricks called Will Goldstone, whose catalogues were packed with fascinating and seemingly impossible feats of magic. I could afford only cheap and easy ones, and sleight of hand was beyond my powers except on the very simplest level. There was a trick with billiard balls that I did master. You showed the audience a single red billiard ball, held it between your first finger and thumb, waved your hand, and a second ball appeared between the first and second fingers. This you repeated until you held four red balls between your fingers. Like all good tricks, it was quite simple; the original ball had several half-shells fitting neatly on to it, and you had only to slip off each of the half-shells in turn and grip it between two fingers with the hollow side facing inwards, and so invisible to the audience.

It was most rewarding to demonstrate a trick to Chegge, Njombo, or to almost any of the Kikuyu, because their natural belief in magic prevented them from turning a stern, sceptical eye on the performance. When I had dumbfounded Chegge and Njombo several times with the multiplying billiard balls, I revealed the secret. Never before had I seen two people so completely convulsed with laughter. They rocked to and fro and rolled about helplessly for about ten minutes, and then staggered off, literally in tears, to tell the joke to their friends. For days afterwards, whenever I saw them they would go off into fits of laughter, choking out the words *mpira ya machanga*, meaning literally 'rubber of the witch-doctor', since there is no word for ball in Swahili, or at any rate in the Swahili we spoke, and the word for rubber had to do instead.

Although these tricks were very cheap, they still required hard cash to be converted into postal orders, and as I received no pocket money, but had to rely on occasional tips and presents, my *repertoire* grew all too slowly. Inspired, perhaps, by my father's predilection for inventions, I strove to devise new tricks for myself. Most of my ideas reached a certain point and then stuck, with flags of all the nations marooned in a canister that was meant to contain a bunch of flowers, or the false egg that should have occupied a magic box still attached to my sleeve by a piece of elastic.

At last, however, I did invent a trick that looked as if it might have worked had I been able to make the necessary apparatus, which included an imitation of the little vest-pocket Kodaks then in vogue. I wrote it all out with diagrams and sent it to *The Magician Monthly*, a magazine I read with fascinated interest every time the mail brought it to Thika. To my great surprise, and even greater gratification, they published the trick in their section devoted to New Magical Suggestions and, in lieu of a fee, gave me credit for two guineas at Will Goldstone's. I spent many delectable hours laying out this sum to the best advantage from the catalogue. After I had calculated from the shipping movements the earliest possible mail by which the tricks might arrive, I rode M'zee to Thika every mail-day until at last, when I had almost despaired of Will Goldstone, the parcel arrived. Enormous strength of mind was needed to carry it home in the saddle-bag, before cutting the string and handling the new tricks as a miser is said to handle his money. I could scarcely hope for another windfall like that, and the problem of how to get hold of ready cash was present in my mind from an early age. Several suggestions had been hatched, examined and discarded before a wholly new idea presented itself.

When it was neither too wet nor too dry, and the farm was ticking over, Tilly and Robin would drive to a place called Makuyu, about fifteen miles away, where an affluent sportsman named Mervyn Ridley had started not only a small club, but a hunt, complete with imported English foxhounds. The ponies went ahead in the morning and as a rule I went with them, accompanied by Chegge, who had been promoted to become a junior *syce*. We had three ponies: the ambling, stumbling M'zee, an adept at that comfortable South African pace called the triple, a cross between a trot and a canter; Hafid the half-Arab with his arched neck and tail and wide nostrils, the most lively and dashing of our stable; and Fair Play, a bony, clumsy but good-hearted animal called after the bank manager. As a rule we stayed the night with the Swifts, in a simple dwelling of white-washed mud blocks heavily thatched. The living-room had been built around a tree whose top had been cut off, and the bole left to help prop up the rafters. After its bark had been rubbed off and it had been creosoted, everyone assumed it to be dead, but in time it came to life again and started to shoot. The Swifts removed these incipient branches with regret, and wondered if in time the tree would lift the roof off its timbers; but it did not grow much in stature, and when they sat on a bench they had made to encircle it, and leant their backs against the bole, they liked to think of the life stirring inside it.

Hunting foxes in Ireland had been Randall Swift's main interest before he came to Africa, although by trade he had been a brewer in Kent. Now he was part-owner of the sisal plantation at Punda Milia. He had married an actress, but she did not look like one; she used no make-up, and although her face was humorous and expressive, and her voice attractive, she was not really good-looking. She had acted in character parts, we were told. She never took to riding, but became heavily addicted to dogs, and surrounded herself by specimens of many different breeds.

To hunt with the Makuyu hounds we got up in the dark, dressed by the light of a smoky safari lamp and emerged as dawn began to fill the sky above the plains. A thin white mist muffled the ground, the sharp air was full of sounds that seemed to creep about as if in carpet slippers: the clink of teacups, an African hoiking, ponies shaking heads and jingling bridles, the woof of a dog. Tea scalded our throats; we hurried to the meet before the sun broke over the straight horizon and flooded a limpid sky with gold. At the meet a knot of restless ponies pawed and snorted, the clumsy and effusive hounds barged about with waving tails (one had to call them sterns), shouted at by the huntsman and his whippers-in clad in scarlet shirts and white breeches. It was important to start the chase while dew still lay heavy on the ground; the scent and the dew evaporated together.

In the mild golden sunlight, while doves pumped their throats in vigorous cooing in the dew-soaked acacias and silvery cobwebs lay on every blade of grass, we trotted quickly to the nearest *donga*, the name by which the many gullies creasing the surface of the plain were known. Jackals were our official prey, and sometimes the hounds picked up the scent of one before we reached a *donga*, and with a few excited yelps and resonant woofs circled the line, converged upon it and were away, the nose of Challenger or Frantic thrust forward as he led the pack at a gathering speed across the plain. Then we would let our ponies out, if they were sufficiently enthusiastic, or urge them on, if they were like M'zee; but even he, at this stage of the game, was prepared to break into a fast canter with his ears pricked and give the semblance of a little buck, to show that he still had a drop of the sap of youth in his blood.

A jackal's scent is strong, so it was the best quarry, but the hounds were just as likely to put up a steinbuck or a duiker. These little buck always waited until hounds or horsemen were almost on top of them before they broke out of their sheltering patch of bush or long grass. One saw a flash of brown, a leaping body with its head laid back, and away it would bound at a tremendous speed, leaving the pack far behind. But the hounds made up in persistence what they lacked in pace. As the sun climbed, the scent faded, and by half-past eight or so the hounds found it difficult to pick up a lost line. If the buck could delay matters until then it was generally safe, but sometimes, of course, it tired, and then the hounds would overwhelm it in some bush place where it had hoped for sanctuary.

Luckily one seldom saw this happen, as the country was broken and the end quick, and I knew it was sentimental to worry about the buck because its natural life was one of continual chase and evasion. If the hounds had not caught it, almost certainly some other enemy would have done so sooner or later – a hyena or cheetah, a lion or leopard or a pack of wild dogs; or else a native snare or trap, or the spear of a herdsman. The Makuyu hounds with their Sunday morning jaunts could not have made much difference to a balance of nature maintained by hunting and guile. But the steinbuck and duiker were graceful, leaping, soft-furred little things, their legs brittle as clay pipe-stems, their horns like prickles on a bough, full of life and energy and altogether harmless, and I was always glad when the huntsman recalled his pack from their vain search among the rocks and brakes of some *donga*, and we trotted home to breakfast while the spent antelope crouched safely in its hiding-place, hearing the retreating noises of the hunters and feeling the earth's vibrations caused by stamping hooves fade away.

Sometimes the hounds behaved in such a fashion as to suggest that the quarry was neither a jackal nor a small buck, and it then became a matter of skill and guesswork to find out what they were after. Mistakes could be dangerous. A warthog, swinging round to back into his hole, would sometimes dart forward to rip the flesh of the leading hounds before he vanished rump-first underground. Once the whole pack set off at a spanking pace, led us at full speed over some broken rocky country and bayed their quarry up a tree. The scarlet-shirted whipper-in tried frantically to drive the hounds away while a frightened and ferocious leopard snarled down from the branches, ready to spring. The Master carried a revolver, but wisely decided not to practise on the leopard, which fortunately remained in the tree. Occasionally the hounds hunted porcupines, which were not at all rewarding, being apt to shoot a battery of sharp quills into their pursuers' faces

So although our country had no fences, no Irish banks or Leicestershire hedges, no stone walls or brooks or posts-and-rails, our hunts were not without excitement of a more unorthodox kind, nor without hazard, of which concealed pig-holes were the most dangerous. M'zee had a genius for sensing the hidden mouth of a pig-hole as he approached it, and swerving at the last instant, often sending me over his head. Tilly's instructions in this event were clear: never let go of the reins. Sometimes, however, these were jerked from my hands, and if I happened to be riding Hafid or Fair Play I would scramble to my feet to see him galloping off with the reins flying, and terrified lest he should get tangled up in them and break a leg. But with M'zee I was quite safe. Even if I did lose the reins, M'zee was not one to lose his head. He would stand a few paces away and nibble grass until I picked myself up and re-mounted. In fact nothing worried M'zee.

By half-past eight or so the sun was hot, the grasses dry and it was time to go home. Thorn-tree scratches on our arms or faces began to sting and sore places to chafe, the ponies drooped their heads and we felt achingly hungry. After perhaps an hour's ride the Swifts' roof came into view, *syces* ran out to take the ponies, we slid off their backs, washed quickly in our tin basins and sat down at a long table on the veranda where Mrs Swift had laid out an ambrosial meal. First came generous chunks of golden, red-tinged, juicy paw-paw, served with slices of green lime; then steaming porridge with thick yellow cream and brown sugar; then platters of fried eggs in a nest of crisp, curly bacon; stacks of warm toast, fresh butter and home-made Oxford marmalade; finally, dishes of bananas and sweet oranges; and big cups of fresh coffee from a sort of samovar. A vigorous appetite brought on by exertions in the open air, a good digestion and no inhibitions about satisfying it, a sunlit veranda in the company of friends with bougainvilleas and morning glories smothering the posts – such pleasures were ours every Sunday morning for about half the year. They never palled; and although one could not boast of their sophistication, I doubt if on their own sensual plane they have since been surpassed.

Among the visitors who sometimes came to share our hunts was the Governor, Sir Edward Northey, a small, dapper, fierce and monocled General who, in the war, had taken a leading part in the local campaign. His fierceness was a shell; he was a man of kindness and goodwill, anxious to do his full duty but handicapped by a lack of experience in politics and bureaucracy. For this reason he later fell out with his superiors and resigned, or was dismissed, from his Governorship, no one quite knew which. Although he seemed to some of the farmers rather stuck-up and formal, and was a stickler for protocol, they respected him because he knew his mind and spoke it, and because they believed in his sincerity. In his home life he was overshadowed by a forceful, high-spirited and outspoken wife from the Cape and by three attractive, independent and ebullient daughters, with whom a great many men were always in love.

The first time he visited Makuyu we had an excellent hunt lasting thirty-five minutes, and it occurred to me that a short description of it might be taken by the *East African Standard*. For anything they published I assumed they would pay, if only on a modest scale; and the chance of a new approach to the Poetry Bookshop and Will Goldstone opened up before me. On sheets torn from an exercise book, in my tidiest writing, I compiled a brief account, and posted it at Thika on my way home with hope, doubt and anxiety. I had to wait until the Tuesday week to learn the fate of my piece. As the days went by my confidence in it wilted until, by the week-end, I had pretty well given up hope.

Our postmaster, the *babu* as he was called, was a handsome Sikh with a turban and a tight little fringe of black curly beard, running from ear to ear, that looked as if it had been stuck on with glue. Although his manner was abrupt and off-hand he would sometimes let me in at the back to help sort the mail. His boy would shake the letters from their sack on to the dirty wooden floor of a small, stuffy room behind the counter, and he and I would put them into their pigeon-holes. The parcels bag was the exciting one. It bulged in odd shapes like a Christmas stocking, and trying to guess what was in other people's parcels was almost as interesting as hoping to catch a glimpse of one's own.

When I went to fetch the mail I generally had a look at the outspan beyond the station to see whether any interesting safaris were waiting there to catch the next train to Nairobi. Although Thika was so small and unimportant-looking, it was the railhead for all the country lying north of Nairobi: even for that distant, enormous and still partly unexplored country of veld and thornscrub and mountain, of sand-river and basalt kopje and lava desert, of camels and nomads and wells for which tribesmen fought with spears and arrows, of long-haired fierce Somali and marauding Galla, that we knew as the Northern Frontier district, and into which only soldiers who guarded it from encroaching Ethiopians, and hunters who sought its harvest of elephants, ever penetrated. In fact, if you came to think of it, Thika station with its little tin-roofed shed, where a wood-burning locomotive stood with its half-dozen carriages on a level piece of hard ground, was the last station you would find, if you travelled north, until you came to Addis Ababa, which had a railway, of a sort, to Djibuti on the Red Sea.

But when I rode down to see whether the *Standard* had printed my report, even the outspan did not claim my attention. I tethered M'zee to a post, claimed our mail packet and tore open the weekly. Thika was all red dust then, except in the rains when it was all thick mud, and cars churned themselves

94

into immobility in the single street that ran between two rows of shoddy Indian stores. There had been rain a day or two before. As I stood by M'zee, a waggon came down the street with the oxen slipping and straining and the red-stained Boer driver cracking his long whip like a maniac, shouting at each beast by name and just flicking its back with the tip of his lash, while a young boy pulled at the rein attached to the leaders.

I was not interested in the wagon, however, but in the *Standard*, which curled up whenever I tried to unfold it, and was full of dull headlines about English politics and a meeting of the Convention of Associations. I went through the whole paper and could not see a trace of my report. Although this was only what I thought I had expected, I found myself stunned by disappointment. To make quite sure I went through it all again, even the Movements of Shipping, advertisements of sales and a list of regulations governing the employment of resident labour. And then, on an inside page, I came upon the headline 'Country Sport', followed by another: 'Makuyu Hunt and Polo Club', and in brackets, the word 'Contributed'. This, indeed, was the story – all there, not even cut. It ran to three-quarters of a column. It was in print. The world changed immediately; the sun was generous but not unkind, the flies bearable, the postmaster's numerous children squatting on the bare wooden steps of his little tin bungalow appealing rather than squalid, the black clouds that had gathered over the Aberdares magnificent and awe-inspiring rather than an indication that I should get soaked on the way home. My only regret was the lack of a letter from the editor expressing his pleasure in receiving so brilliant a contribution, and enclosing a postal order for at least five shillings, if not ten.

Chapter 8

WHEN I had read the story three or four times, and the excitement had faded into a comfortable glow, I unhitched M'zee and prepared to ride home. Meanwhile an unknown young man had arrived at the post office. He wore clean, well-pressed shorts and the crest upon his shiny shirt buttons indicated some kind of official: but not the ordinary administrative sort, who wore a khaki topee with a prancing brass lion in front. This young man had a soft *terai* with one side turned up and pinned back by a badge. He smiled in a friendly manner and asked me if I knew the way to the Clewes'.

'They're our neighbours,' I replied.

The young man smiled even more politely. He was tall and thin with sandy hair, a fair moustache, a small snub nose and the kind of scooped-out face known among cattle as dished, and seen often in Jerseys. His face and arms were burnt the colour of egg-yolk.

'They've asked me to stay the night,' he explained. 'I'm on my way down from Archer's Post.'

The very words Archer's Post always made me long to go there; I thought of a stout stockade on the crest of a rocky hill defended from encircling savages by archers with longbows, although I knew that in reality it had nothing to do with bows and arrows but was called after the man who had first camped there.

'Have you shot many Abyssinians?' I inquired.

'Not many, really, but one keeps on trying. Will you show me the way to the Clewes'?'

First he returned to camp to collect his kit, and to give instructions to his corporal. His porters were wild-looking men wearing pigtails fore and aft, done into a queue with sheep's fat and red ochre, and clad in short cotton cloaks dyed with the same pigment. They were looking about them with a mixture of disbelief and contempt; they had never seen before such things as a row of shops, a T-Model Ford that lurched along the road, least of all of a train that ate logs, spat sparks and grunted like some fabulous beast. If such things did not exist, their attitude implied, beyond the slopes of the great mountain, the extremity of their universe, it was because they were undesirable, and no sensible man would look at them too closely. So they turned their backs on the township and went off with pangas to chop firewood, or in a languid fashion restacked their loads. The askaris belonged to the King's African Rifles. They were walking about with an arrogant and superior air, now and again shouting an order at the porters and doing no work themselves; but when they saw their officer they brought their sandalled heels together with a smack, stood rigid as pokers and gave him a quivering salute. Their forage caps had khaki flaps hanging down behind, over the neck; a form of headdress worn only by those serving in deserts, and speaking of distant, dangerous frontiers.

The young man told me that his name was Captain Raymond Dorsett, and trotted beside me on a mule over the bridge above the Chania falls, past the Blue Posts and up the hill towards the farm. His long legs almost touched the ground and he looked rather absurd on his small mule, so I did not feel so ill at ease as I generally did with strangers. He told me that he was on local leave and that Harry Clewes, an old companion from the war, had invited him for a few days on his way to Nairobi.

'Then I'm going to the coast,' he added. 'The one thing you pine for after all that desert is the sea. I believe some people think the desert's romantic, but all it is really is hot, waterless and damned uncomfortable.'

'There are Abyssinian raiders,' I suggested.

'All *they* are, are camel-thieves and slavers. I don't know why it's more romantic to pinch camels than the family silver, still less to capture helpless children. If they find an undefended camp they slaughter everyone who can't be carried off, including the babies.'

Captain Dorsett seemed determined to destroy my illusions, and added that rhinos were more dangerous than raiders; they had playful natures, and would charge up and down a string of porters just for fun, to see them all throw down their loads and bolt, sometimes up prickly thorn-trees.

Behind us, on another mule, rode Captain Dorsett's personal servant. He was tall, slim and proud, wore a splendid red turban, had a short aggressive beard and was a Galla, so his master explained. Although the Gallas had been conquered by the Ethiopian Emperor, and were ruled by Rases, or governors, they believed themselves greatly superior to their Christian overlords, if only because they were circumcised Muslims; and, of course, immeasurably superior to the pagan savages of the south. Deslin, as he was called, looked with extreme disdain upon the ground his mule trotted over, and had the unshackled look of a kestrel. I felt my escort to be impressive, and began to wonder whether the arrival from the north of Captain Dorsett would make a news item for the *Standard*.

'I've never met Mrs Clewes,' Captain Dorsett said. 'She'll be the first white woman I'll have seen since I left Nyeri on the way up, fifteen months ago. I hope she won't expect too much of me. I've forgotten my party manners and I never did have any parlour tricks. Is she very – well, you know, posh and swagger? Changes for dinner and that sort of thing?'

'We all wear pyjamas for dinner,' I said.

He looked rather disappointed; perhaps he had hoped to see his first white woman in something more glamorous.

'I daresay Miss Cooper puts on a dress,' I suggested.

'Miss Cooper? They've got a guest?'

'Well, not a guest exactly. She looks after the children.'

'Oh, I see. Is she – well – what sort of age is she?'

'My mother says she might be any age. Mutton ...' I paused, realizing that this was unkind. Obviously she would lose no time in going in full cry after Captain Dorsett, and although she irritated me, I had no wish to queer her pitch.

'Mutton?' Captain Dorsett inquired, with a slight frown. Luckily he did not seem to be very quick in the uptake, having spent so long by himself, or in the biblical society of nomadic tribesmen.

'She's very fond of mutton,' I added lamely, and hurried on. 'It's something to do with her religion. Not that she's a heathen, or anything. It's a sect. She wears a lot of bangles, and prays to the moon.'

Captain Dorsett looked at me with a tinge of suspicion, but just then M'zee stumbled badly and created a diversion. 'Mrs Clewes is nice too, although she talks a lot. It's not just that she talks, she runs everything together, like a painting when the brush is too wet. But she's quite kind.'

Despite his air of authority, his haughty escort and his contempt for Abyssinian raiders, I suspected that Captain Dorsett was growing nervous as we approached the stronghold of his unseen hostess.

'I hope Mrs Clewes will make allowances,' he repeated. 'Deslin did his best with my hair, but I'd lost my only pair of nail scissors and he had to tackle it with a razor blade, and it had grown so long I looked like an Old Testament prophet or something. I let it grow on purpose, I thought it might keep off the wild bees.'

When we reached the turn-off to the Clewes', Captain Dorsett kicked his mule into a reluctant jog, intending no doubt to get over the sticky patch as quickly as possible, and proceeded up an avenue of young jacarandas, followed by the faithful and imperial Deslin, to face an assault which I supposed he would find a good deal more deadly than anything the Abyssinians had been able to mount.

At teatime I put the *Standard* in a prominent position on the table, hoping that one of my parents would pick it up, browse through it and remark: 'There's an awfully good account here of our hunt last Sunday week. Whoever can have written it, I wonder?' This would have been my big moment; and I was prepared to parry with an unaffected modesty the proud congratulations that would have been heaped upon me. I should have known better, of course. The *Standard* sometimes lay about for several days before anyone did more than glance at the headlines. Our small world seemed altogether remote from the larger one outside, even that of Nairobi, and if some event of moment had occurred we generally heard about it. Alec Wilson had a private line to the bush-telegraph, Harry Clewes often went to Nairobi in his Dodge, and one had only to call at the Blue Posts for an up-to-the-minute, stirring and always accurate account of whatever piece of news was of interest at the time.

The *Standard*, therefore, remained unread, while Tilly opened a letter from Nairobi addressed in green ink, in a sprawling hand, on a thick cream envelope.

'Well, now, just think of that,' she exclaimed when she

99

had read it. 'Whoever do you think is in Nairobi? The last person I'd suspect of wanting to visit the colonies.'

Robin was sitting with his head slightly on one side and his eyes screwed up, staring out over the stoloniferous lawn, the flowing shrubs and grapefruit trees and the bush beyond that ran down to the river, an expression of great wisdom and concentration on his face. This sometimes denoted that a new scheme or invention was under mental examination, sometimes that he was in a rosy dream about its fortunate outcome, or sometimes that he was just sitting and enjoying his tea. He paid no attention to her remark.

'Cousin Hilary's in Nairobi,' she said in louder tones. 'He wants to come and stay.'

Robin stirred and came to, looking a little apologetic.

'Do I know him?' he inquired.

'Considering we stayed with him twice in Ireland, and he was always in and out of my father's house when we were engaged, and he gave us that gilded bird-cage with the automatic songbird for a wedding present ...'

'Of course he did,' Robin said, showing interest at last. 'Whatever happened to it? You know, it might be very useful here. If I could have taken it on that recruiting trip to Kavirondo, I think they'd have come in *droves* to see it, and we could have signed them on ...'

'You forget the sale,' Tilly said shortly. 'Anyway, it's Cousin Hilary who wants to come and stay, not the automatic bird. He says he's here on a trip to see the country, though I can't imagine what he wants to see it for; I thought he was too busy writing plays and recording Irish folk songs and collecting early Persian pottery. Still, it will be fun to see him; I must get the herbs out of the spare room.'

'Why is the spare room full of herbs?'

'All the other rooms leak.'

'That reminds me, there's no bath water. The boys managed to smash one wheel of the water-cart this morning and then hid it in some bananas; they must have gone at it hammer and tongs with crowbars I should think. I'm afraid it means another wheel, and just at the moment the overdraft ...'

'Surely you could get the ram going,' Tilly said. This contrivance, a form of pump, had been sitting in the store for months, waiting for Robin to install it in the river, whence it would convey all the water we needed. But first he had to build a small dam; this called for cement, which in turn called for hard cash.

'Harry Clewes would lend you some cement,' Tilly added. 'He always seems to have plenty.'

'I have no wish to gather crumbs from his table,' Robin said with dignity.

'That's not the same thing as cement from his store.'

So the conversation about Tilly's cousin ended in cement, and that seemed to be the fate of many of our family talks. We started with the latest book from England, or a critique of a play sent by Tilly's sister Mildred who lived in London, and ended with a drench for Hafid's colic or the price of corrugated iron. But I supposed that everyone's life was like that.

Meanwhile no one even looked at the *Standard*, and when I told Tilly, in the evening, that it contained a report of our hunt, she was not at all interested. I cut the story out to stick in a book, and never did mention my authorship. Clearly it was a subject, like illness, of intense interest to oneself, but absolutely none to anyone else.

Arrangements were made to fetch Cousin Hilary from Nairobi, but these were never carried out, as one afternoon we got a message to meet him at the Blue Posts. We all drove down in the Chevrolet in some apprehension, for the road was deep in ruts and quagmires, and the streams lapped at their log bridges. You could generally get down, unless one of the bridges had been washed away; getting back, up the hill, was the problem.

At the hotel we encountered the Clewes and Miss Cooper, who had just seen Captain Dorsett off to the frontier. But he was coming back, they said, for Christmas; he had cancelled his trip to the sea.

'I've never heard of anything so foolhardy,' Betty Clewes said to Tilly, while Miss Cooper was out of earshot with the twins and Robin in the bar collecting gossip. 'But, of course, when Harry asked him and he jumped at it I couldn't very well tell him it would be *lunacy* to come anywhere near us again. The poor young man doesn't realize that he's in *far* more danger now than ever before, but I suppose you can't look for sense in a young man who's seen nothing for a year but savages and thorn-trees, so prickly and uncomfortable, I expect anything female looks irresistible; Miss Cooper is positively *licking* her lips, my dear. There ought to be a sort of acclimatizing period, like the room that cools you off after a Turkish bath. How are your dahlia roots doing, Tilly dear; mine are rather sickly but I think alive, though one never knows with roots, does one; I remember my father brought a tree back from the Holy Land, a cedar I suppose or it may have been an olive, one day a friend came over to see us, that was Rupert Holloway, perhaps you knew him, he was *such* an enchanting person and so good-looking, like a *god* my dear, of course he was old enough to be my uncle but nevertheless he was a little *épris*, though he was married to one of the Gawthorpes, the one with the lisp who was always *said* to have been a friend of King Edward's, I don't believe it because after all whatever you may say about him, he did have good taste in women, and I believe in cigars, though not in other things naturally, one wouldn't expect it. I expect he – now whatever are the twins up to, Vicky stop teasing that monkey at once or it'll bite you, how would you like it if I kept snatching your food away every time you had settled down to a meringue, and Simon whatever have you got on your hands, you mustn't speak like that to Miss Cooper and now you must all get ready as we're going home.'

'Miss Cooper's got her best bangles on,' Vicky observed, 'and she's washed her hair.'

'Now, Vicky, don't go telling tales out of school,' Miss Cooper said. 'Besides, they aren't my *best* bangles; they're just bracelets I'm rather fond of, they were given me by an admirer before I came out here to remind me of happy days and old friends, he said, such a nice gesture. "Wherever you go, I know you will leave the imprint of your personality," he said – I always remember those words. At least no one could say I'm a nonentity.'

'I think Simon's hands, Miss Cooper ... And then we must start back, it's nearly teatime. Won't you come with us, Tilly, and have a cup of tea?'

Tilly explained that we had come to meet a distant cousin she hadn't seen for ten years.

'How exciting!' Miss Cooper exclaimed, amid a tinkle of bangles. 'I always say there's nothing like a new face to liven things up. Although my friends at home think it brave and adventurous of me to come to Africa, life can be very dull for those of us not fortunate enough to be always going on safari, or to Nairobi for the races, or something like that. And then the people one meets, although no one could be less of a snob than I am, I'm very broad-minded in fact, and take people as I find them, but some of them are not at *all* the sort of people I'm used to mixing with at home. So it's all the more delightful when one comes across a person who's really *congenial*. We've just seen off a quite presentable young man, perhaps you met him, a Captain Dorsett.'

'I didn't meet him,' Tilly answered, 'but I wondered if he was quite all there; I heard he grew his hair long to keep off bees, but I should have thought it would only have entangled them.'

'His hair was quite short when he stayed with *us*,' Miss Cooper said severely. 'I expect he had smartened himself up for the ladies – although he'd been living such a rough bachelor life for a whole year, I must say no one would have known it, he was a gentleman in every sense of the word. Of course, I know he hadn't come to see *me*, in fact he didn't even know that I existed, but no one could have been more affable, indeed he seemed to like my company and told me a great deal about himself that I daresay he didn't tell to other people. But then I've always been told that I'm a sympathetic listener, and though like all bachelors who've lived alone so much he was shy and rather tongue-tied at first, I soon found a way to get over *that*. You've heard that he's changed his mind about going to the coast, I expect, and coming back for Christmas. Perhaps he was only flattering, but he certainly hinted that I had something to do with that!'

'Now I think we really *must* be going,' Betty Clewes said, 'and perhaps everything will work out for the best. Simon dear, do go and wash your hands, and Vicky, you will never catch a lizard, they're too quick for you and anyway I don't think it's true about their tails. Run and tell Daddy we're ready to go, I'm sure he's settled the whole future of the country with Robin by now, and if they go on talking much longer they will start a company to dam the Nile or put the whole country under rice, such a very dull thing I always think except, of course, for risottos, I remember once in Naples . . .'

It took the Clewes a long time to collect themselves, they fussed about like a flock of starlings in a tree, except for Harry, who strode masterfully from the bar in the well-cut riding breeches and shepherded them efficiently into the car with several cutting remarks about chattering women, the grubby children and the general waste of time involved in such social and domestic outings.

'A little of Betty Clewes goes a very long way,' Tilly observed as they finally departed, leaving us in a delightful peace on the veranda to await our guest.

His arrival, when it came, was unexpected. We heard at first distant shouts from the direction of the bridge above the falls; then a garden-boy, who was gently lopping grass-heads with a piece of bent iron shaped like a hockey stick, became infused with sudden animation and disappeared down the road, followed by several other Africans who had been dozing in the shade.

'Someone must have fallen into the river,' Tilly remarked.

'Perhaps they will be eaten by a crocodile,' I said hopefully.

The sounds died down but we were conscious, in some indefinable way, of an impending event. The silence that flowed back after the shouting was brittle, the doves had stopped cooing and there was no one in sight. A hedge of prickly kei-apple obscured our view of the road. Presently the silence was broken again and it was evident that something was approaching up the slope from the bridge.

'Perhaps it's some kind of animal,' Tilly said: and she

was right. Four zebras rounded the corner and galloped into
the forecourt of the hotel. They were in harness, and drew
an open buggy with large spindly wheels bearing two figures,
one of whom was standing up with a coaching whip in his
hand. I recognized him as one of the successful hunters of
the day, a hard-bitten, middle-aged man called Jock
Cameron. He reined in his team with a lot of whooping,
jumped down and ran round to grab the bridles of the
leading pair.

'Well, if I wasn't stone cold sober ...' Robin remarked.
'This will give some of the regular customers a turn.'

The zebras were now standing rock-still with their ears
laid back, their teeth showing and a look of implacable ferocity.
Like all zebras they were fat, but they did not look at all
reconciled to their lot. Several people had tried to tame
zebras, always without success until Jock Cameron had collected a number of foals, brought them up from infancy and
accustomed them to harness. The survivors had learnt, in
time, to pull a buggy, although no one but their master
could control them, and he sometimes failed. They had become quite a famous sight in Nairobi, trotting in style down
Government Road. Their photographs had appeared in many
British and American papers and they had brought him a
great deal of useful publicity.

Meanwhile a remarkable figure was beginning to disengage
itself from the passenger's seat. It was muffled from head to
foot in so many garments as to be virtually invisible, and
sheltered under an enormous topee to which was attached a
long purple scarf, floating down over the back. Under this was
a spreading spine-pad made of kongoni hide lined with red
flannel. The face was concealed by large black goggles, and
over all was held a huge striped sun-umbrella. So heavily encased was this individual in protective clothing, hides, scarves
and goggles that Jock Cameron had practically to lift him
down. Clutching the umbrella, he hurried into the shade of
the veranda and cautiously began to divest himself of some
of his casings.

'Thatch *over* corrugated iron,' he remarked. 'That is a step
in the right direction, but there should be two thicknesses of

bituminized felting between the tin and the thatch. I think, however, I can venture into my lighter headgear.'

'Hilary!' Tilly exclaimed.

'My dear cousin, how delightful to meet you again! What a refreshing pleasure at the end of such a tedious and risky journey! It makes everything *more* than worth-while. But do you think it safe to stand in this veranda without a hat? And that blouse – charming, becoming, but nothing there whatever to keep off the actinic rays!'

'Do take off those goggles,' Tilly said. 'I can't see if it's really you or an impersonator.'

'What a really dreadful journey,' Cousin Hilary went on, gradually emerging from his cocoon. 'Never again, not for all the tea in China; all that way over these dreadful tracks, with those appalling beasts likely at any moment to dash us to destruction, I don't suppose I shall *ever* be the same again. I'm dreadfully afraid some of the actinic rays may have penetrated my defences, despite all my precautions; we've been exposed to the sun for five hours, five hours my dear, not counting a break for lunch. I hope you have a nice, cool, dark room, Tilly, with proper roofing – bituminized felt is the best – where I can rest? I shall be done up for days after this journey.'

'You look as fit as a flea,' Tilly said, as soon as she could see him. 'You always were pale, and rather anaemic looking, although as tough as nails underneath. How are you? And how's Aunt Constance?'

'Still in bed, my dear. Ten years ago, you know, she caught a chill when salmon fishing and had to go to bed; she found it so enjoyable, and got so much attention, that she's never left it since. I'm only waiting to find a bed that looks sufficiently comfortable to do the same myself.'

'I'm afraid ours is very hard and most of the springs are broken.'

'Who is this child?' Hilary inquired abruptly.

'Mine, of course, and Robin's. She won't bother you; she spends most of her time on ponies or missing pigeons with a ·22 rifle, and is supposed to do lessons which will keep her out of your way.'

'That's the main thing with children – scarcely ever heard and never, never seen. But she's *very* improperly dressed. You should be much more careful, Tilly; you know the sun affects the spinal fluid and damages the ganglia, and in the end will certainly send you mad. And, of course, combined with the altitude and the ultra-violet ... Oh, be careful there, for Heaven's sake stop that savage from *hurling* my precious cameras about as if they were assegais; Robin, do something – I can't move – Tilly, my sunshade, my goggles, my spine-pad, quick ...'

The crisis was averted by Jock Cameron, who was trying to get a large number of bulky packages unloaded and at the same time to keep the zebras from kicking and biting each other and from getting their legs caught in the traces. Clearly the zebras had unpleasant natures, even allowing for their natural resentment at being made to pull a buggy, whereas Cousin Hilary, I decided, had an engaging nature, and a sort of animation that went on and off like a light. He was good-looking in an unusual way, or at any rate unusual for Thika. His skin was pale and delicate, almost translucent like a petal, his eyes grey and deep-set and remarkably bright, like a bird's, his hair curly, his face full of interesting shadows and hollows and its bones delicately moulded. His wrists and ankles were slim and his hands, instead of being calloused and red, were white and soft, that is for a man's. That he had written poetry was exciting, although I was disappointed not to have found any of it in the Georgian collections. I had only met one poet in my life, a man called Basil Brooke famed less for his verse than for having crawled into a cave, armed only with a spear, to dispatch a wounded leopard; he had written stirring frontier ballads, and been killed in the war. It was obvious that Cousin Hilary was a poet of quite a different kind.

He had a great deal of luggage, including trunks of clothes, photographic apparatus, a butterfly collection, a heavy box containing bits of Persian pottery and a small crate harbouring a water-filter.

'I must have the water filtered and of course *boiled*,' he told Tilly. 'One ought to boil the bath water too, but to save trouble I've taken to washing in olive oil. Very nourishing for the skin and affords some protection against mosquitoes. I hope you have no mosquitoes, Tilly?'

'Oh, no, nothing like that,' Tilly assured him. 'And no malaria.' In fact, people often got malaria – Robin had suffered from several attacks – but it was an article of faith that the infection never arose on the farm, but was contracted elsewhere, for instance in Nairobi, or down on the plains. Our mosquitoes were supposed to be harmless, not *anopheles* that carried the malaria parasite.

'And no scorpions either, I hope,' Hilary added, 'or hornets, or hunting spiders which are worse than tarantulas, or ticks, or jiggas – the number and variety of dangerous, hostile insects that exist is quite unbelievable. In my opinion, God didn't *want* this continent to be inhabited by human beings, and everyone who tries to live here, black or white, is committing mortal sin. Now where is my medicine chest, and my case of geological specimens, and where is the bag containing largesse? Tilly, I have a present for you – I have brought a box of presents for each of my friends. I feel very much like the redoubtable Stanley or the scurrilous Burton, advancing through the wilds with beads and calico and copper wire for the savages, and indeed beads and calico, in one form or another – a diamond necklace, for instance, or a dress from Worth's – remain the basis of so many gifts. Not that I have brought you diamonds and dresses from Worth or even Gorringe's, but a few little parcels from Fortnum's, enough I think to last while I am staying with you; at any rate I can always leave when they are finished. My digestion will not stand ancient hens worn out by egg-bearing, and rancid stewed goat.'

'Robin would have been delighted if you'd brought him some copper wire,' Tilly agreed. 'He seems to put as high a value on it as any Masai does.'

'But of course – one is bound to absorb the values of one's surroundings; we are just so many pieces of litmus paper, turning pink or blue according to where we find ourselves. That's why you're so terribly rash, Tilly, quite apart from the ghastly dangers to your health (though I don't see how you can cease to think of those for an instant) to live among savages; you will become just like them, rings in your nose I daresay before you've finished and at the very least terrible lacunae in your mind, which instead of being filled with thoughts of beauty and the gentler vices will become a ghastly repository of crude beliefs, absurd prejudices and dreadful bits of information like how to cure a sick sheep or build a pigsty out of barbed wire and cow dung. And your house full of ink-wells made of bovine feet, and rugs with great toothy moulting heads and –'

'The boy's just dropped a case marked Fragile,' Tilly said coldly. 'I hope your medicines haven't got broken. All we have is Epsom salts, calomel and quinine.'

With a little cry of dismay Cousin Hilary started towards the buggy, but recoiled at the veranda's edge, having too little protective clothing on to venture farther. Jock Cameron was in difficulties trying to suppress the fury of the zebras; as soon as the last case had been tumbled off the buggy, he leapt on to the driver's seat and away they went in a flurry of hooves and tossing heads, plunging and kicking as if a lion was at their heels. A little farther along the road they stopped stone-still, dug in their heels and refused to budge, making vicious snaps at each other.

'For one who likes his comforts that seems an odd way to travel,' Tilly observed.

'It was not my choice. Jock Cameron said they were quieter than mules and more reliable than motors; besides, they are clearly photogenic, and I hoped for some unusual slides. And their *fatness* excites me, they're like seals with legs.'

'I always wonder at it too,' Tilly agreed, 'because I'm told their insides are stuffed with parasites.'

'My dear Tilly, it's worse than I thought; your mind has already retreated, perhaps beyond recall, into a visceral abyss; I doubt if even my presence for a few weeks will suffice to save you. And to think of this unfortunate, doomed child, condemned forever to the pit from which a few Greeks once clawed their way into the first pale sunlight of the intellect . . . I am so glad to see the last of those heraldic but repellent beasts. How do we proceed, Tilly, to your kraal? Have you a retinue of porters? If so I shall insist upon a hammock, a very sensible way to get about, but, of course, it must have some kind of shelter over it; perhaps two bearers each with an umbrella would be sufficient, now that the sun is well below the meridian.'

'I'm afraid we shall have to go in a dilapidated car, and that you may have to get out and push.'

Cousin Hilary winced. 'I have never pushed anything, not even shares. I feel like the Bellman – forty-nine boxes, all beautifully packed – I trust, however, that none of them will be left behind on this dreadfully primordial beach.'

'We can't get them all in at once, Hilary. We'll send the scotch-cart tomorrow for the less urgent ones.'

'They are all urgent, as you put it; what is the point of travel if between the thing seen and the mind one inserts a layer of petty anxiety? It's absurd to travel at all if one does so without all one's comforts handy, and every need foreseen. After all, I am not travelling to *get* anywhere; that would be a very poor reason to leave home.'

'I've wondered why you *are* travelling, ever since your letter came,' Tilly observed.

'It is clumsy to act always in character; one must surprise oneself now and again, if only to enjoy the pleasures of the expected. No, no, that one is *essential*,' Hilary cried in distress, as Tilly directed to the unwanted pile a trunk about to be heaved into the car. 'It has my moths and butterflies, and I must show them to you; they are superb, some as large as saucers – in all honesty I must add, the saucer of a coffee cup. I am looking now for miraculous insects, such as Pliny described, I am sure quite correctly, for he was a most accurate man; Indian ants for instance, as large as an Egyptian wolf and cat-coloured, who dig gold in the winter, and are robbed of it in summer by the base Indians when the heat forces them to take refuge in their holes. Sometimes, I am glad to say, they caught a whiff of Indian and sallied forth to attack their despoilers, who kept swift camels poised for an escape. I suppose you have no insects of that nature, Tilly, or fish that wear their scales backwards, or mares that are fertilized by the west wind?'

'We are rather short on marvels,' Tilly said, with a trace

of regret. I could see that Hilary amused her. It was always touch and go with people like him – not that we had encountered anyone quite the same, but people out of the ordinary, who talked a lot. Hilary had a twinkle in his eye, a silvery voice and a great deal of charm, and I felt sure we were going to enjoy his visit.

Chapter 9

ROBIN had been a little grumpy about the prospect of entertaining Cousin Hilary. He was very busy with the coffee, short of labour, in trouble with the overdraft, and he had veld sores, painful afflictions for which no cure was known. However, when Cousin Hilary arrived and had climbed out of some of his coverings, he won Robin's heart by walking over to inspect a picture that hung above the fireplace, and making an appreciative remark.

'Not a bad little thing,' Robin agreed in an off-hand manner that deceived no one, narrowing his eyes. 'I picked it up in Spain. The fellow I got it from *said* it was a Goya, but as you know, they'd say it was a Leonardo if they thought you'd believe 'em. Not that he was a dealer, he was a well-known connoisseur who used to advise the King and the big collectors. He *swore* that Goya painted it, and certainly it's very like him in his early period.'

Robin was wholly convinced of its authenticity and nothing wounded him more than any suggestion to the contrary. It was a rather blurred painting of two figures by a seashore, dark, cracked and badly in need of restoration, and probably no one could have told whether or not it was a Goya in that condition.

'A charming piece,' Hilary said, 'all the more so for being unexpected; I see you have several reminders of Spain.'

Robin's active service in the war had ended when he was blown up by a bomb on November 5th, a date his friends felt to be characteristic. After his recovery he had spent two years as Military Attaché in Madrid, where his romantic leanings had been stimulated by the intelligence work in which he had been involved. An atmosphere of codes, cyphers, secret agents and passwords delighted him; there had even been talk of burgled safes, disguises, invisible ink and beautiful ladies decoying officers and diplomats to luxurious apartments. Spying in the First World War seemed to follow closely the lines laid down by E. Phillips Oppenheim, and I think Robin had always hoped that one day a beautiful, scented lady in a diaphanous négligé would endeavour to unlock the miltary secrets in his breast; unfortunately, so far as I know, this was never his lot.

Tilly had found the diplomatic receptions so tedious and stuffy, and the strain of being polite to neutrals who clearly hoped for a German victory so great, that she had left him to take his chances with the beautiful spies and retreated to Britain to help run the Land Army, which was more in her line. She had been exposed, she said, to much more danger than Robin's among spies, for she had to carry out recruiting drives, and lived under the constant threat of attack by infuriated ladies whose last remaining parlour-maid had been swept by her eloquence into the farmyards of England; besides having to get about winter roads on a motor-cycle. Robin's reminders of Spain included the Goya, a large leather chair which lived on the veranda and was gradually chewed to pieces by dogs, and a signed portrait of King Alphonso in a silver frame that lived on the writing table.

The house that had been started before the war had at last been completed, although it was not as grand as Robin had intended. But it had wooden floors, two Dutch gables and a tin roof on which thatch had been laid. This reassured Cousin Hilary, and he was able to take off his topee, his kongoni skin, spine-pad and goggles. It also had a spare room inside the house, rather than a rondavel outside for guests, so that he could be accommodated under the sun-proof roofing, and in a residual aroma of herbs. Our old grass house, where we had lived so long and where I still had my school-room, horrified him because of the refuges it offered for snakes, scorpions and hornets, and because a single layer of thatch, in his opinion, offered meagre protection against actinic rays which constantly threatened our lives and sanity.

'The child ought never to take her hat off, and to wear goggles,' he advised. 'Sitting there with the door open and the sunlight pouring in! It's sheer suicide. If she isn't killed outright, she'll suffer from degeneration of the brain cells and become a drooling idiot. What are you learning in this death cell, may I ask?'

'Well, at the moment I'm studying the Illuminati, and a commentary on the prophet Isaiah,' I replied.

'That seems an unusual combination,' Cousin Hilary observed.

'Isaiah was intentional,' Tilly explained. 'We had been neglecting divinity; but the Illuminati was an extra. An old uncle with bees in his bonnet sent Robin a two-volume history, proving the members to be devil-worshippers practising the rites of Baal and in control of the Freemasons, as well as being behind the Risorgimento, the Easter Rebellion and the Russian revolution – in fact practically everything untidy that has happened in the last hundred years. I expect very few children will know as much about the Illuminati as she does when we've finished – we're only half-way through volume one. It will be an unusual accomplishment.'

'You're right,' Hilary agreed. 'It will give her a topic of conversation. When I was young I was ignorant of how to broach a conversation, until an aunt experienced in these matters gave me some advice. 'Think out in advance a couple of openings,' she said, 'and cast them like flies on the water.' One that I have found useful is: "I understand persimmons are in season; served with peacocks' tongues and stewed in Bactrian honey they are more appetizing, don't you think, than pomegranates, with all those tiresome seeds?" The other was about the habits of the mamelukes and went better in French. I found them very useful, and have had no trouble since.'

My curriculum was erratic. In part it depended on the rival calls on Tilly's time, in part on books sent from England and in part on whatever topic had, for the moment, taken her fancy. Thanks to the demands of the farm and the Kikuyu, I spent a good deal of time on my own, either reading books which I seldom remembered, or carrying out projects Tilly invented to keep me quiet. I had just finished designing an ideal capital instead of Nairobi, learning Old English lettering and paraphrasing the speeches of Alexander Hamilton. Unbeknown to Tilly, I had also written a play about Philip of Macedon and Olympias and wanted badly to show it to Cousin Hilary, but I could not screw myself up to the point. I asked him instead whether he had any of his own poems he would let me read.

'I'm going in for long, dramatic plays in alexandrines at the moment,' he said. 'They are most unfashionable and will never be performed, or probably read, but they are becoming more and more pompous and orotund and I have already been called the Irish Racine. When I'm established as an unbearable bore with impeccable syntax I shall write a play in nothing but colloquial obscenities about stokers on an Orient liner, in the hopes that no one will notice and the Board of Education will set it for examinations in the elementary schools.' He lent me a book in soft green covers containing satirical ballads in conventional rhyme about people I had never heard of, so I did not understand them, and a delightfully bound, nutty-smelling copy of Baudelaire's *Fleurs du Mal*, whose French was beyond me.

Hilary was a difficult guest. Even the water for cleaning his teeth had to be boiled as well as filtered, he would not venture on to the veranda without a sort of robing ceremony in the house, and tremendous mosquito-hunts took place at nightfall, accompanied by so much anointment with insect-repelling fluids that you could smell the house as you approached it in the dark. The first time he ventured out on horseback his appearance so startled the ponies that they snorted and backed away from him, as if he had been some alarming animal; even M'zee pricked his ears and looked concerned.

'That bwana must be a great chief in his own country,' Njombo remarked, with some awe.

'Why do you think that?'

'He has such a very big hat.'

Tilly scarcely knew whether to be amused or exasperated. Few of the usual pursuits of guests appealed to Hilary, and he was fussy about his food, but on the other hand he occupied many hours in photography. This was no matter of pointing a camera at a group of friends or at a pony, dog or view, and taking a snap. Hilary's camera was a huge, heavy object on legs whose siting was a good deal more elaborate, Robin said, than erecting a machine-gun post. A number of Africans had to be employed in this, and in carrying about the camera and its accessories, including a level used to see that it was not tilted even to a minimal degree.

And then his choice of subjects was not at all what we were used to. The waterfall just above the coffee nursery, the view from a bluff above the pulping shed, even the new house with its smart Dutch gables, none of these stand-bys, normally so attractive to our visitors, aroused even the mildest interest in Hilary. He was fascinated by a chameleon on a shrub, by the flowers of a passion-fruit creeper on a low wall, by the nests of a kind of weaver that built in a swamp. These nests hung down like little pockets attached to the reeds' heads, and were extremely difficult to get at, for the swamp was deep and treacherous. Hilary thought he could best reach the nests by boat.

'There are two objections to that,' Robin pointed out. 'The swamp's too thick to get a boat into, and anyway we have no boat.'

'Then we must borrow one,' Hilary said.

'But no one else has a boat, either.'

'Surely the natives have dug-out canoes?'

'Not these natives. They are a landlubbing tribe.'

'Other tribes, then. I have seen far too many prints of natives shooting rapids in dug-out canoes, with or without an explorer on board, to be taken in by such excuses. We must find a dug-out canoe.'

'Even if we did find one, you couldn't push it through those reeds,' Robin insisted.

Hilary eventually decided to go on foot, despite dangers from leeches, crocodiles, pythons and other aquatic enemies, on which he dwelt with hair-raising inventiveness. The expedition involved nearly as much preparation, planning and publicity, Robin thought, as Stanley's search for Livingstone.

Several bearers, who cast aside their blankets and advanced naked into the mud, clasped the tripod's legs while Hilary struggled to change plates under a canopy of black cloth and his enormous topee. He emerged dripping, exhausted but triumphant, to subside into a hot bath and drink spiced rum to keep away the chill he feared he might have contracted, although the temperature must have been well over a hundred degrees in the sun.

Encouraged by this display of hardihood, Tilly decided to take Hilary to see something of the life of the Kikuyu. The ponies went ahead to an Italian Mission four or five miles inside the reserve where we left the car, and took to the saddle. The country here was much more hilly than at home, the ridges steeper, the soil redder, and everywhere little shambas scooped from the bush showed up like fragments of milk chocolate. Maize and millet crops were knee-high and the women were out all day weeding, their babies bobbing about on their backs. They planted all their crops mixed up together, maize, beans, sweet-potatoes, groundnuts, millet all in one patch; everything took its chance in a free-for-all, and so fertile was the soil that everything germinated and found a place in the sun.

Each homestead then was separate, sheltered by bush from the eyes of strangers and shielded by a wooden stockade with only one entrance, so that anyone approaching could be seen in good time, and thieves and hyenas kept at night from the sheep and goats, the wealth of the family. These slept in the huts, under beds made of poles lashed together with strips of bark. In most huts, a brown ram was fattening for a feast under one of the beds. All day long he nibbled sweet-potato tops, getting fatter and fatter, especially in the tail, which would weigh ten or twelve pounds by the time he was ready for slaughter.

It was remarkable to think how different were Kikuyu lives from our own, and not surprising that they often found our ways wholly arbitrary, and forgot that salt, mustard and pepper pots should all be grouped together in two clusters on the table, and that pudding spoons should point in one direction and forks in another. Europeans rarely questioned their own customs; what they did was right and civilized, what others did was savage and stupid. No doubt all people think like this about their own habits. The Kikuyu probably accounted for most of ours as a form of magic. One of Betty Clewes' house-boys persisted in laying hot-water bottles on the floor under the bed instead of between the sheets, no doubt because he regarded them as charms to keep off evil spirits, and the proper place for charms was underneath a bed, not inside it. It was beliefs that divided us, of which colour was the symbol, not the other way round.

We had brought a picnic lunch, a venture which Tilly regretted. First the grass round the fig-tree selected to shelter us had to be cut, and the nearby bush whacked with sticks to dislodge any lurking snakes or rodents. Although instant death was believed by all to claim any white person who exposed his head to the sun between nine o'clock and four, a few bolder spirits did remove their topees or *terais* under trees if the shade was dense enough. This was not Hilary's way. Natives, according to him, had skulls of double thickness to protect them, as well as their pigment; even then, the actinic rays had so impaired their brain cells as to render them incapable of the intellectual growth achieved by races native to the temperate zones.

Chegge, our assistant *syce*, had volunteered to take us calling on his family. He looked as frail and skinny as a plucked snipe, with eyes as round as a bush-baby's; he was devoted to the ponies, especially to M'zee, with whom he would carry on long conversations. I often wondered what they were about. Chegge said vaguely they were stories his mother had told him, but he would not pass them on to me.

We approached his home along a path which, like all Kikuyu paths, wound secretively among the bush as if perpetually avoiding some invisible obstacle, as a cat often does when crossing a room. The entrance was cleverly concealed among trees and creepers. We found ourselves unexpectedly standing in a sort of archway, confronted by a clearing encircled by five huts, each flanked by its granary – another hut in miniature, standing on poles about four feet high. One of the simpler suggestions made by Europeans was to fix discs of tin round these poles, like collars, to prevent rats from running up them. Rats and fires were the great enemies.

Chegge was quickly surrounded by several women, ranging in age from an ancient, toothless person whose wizened breasts hung down to her waist, to a girl glossy and plump with youth, a round patch of wool on top of her head indicating that she was not yet married. All wore leather aprons, heavy coils of beads, and wire in their ears. One of the older women brought us, in a calabash, a handful of heavy greenish dough, made from millet flour and pounded plantain flavoured with a kind of spinach. After the greetings were over the young woman returned quietly to her pounding millet in a hollow log with a heavy wooden mortar. The muffled thump, thump of this rhythmic pounding, often done by two women in unison, was as much a part of the landscape of sound as the cooing of doves and tinkle of goat-bells.

Wherever you went, you never saw a Kikuyu woman idle; even grandmothers sitting with their legs stretched out in the sunshine, leaning against a hut, would be busy making one of the close-woven fibre bags used for carrying grain. On the other hand you seldom saw a man at work. Elders spent their days in beer-drinks or sitting in *kiama*, the council of elders, hearing disputes about goats and bride-price, and younger men seemed only to loaf about, although before the rains they might break ground for a new shamba. Sowing, cultivation and harvesting of crops they left entirely to the women. Sometimes you would see them squatting in the shade to play an interminable, complicated game with beans dropped into shallow holes made in a flat piece of wood, or if necessary in the dusty ground. Njombo had tried to teach it to me several times, with poor results. It involved a far greater skill in mental arithmetic than I was ever likely to muster, and it seemed to me (perhaps wrongly) that the rules varied on each occasion.

Despite the germs, insects and parasites that obviously abounded in Chegge's home – the children's eyes were plastered with flies, the women's aprons stiff with dirt and grease, and everyone undoubtedly had worms, whose eggs were said to lie concealed beneath all Kikuyu fingernails – Hilary was so fascinated that he almost forgot the deadly perils to which his health was exposed. He even entered a dark hut, quite without windows and with a fire smouldering in the centre, the floor caked hard by goats' urine and the rafters encased in soot, and was disappointed when smoke drove him out before he could set up his camera for a flashlight photograph. But the sight of ripe gourds on a vine clambering up one of the huts consoled him. These were of all shapes and sizes, long and thin, round and fat, large and small, and of many shades of orange, brown and yellow.

It was their shapes that delighted him and inspired prolonged photography. His eye then fell on a woman making pots. She had no wheel, but moulded the wet clay with her hands; nor did she fire the pots, but simply left them to dry in the sun covered with banana leaves. To everyone's astonishment he took a number of exposures merely of her hands moulding the clay. My idea of portraiture, like everyone else's, was to line people up, not quite facing the sun, where they stood at attention and were preserved on film in *toto*, from head to foot. Just to take a bit of someone seemed pointless, but Hilary went into raptures about the curve of the knuckles, and said that there was poetry in the prehensile movement of the fingertips. During the photography he evolved a theory that the Kikuyu were offshoots of the Celts, or at any rate that both races shared a common origin. Some of the squiggles on the rims of the pots, he said, had a Celtic fluency and eloquence, and both races were feminine in their artistic approach. In fact he thought the Kikuyu were a feminine people (this was not the same, apparently, as effeminate) and that was why they got on well with the British, who were thoroughly masculine.

Tilly thought they had no artistic feelings, or at any rate no arts; they never sculpted or painted, they had no architecture, they did not carve designs on stools or implements, and the little beadwork they did indulge in, such as belts and edgings to cloaks and aprons, while pleasing, was copied from the Wakamba. Although Hilary looked round carefully, he had to admit that he could see no sign of creative art in Chegge's household, beyond the squiggles on the rims of the pots. He felt sure they must have musical instruments, and tried to question Chegge about this, but our basic version of Swahili lacked words more precise than 'thing to make a noise in play'.

Chegge and his relatives looked blank when this question was put to them.

'What sort of noise do you want to make?' Chegge inquired.

'*I* do not want to make a noise,' Tilly explained. 'The bwana asks whether the Kikuyu have things of this kind.'

'Things of what kind, memsabu?'

'Things that make a noise while people dance.'

Chegge shook his head and Hilary, putting up both hands, waved his fingers in the air in front of his mouth. I could see that he was miming a flute player, but to anyone who did not know about flutes it would have looked very strange. Several of the women began to retreat towards their huts and one of the children burst into tears.

'A piece of wood with several wires, and people hit the wires with their fingers,' Tilly hopefully suggested. Hilary cradled his left arm, and plucked at the air with the fingers of his right. Giving a low moan, one of the women turned and drove the children hastily towards the huts like so many chickens. In a moment everyone had disappeared but Chegge and even he looked anxious for flight.

'Brass, perhaps,' Hilary said. Cupping his hands, he let fly a resonant bellow. Chegge edged away, his eyes wide with terror. It was obvious to everyone that a spirit had taken possession of Hilary's body. All such spirits were harmful, and one strong enough to possess a white man would be even more harmful than usual.

'I really don't think we're getting anywhere, Hilary,' Tilly said. 'We can ask the Italian fathers at the Mission. Now I expect Chegge's family will have to send for a witch-doctor to get the place cleaned up.'

'An excellent suggestion!' Hilary exclaimed. 'And it would be only right for me to defray the expense. What is his fee likely to come to?'

'Probably a goat.'

'Oh, six or eight shillings.'

'Then let us buy a goat immediately, and hire a practitioner. To see one at work is one of my dearest ambitions. Tell this boy, Tilly, to fetch us immediately the best witch-doctor in the neighbourhood, the very paragon of Harley Street, and I will buy the largest goat we can find.'

'It isn't as simple as that,' Tilly objected. 'They'll scarcely admit they have witch-doctors at all these days, much less produce one openly.'

'Then they've certainly managed to keep their medical profession under better control than we have. But they *have* witch-doctors, all the same?'

'Of course. It's the Government that tries to control them, not the Kikuyu. Egged on, of course, by the Missions.'

The official view, Tilly explained, was that all magic was superstition, and all superstition backward and wrong, and an obstacle in the path of progress and civilization. It must therefore be ended, and to this purpose laws had been passed by Europeans in Nairobi. It had now become an offence to practise witchcraft, however beneficial its intention might be. If people fell ill, they should go to a Government dispensary or Mission. Witch-doctors could be fined and imprisoned even when, by African standards, they were doing nothing but good. Could a dispensary placate umbraged spirits, and protect people from harmful spells? And then, if a sorcerer was detected, an enemy of society, he should be put to death at once in the interests of the community. In British eyes this was murder: in African eyes, the execution of a dangerous criminal. All this had naturally led to secretiveness among the Kikuyu about their witch-doctors, although such individuals were consulted as freely as ever. But it was no use asking Chegge to produce one.

'I'm disappointed,' Hilary said. 'I'd hoped to learn some of their methods, which in essence are probably much the same as those our own physicians practise, though certainly not for a fee of six or eight shillings.'

'They always involve hideous cruelty to a goat.'

It had always puzzled me that, while the Kikuyu treasured their goats above everything, spent their days herding and tending them and slept in their close proximity at night, and would pursue lawsuits lasting for years about the fate of a single one, they did not by a flicker of an eyelid reveal the slightest concern when one of these harmless beasts was tortured to a lingering death as part of a magical or religious practice. Chegge was devoted to M'zee, and spent hours in his box, and for his part M'zee trusted and respected Chegge; yet I sometimes wondered whether Chegge would show any emotion if M'zee was hurt. Perhaps, if it were an accident, he would, but if someone decreed that M'zee had to be sacrificed, I believed that he would accept the ruling without protest, and even watch the pony's agony unmoved.

Chapter 10

ONE day towards the end of Cousin Hilary's visit, Robin came in to breakfast – Hilary had a tray in his room – and said: 'There's a dead rat in the store.'

'I hope you didn't touch it.' Tilly looked disturbed.

'Of course not. I hooked it on a long stick and it's been burnt.'

'Perhaps it died a natural death,' Tilly said hopefully. 'Or perhaps Sinbad killed it.' Sinbad was the cat.

The reason for their concern was fear of bubonic plague, whose first sign was generally a dead rat or two. Outbreaks of plague could be checked by an injection, but the medical authorities often took some time to go into action and the infection spread with alarming speed.

'We ought to get inoculated,' Tilly said.

'What about Hilary?'

They looked at each other blankly. 'If we told him we'd got Black Death on the farm, he'd have an apoplectic fit. It may not be that at all.'

'We'd better send chits to all the neighbours and find out if any of their rats have died.'

The replies were reassuring; no one else had seen a dead rat, although the Judds reported a rumour of an outbreak in the reserve.

There was only one Judd really, a large beefy man who

wore shorts and a black beard and had been a sergeant-major, which had left him with a habit of barking rather than talking when he wanted things done. Perhaps for this reason he was always having labour troubles, although he was a kind man at heart and fond of children, for whom he would buy sweets and dole them out to any Kikuyu children bold enough to approach. He studied all the pamphlets, books and articles on coffee growing he could get hold of, and always had some new theory about pruning, fermenting or controlling disease. Tilly had put him in the plural because he had told us so much about his tapeworm that we felt we knew it personally. It was a punctual nematode, and grew restive if he postponed his midday meal later than one o'clock. It did not like milk puddings, but delighted in bacon and eggs, and Mr Judd had grown quite fond of it – at any rate, as Tilly said, it was strongly attached to him.

While the bubonic plague scare died down, Robin's veld sores were causing trouble. Arising like ordinary boils, they spread into great angry gatherings that burst and then became deep, suppurating sores all over his body. Doctors treated them with arsenic injections to which they seldom yielded. When they were at their worst, an English mail arrived with a small, interesting packet from Portugal for Robin. We speculated about the contents while he opened it at teatime. It was too small to contain a bottle of port, even a miniature; Tilly suggested a sample tin of sardines, and Hilary a saintly relic, an eyetooth of St Polycarp perhaps, or a shred of the shift of St Babylus.

Robin stripped off the wrappings to reveal a neat little leather case. This was lined with padded white satin, and inside lay a shining medal and clasp, attached to a gay watered silk ribbon, as magnificent as it was mystifying. Robin's name was stamped in gold letters on the lid of the box, so there could not have been a mistake. He examined the medal more closely, and a look of absolute astonishment came over his face.

'How could they possibly have known?' he exclaimed.

'Known what?'

'About my sores!'

'How could who have known?'

'The Portuguese Government.'

'What *are* you talking about?'

'This,' said Robin, holding up the medal, 'is the Order of St Lazarus.'

And indeed it was, although two saints were involved, St Lazarus and St Michael. In a separate envelope was a letter written on thick, crinkly paper, full of official seals and flowery addresses, telling Robin he had been awarded this Order for his valiant and faithful services to Portugal during the recent war. Robin scratched his head reflectively and puffed at his cheroot.

'But *what* services?' Tilly inquired.

'The only thing I can think of is that a report of mine had some influence in keeping Portugal out of the war, on our side, for six weeks.'

He never did hear what the Order really was awarded for, but from that day his sores started to mend, and within a couple of months they had healed over.

Our respite from the threat of plague was brief. More rats were found, and reports of deaths in the reserve confirmed. A doctor was encamped there injecting everyone, but he could spare no time for labour on the farms, so Robin sent to Nairobi for supplies of the vaccine, Tilly boiled the syringe normally used for ponies, cattle and dogs, and a parade was ordered of every man, woman and child living on the farm.

The problem was how to keep all this from Cousin Hilary. Tilly sent chits round to all the neighbours to warn them not to mention plague in his presence, but feared that someone would be sure to forget. The other difficulty was that Hilary ought to be injected. Either he must be told, suffer and be safe, or he must be kept in ignorance and peace of mind, with the possible risk, however slight, of infection. The decision was a great responsibility for Tilly and Robin. The risk did, indeed, seem very slight. Plague-infected fleas were supposed to leave the rats only when their hosts died; unless you had contact with a dead or dying rat, you ought not to be in danger. But, as Robin said, it was rash to build too much on the habits of fleas, or rather on medical knowledge of these habits. Fleas, like other creatures, might have whims, or make mistakes; somehow or other, one might go astray and hop on to Hilary. After much discussion it was decided to do nothing unless there was a case of plague on the farm: if this were to occur, he would have to be injected.

As the entire population of the farm could not be mustered and injected without Hilary's knowledge, Tilly asked the Clewes to invite him over for the day. Harry Clewes did better, and took him off to the Athi plains for two or three days' shooting. Not that Hilary was a shooter, but he enjoyed collecting plants and butterflies and looking for the traces of the lost civilizations he was convinced must exist somewhere on this savage continent. While he was away, everyone was injected. The Kikuyu endured the unskilled jabs with stoical impassiveness. It was odd how, from the very first, they had taken to injections with avidity, or at least the men had done so; the women hung back, and had to be hunted out by Mugu, and some had taken refuge with relatives. The women's fear of the unknown was deeper than the men's, and they became their own jailers in the subjection in which they were held.

Hilary returned from his excursion with several new butterflies, and in hot pursuit of the tiny red ticks that had got through all his defences in droves, and called for a bath in methylated spirits. Although his stay with us had been a long one, when the time came for him to go, everyone was sorry. We had grown used to him, and yet he remained unpredictable. Tilly was the sorriest, because she liked nothing so much as a laugh, and Hilary constantly provided them. My own feelings were mixed. He had given me one or two lessons in French, an experience equally painful for us both.

'The accent is excruciating,' he exclaimed. 'Far, far worse than a knife squeaking on a plate. How can this have come about?'

'Perhaps it's my fault,' Tilly said.

'No, no, that's impossible. It's the same in all the colonies. As soon as a place becomes a colony, something in the air ruins the accent.'

'I don't see the point of learning French anyway,' I said

crossly. 'No one speaks it here. It would be far more useful to learn Kikuyu.'

Hilary closed his eyes and a look of intense suffering contorted his face. 'Have you no idea, child,' he demanded, opening them and gazing with his grey, flecked eyes into mine, 'what it means to be civilized?'

'We're civilized, and the natives are not.'

'That is only half true. The natives certainly are not.'

'Perhaps it's just as well you're going home,' Tilly said, 'since you despise us rough colonials so much.' Although her tone was light, Hilary had hurt her feelings.

'I ought to take you with me,' he said, more seriously than usual.

'Thank you, Hilary. In what capacity?'

'A damsel in distress, rescued from a fate worse than death.'

'What makes you think I want to be rescued?'

'That's just the trouble,' Hilary said sadly. 'I'm afraid you don't. There it is, creeping up without realizing what's going on: that dreadful French accent, the *Revue des Deux Mondes* pushed into the garden-house, ink stains on the embroidery ... Do you recall "I don't remember the Italian for window or ceiling!" – spoken by Irina? One of the most poignant, heart-rending cries in all literature. Only one thing would have been worse – if she hadn't *known* that she'd forgotten it. But you, my dear, you're in mortal peril, and you don't even realize the fact.'

'In that case it hardly matters,' Tilly said. 'Thank you for your chivalrous intentions, but I'm quite happy where I am.'

'Perhaps you'll miss me a little?' Hilary asked almost sadly, and without his usual obliqueness.

'I shall miss you very much, Hilary.'

'Thank you, I shall remember that – it will be like a glass of very old Madeira on a cold day. Even though it isn't true, or won't be for long; there'll be a sick pony, or a temperamental incubator, or a wonderful new crop that's going to make your fortune in a few months. Once I was engaged to a beautiful creature who jilted me for an Armenian violinist; he died young of some horrible disease. She was right: he

126

played superbly. But to be spurned for a cavalcade of ticks and blights and veld sores, for a life where the sunshine's full of poison and the bath water of tadpoles, where everyone talks about glanders and neck-moults, and where parchment is part of a coffee bean and not an ancient document ... You won't take me seriously. But I am serious, you know.'

Tilly was looking at him in a quizzical sort of way, almost tenderly; she was not displeased.

'Never mind; Mugu has organized a crate to take your photographic plates and butterflies; would you come and tell him how you want everything packed?'

'We must make them airtight somehow, to resist the humidity in the Red Sea.'

Hilary spoke in a resigned way, and I was half sorry for him, and half glad that he was going. Although I liked him I never felt at ease with him; I knew he thought I was a kind of savage, and he seemed to represent, in an indefinable way, at once a criticism of our existence and a threat to our security.

Meanwhile I had been planning a farewell surprise. By now I had mastered quite a *repertoire* of conjuring tricks, and felt the urge to give a small performance. Conjuring, like any other art, cannot indefinitely be practised in private; the time comes when you feel the need to offer your achievement, however meagre, to the world. I knew that my finger-work was clumsy, my patter crude, and that things might well go wrong, but all the same I wanted to see how my tricks worked on an audience more critical than Kigorro, Chegge and Njombo.

First I had to consult Robin. Several of the tricks called for sleeves to conceal pieces of elastic, and for inside pockets, so I needed a man's coat, and also a top hat. Robin pointed out that top hats were not to be found on African coffee farms.

'Won't a topee do?' he asked. 'Are you going to pull out a rabbit?'

'No, not a rabbit. I'm going to mix a cake.'

'What, in the hat?'

'Yes, but it won't hurt the hat.'

'Well, I suppose one could wash it out. But I haven't got a topee. You'll have to borrow Hilary's.'

The cake was to be mixed in a black tin container, made to fit invisibly into a top hat, that had come with the trick. This was useless for a topee, and the best I could do was to get a pudding bowl from Kigorro and make a sort of jacket for it out of red material, the insides of topees being lined with red. It made the trick even more difficult, and the preparations more prolonged.

Robin lent his dinner jacket with reluctance. It was fifteen years old, and he did not think that conjuring would improve it. I had, indeed, to sew bits of elastic to the armpits and make a false pocket for the inside. It was puzzling to know what to wear under the dinner jacket. It hung in folds and reached almost to the hem of my dress, and bare legs beneath looked, even to my uncritical eyes, somewhat incongruous. The only solution I could think of was a pair of riding breeches, worn with long mosquito-boots. I arranged my apparatus at one end of the living-room and the chairs at the other, as far away as I could, and invited Alec Wilson, the household staff and Njombo, who could be trusted to applaud.

I cannot remember the *repertoire*, but it went quite well. There was the trick with the billiard balls, several with a hollow egg into which I stuffed coloured silk handkerchiefs, and one that I always liked with two bowls and rice which first doubled in quantity, and then turned into water. The cake trick came at the end. It was rather complicated, and involved a good deal of juggling. A chair facing the audience had a little shelf fitted to the back on which I stood the pudding-bowl, and a sponge cake provided by Kigorro. I had to conceal a watch, borrowed from one of the spectators, in the centre of the sponge, and I asked Robin for his. It was a treasured possession, a gold half-hunter given him by his father on his twenty-first birthday, I think inherited from a grandfather before that. I bore it back with me to my end of the room, stumbled, appeared to drop it to the ground, and picked it up with a contrite air and many apologies. The glass and hands were smashed, I said, and it had stopped ticking.

There was a shocked silence, and Robin looked as vexed as I had ever seen him. I could feel a cold wave of displeasure coming from the audience. No one actually said anything, and that made it worse. Alec came to my rescue with some frivolous remark, and I proceeded to break two eggs into Hilary's topee, and to add flour, sugar, butter and milk. Tilly remarked that the cake would be a very heavy one. After a good deal of stirring and waving of wands and stilted patter, I managed to exchange the bowl of ingredients for the sponge cake, which I pulled from the topee. I could tell that this impressed my audience, even though they still mourned the breakage of the watch.

Slightly restored, I advanced upon Robin and asked him to cut the cake, but he shook his head. He was still huffy about the watch.

'I'm not hungry, thanks,' he said.

'You needn't eat it. Just cut a slice.'

'No point in spoiling it. Keep it for tea.'

'But please do, I want you to see it's a real cake.'

'I can see that without cutting it.'

This spoilt the whole effect of the trick. Nor did Tilly seem inclined to come to the rescue. She had the dachshunds, Bluebell and Sunflower, on her knee.

It was Bluebell who saved the situation by lifting her head, craning her sleek neck towards the cake and then, throwing manners to the wind, extending a long, pink tongue to lick the nearest side. Tilly pretended to scold her, but Bluebell could do no wrong.

'Now you'll have to cut it,' I said firmly.

'Oh, well, all right. Though I don't know why you're making such a fuss.'

The knife blade struck something hard and there was the watch, safe and sound and ticking. This was a small triumph; everyone had been taken in, even Hilary, whose topee had only a few splashes of egg.

'You have started on the right lines by practising deception,' he said. 'I hope you'll keep it up. To deceive gracefully is the very essence of social life. One must start by deceiving oneself, and make a lifelong practice of deceiving others; if one does it well enough, in time one might even become an artist, the greatest illusionists of all.'

'Do stop practising epigrams on the child, and filling her

up with a lot of nonsense,' Tilly said. 'Tell me: of all the things you've seen and done here, I mean in this country, what have you enjoyed most?'

Hilary took her hand and kissed it, and instantly replied: 'Your company, my dear cousin.'

'I made you a present of that opening, didn't I; luckily you'd given fair warning that you only tell lies.'

The next few days were fully occupied with preparations for Cousin Hilary's departure. He possessed even more boxes, crates and cases than when he had arrived. The cameras had to stay unpacked until the last moment, in case some scene or subject caught his eye. This turned out to be unfortunate, because it was only at the very last moment that his eye was caught, just when all the preparations to take him to the station had been made. That there should be no hitch was important, because the whole operation had been carefully timed. To avoid staying a night in Nairobi, Hilary was transferring himself and his baggage direct from our local train to the boat train, which left the capital at four o'clock the same afternoon. So if he missed the train at Thika, the whole logistic exercise would miscarry, and he would be stranded for weeks, if not months, at a hotel in Nairobi.

A number of Kikuyu were standing by to push the car if it refused to start, and Kigorro, Njombo, Mugu and the houseboys were assembled to wish Hilary God-speed. Alec had ridden over for the same purpose, and Harry Clewes had sent a box of cigars. Most people came and went without ceremony, but whenever Hilary made a move it became an event – like a Royal Progress, Robin said, in the seventeenth century.

Robin looked at his watch. 'Time to be going,' he said briskly. Although he was always polite to Hilary, and amused by him, I did not think he was really sorry to see him go. He had mentioned an old Chinese proverb saying, 'Guests and fish stink after three days.'

Tilly sent a message that the car was ready. We all went on waiting, but after five or ten minutes Hilary still had not emerged from his bedroom, where he was ensconced behind closed doors.

'What on earth can he be doing?' Robin wondered. 'If he misses the train . . .'

'We might be able to catch it up at Ruiru.'

'Not with that swampy patch where they drowned the camel.'

'I'd better go and see what he's up to.'

I followed her to the spare bedroom door. Her knock was greeted at first with silence and, when repeated, with a sudden hiss like a snake's, only much louder. Was it a cry for help or a prohibition? Tilly stood irresolute. The car's horn tooted anxiously.

Tilly entered to find Hilary on hands and knees, his head and shoulders invisible beneath a black tent in whose shelter he operated on his camera. The camera itself was aimed at a washing-stand under the window where Sinbad the cat was endeavouring, for some wayward reason, to drink from a tall enamel jug. His forepaws were in the rim and he was craning his back to reach into the jug.

'My dear Hilary, are you all right?'

Hilary rose slowly to his feet and dusted his knees. 'The light from the window is rather brilliant, but I hope that I have succeeded in filtering it down.'

'Do you realize that you may have missed the Thika train, the boat-train *and* your ship?'

'A successful picture would be worth it. I have seldom seen anything more exquisite than the curve of Sinbad's back against the light as he bent towards the water, like the trumpet of a velvet tiger-lily bowed before a gentle wind.'

Tilly, for once, was defeated. She gulped, and said in a strained voice: 'Hilary, either we must go at once and drive like fury, or you must book yourself for three or four weeks at the Norfolk Hotel.'

'It is accomplished; I am ready to go.'

Hilary distributed his tips like a monarch awarding orders, and spent another five minutes arranging his cameras in the car. Robin was silent, and drove like a demon all the way to the station, shaking everyone to bits. We heard the whistle blow as we charged along the rutted street between the *dukas*, bucking in and out of holes and hooting to attract the guard.

He saw us, and checked his arm just as he was about to raise his green flag. Hilary's cameras and the rest of his baggage were hoisted and slung into one of the carriages; with remarkable agility, he pulled himself up after them, veils flying behind his topee, his kongoni skin spine-pad in place over a shirt of khaki shot with red, and leant out of the window to wave gaily as the train, packed with gesticulating Africans, puffed importantly away.

The house seemed quiet and ordinary without him, but in a few days the impression he had, as it were, imprinted on the air grew nebulous. Some months later we received a photograph on a large black mount of Sinbad drinking from our white enamel water-jug. The curve of his back was indeed bold and sweeping, balanced by a lesser curve in his tail. For a while the photograph was propped up on a bookcase, but it gathered dust, grew tattered, and eventually disappeared.

Chapter 11

WHEN a number of farmers in our district made plans to gather at Makuyu over Christmas for three or four days of sport and festival, they decided to put up *bandas* to house everyone who came. You made a *banda* by tying sisal poles together with strips of bark and arranging bundles of dry grass, cut from the veld, to make the walls and roof. You left a gap for the doorway, and perhaps a window aperture. The grass, poles and bark were free, and so the only expense was the labour; and a good gang could run up several in a day. *Bandas*, therefore, appeared very quickly at Makuyu to shelter the farmers, their ponies and their ponies' *syces*, one *syce* to each animal. This was a custom imported, we understood, from India. Africans soon got the hang of it, and no *syce* would look after more than one pony. His duties were light, and his status superior.

After the Christmas party had been fixed the rains came back, entirely out of season, and turned the whole plain into a soggy, treacherous, waterlogged morass. The mud, the leaking thatch, the sodden state of everything was taken as a joke, at least for the first day or so. A polo tournament was arranged for a cup presented by Sir Northrup Macmillan; teams arrived from several districts, more ponies than I had ever seen at one time were assembled, and *syces* of all kinds were exchanging details of each other's names, families and life histories. Most were Kikuyu: those who were not looked morose and ill at ease. Everyone else distrusted the Kikuyu, and half expected to be poisoned or cursed.

We all brought our own food and camp equipment, and fed in a communal *banda* furnished with trestle tables. I was hoping to report the polo matches for the *East African Standard*. Some of the players had scarcely wielded a stick before and few of the ponies knew what they were up to, but polo is a simple game in essence, started in Persia by posses of warriors riding at each other – in Japan it had been played with thirty-six balls – and the Kenya version, though played by only four a-side with one ball, must have somewhat resembled this embryonic form.

The Beatties came down from Nyeri for the tournament, all except Alan, who had been engaged by Jock Cameron as an unpaid bottle-washer to help conduct a party of Maharajahs in pursuit of elephants. If he shaped well, Jock or some other established figure in the safari world would very likely take him on as second hunter, and one day he would take out parties on his own. The best hunters received a hundred pounds a month, a salary that to most people seemed immense; but, like actors, they often had to wait between engagements, or go in search of ivory. It was a disappointment not to see Alan, even though he was generally rude to me, but he had remembered to send the cheetah skin. It was better cured than any skin we had ever treated, and gave a touch of splendour to the *banda*, but it soon began to get muddy and I rolled it up and put it under my pillow, the only place I could depend on to be dry.

Every afternoon it poured with rain, the camp became a mass of slithery mud, people played bridge, moving their chairs about to avoid the drips, singing the choruses of music-hall songs and drinking whisky to keep out the cold. On Christmas Eve there was a great carousal, and next morning Robin was heard to remark that the only dry thing in the camp was his mouth. Christmas Day started with an early jackal hunt across the plains and continued with a service in the dining-*banda*, taken by a young parson fresh from England. Missionaries were interested in black souls, not in white ones, so whereas Africans got their Christianity free, Europeans had to pay for theirs. Few were prepared to pay as much for their religion as for their recreation, but in this they were not exceptional. They had raised by voluntary subscription a Chaplaincy Fund to bring out the parson, and were now collecting money for a proper church, which in due course arose at Thika. The Christmas offerings were to go to this cause, and, as the worshippers had brought little ready cash to Makuyu, they were asked to put chits into the plate. This was a shrewd move. The spirit of generosity, curbed by shortage of cash, thrived on chits, and the parson was able to announce that a record sum had been pledged towards the building fund.

After the service there was time for polo while the turkey and plum pudding were roasting or boiling in *debes* on the three stones with which the cooks miraculously contrived to make anything from a curry to a soufflé. I had resolved to conceal my trade as a reporter and to sign my contributions with the pen-name of Bamboo. I had to follow the play with close attention but not to give myself away by taking notes, and in the afternoons to find seclusion in which to write my reports. I was also allowed to play in practice chukkas, though not, of course, in the tournament. Almost everyone who could ride, male or female, young or old, was roped into make up sides, and so with the mounts – even mules took part. Many of the ponies naturally disliked being hit about the legs with mallets, or in the face by a bouncing wooden ball. They often stopped, jinked or shied, unseating their riders, so the practice games were slow and precarious, but exciting.

Either M'zee had taken part before, or he grasped the idea at once. He watched the play carefully and would often stop and start to turn – he was a neat-footed turner – before the player ahead of him hit the ball, either because he could see that the shot was to be a back-hander, or because he knew from experience that the player concerned was sure to miss. As a polo pony he made up in wiliness what he lacked in speed. He refused to be hurried, and when it came to riding off other ponies he was cautious rather than bold. I felt safe on his back in the reassuring conviction that he knew much more about the game than I did, and that if I did not hit his fetlocks, which made him sulky, I could safely leave most of the tactics to him.

The reporting was difficult, but had its compensations. I enjoyed remarking that my father had missed several easy chances and should improve his back-hand, and that Colonel Beattie had thrown away a goal by failing to mark his opponent. The Colonel galloped about at a great speed shouting at Commander Strudwick, who, after so much practice in the cage, had a beautiful style and could hit a ball magnificently provided he was stationary, but nearly always missed it when his pony was in motion. He was therefore apt to pull up when he approached the ball, and this resulted in his being run into from behind and bellowed at by Colonel Beattie to stop behaving like an equestrian statue of the Duke of Wellington.

The Clewes were of the party, together with Miss Cooper and Captain Dorsett, who was spending the last few days of his leave as their guest. Miss Cooper was all a-bobble with necklaces, bangles and ear-rings; Captain Dorsett followed her about like a spaniel and had even been observed holding her knitting wool. Whenever one of her arch pleasantries popped out he smiled inanely as if at a great witticism. Despite their foolishness, I felt sorry for them both because so many jokes were made behind their backs, and sometimes, indeed, to their faces. These gratified Miss Cooper, but very much embarrassed the Captain.

'In some ways I shall be glad to get back to the Frontier,' I heard him remark to Alec, when out of earshot of Miss Cooper. 'Want to see how all my fellers are getting on. Shouldn't be surprised if the Havash hadn't been getting uppish again. Ticklish customers, those Havash, you know.'

The Havash were brigands who emerged from Abyssinia to raid the Kenya tribes for camels and slaves.

'It's no good thinking you can just slip up there and hide behind the camels and Somalis,' Alec replied. 'If a woman's after you she'll go through them like butter. You're a lost soul, old man.'

'Oh, tommyrot.' Captain Dorsett laughed nervously. 'You flatter me, my dear chap. I'm no ladies' man. But give me the day's trek and the open sky and my blokes yarning away at night by the camp fire and I'm in my element. You keep fit up there, too. None of these grains to make you flabby. I bet you've never seen a flabby Galla or Somali. It's the camels' milk that does it. Have you ever tried living on camel's milk?'

'Never.'

'Well, you should. It's awfully good, and you'd be astonished what it does for your stamina. You can go all day on a good swig of camel's milk. It's got to be fresh, of course. High sugar-content. Straight from the camel.'

'A simple form of housekeeping.'

'No housekeeping there, old man. No houses.'

Captain Dorsett spoke with surprising warmth and feeling about his northern deserts. Alec said this was like the last despairing convulsions of a chicken whose neck has just been wrung.

Deslin the Abyssinian was with his master at our camp, unbending as a winter cliff. He would not associate with the Kikuyu, for whom his contempt was bottomless, nor with any of the other *syces* and servants, but slept outside the door of Captain Dorsett's *banda*. When it rained he got soaking wet and refused to go inside, or to take refuge in the stables. Obviously he missed the camels' milk, and would not touch the maize-flour provided for the retainers.

'You'll have trouble with that cut-throat of yours,' Alec said.

'Oh, I don't think so. He's a devout Mohammedan. Absolutely T.T.'

'The more devout, the more trouble. A universal rule.'

Alec was right, as he so often was over these affairs. On Christmas Day a bullock was presented to the Africans, who roasted the meat on spits and sticks round open fires that night. They were not supposed to have beer in the camp, but, of course, they did, and no one inquired too closely, hoping they would get through the night without a scrap and sleep off the worst effects by morning.

I retired late and went to sleep with the swampy scent of wet grass and earth and the slight, dry smell of mosquito-netting in my nostrils. What woke me I do not know: shouts perhaps, or a sudden stilling of the hum of voices from the dining-*banda* and the *syces'* camp fires. Something was wrong. Slipping on a dressing-gown and mosquito boots, I hurried out to investigate. The *syces*, amid angry shouts, were dragging a fuzzy-headed man towards the dining-*banda*. Something red, I thought at first a stream of blood, appeared to be a shawl flying loose; a moment later, it vanished into the mud. Several Europeans ran out of the *banda* and a raised safari lamp illuminated the advancing knot of men. I recognized Deslin without his red turban, struggling like a trapped animal in the grip of half a dozen stalwart *syces*.

How the fracas had started, none could tell. Perhaps someone had shouted an insult at Deslin, aloof from the feast, or perhaps he had begun it with a gesture of contempt. At any rate he had been insulted: in the splinter of a second he pulled his dagger and hurled himself upon his accoster, who crumpled with a cry into the fire. Another man who went for Deslin recoiled with a slashed arm and half-severed fingers. The rest did not dare to touch him as he stood with his dagger dripping and his wild, handsome panther face twisted with fury. But two others jumped from behind and pinioned him. Then Deslin was very nearly hacked to bits. A panga slashed into his ribs, but his attackers pressed in so wildly that they fell over each other, and help arrived in the nick of time to rescue him from the fate of a buck pulled down by the hounds.

Maggy Nimmo, helped by Tilly and several other women, went into action with bandages and iodine. Once his rage had ebbed, Deslin lay absolutely still and rigid and did not flinch even when the disinfectant stung his wounds, or when his bruised bones were handled in search of fractures. One of the *syces* had been severely burned, another gashed and in need of stitches. The native method was to pin a gash together with thorn prickles, but Maggy Nimmo tackled the job with an ordinary needle and thread.

Next day, at the inquiry, so many witnesses came forward to name Deslin as the aggressor, and he himself remained so taciturn, that the inquirers had little choice but to find against him. Normally, the penalty would have been a severe flogging. This was then the quick, harsh but accepted unofficial punishment for breaches of the peace, theft and flagrant disobedience. Most of the men who imposed these sentences had themselves been beaten when young, and did not regard the whip as an insult to a man's dignity but as a valid, indeed indispensable, way to enforce order. But Deslin was in no condition to be beaten; nor did anyone wish to hand him over to be ground to pieces in the mill of authority.

Captain Dorsett acted with vigour as the prisoner's friend. Clearly he thought Deslin the aggrieved party and the *syces* in the wrong. At the same time he felt responsible, as if he had been the owner of a tame lion who had turned and savaged a child.

'What are we going to do with this fellow?' Randall Swift inquired. 'We can't just leave him as he is. Either one of the *syces* will try to finish him off, or he'll try to get his own back on them. We'll have to tie him up, even if he is injured.'

'You can't do that,' Captain Dorsett objected.

'What can we do, then?'

'I can put him under military arrest.'

'But you haven't any askaris.'

'I could shoot him if he tried to get away.'

'It isn't his getting away that I'm worrying about,' Randall said. 'It's his spirit of revenge.'

'If I tell him he's under military arrest, I'll guarantee he won't make any trouble.'

'And if he was under ordinary arrest, not military, do you think he would?'

'He wouldn't feel bound.'

'Well, make the difference quite clear to him,' Randall said.

Captain Dorsett addressed him in some tongue assumed to be Galla. Deslin remained completely wooden and without emotion. He was standing to attention despite wounds which would have kept a European a week on the danger list and months in hospital.

'He understands,' Captain Dorsett said. 'Until we leave, he's under arrest; and he'll be charged when we get back to the Frontier.'

'But you won't have any witnesses.'

'I'll see he's fairly dealt with there.'

'I object to that,' said Harry Clewes. 'That's not justice. This man has made a savage attack on a peaceable civilian. He should be punished for it. I still think he should be beaten, but at the very least he should be handcuffed and kept in proper custody and then handed over to the authorities.'

'He would never agree to that,' Captain Dorsett said. This infuriated Harry Clewes.

'Damn it, no one's asking for *his* agreement! Anyone would think he was as innocent as a newborn babe. He's the one who –'

'I don't agree with that. If the *syce* hadn't provoked him –'

The argument nearly started another fight, this time among the Europeans. Captain Dorsett had become quite a different man from the meek swain content to hold knitting wool. He had the rest against him, but no one felt prepared to interfere when Deslin marched away, holding himself very stiffly as if a touch would collapse him, to his master's *banda*. No one saw him again until he departed with his master two days later. Captain Dorsett kept himself somewhat aloof after the incident, with a hint of sulks, although everyone else forgot about the difference of opinion in the excitement of a buffalo-hunt that unexpectedly took place on Boxing Day.

It had been arranged for the Captain to take a new draft of askaris with him to Archer's Post, and another officer was to hand them over to him at Thika station. We had to get back to the farm the same day, so we rode with him as far as the station, while the Clewes, and, of course, Miss Cooper, came by car to see him off. We all arrived before the train, and had one of those awkward pauses at the Blue Posts, trying to think of things to say. The Captain and Miss Cooper sat in melancholy silence, obviously wanting to hold hands but not liking to. He gazed at her face with moist, glassy eyes and slightly parted lips and seemed to have shrunk into quite a weedy, insignificant person.

'You will write, I know,' Miss Cooper said. 'I shall be interested in every detail. Although, of course, I've never been to such a wild, romantic sort of place, I have a vivid imagination, and I shall be able to picture it all.'

'You must write to me, too.'

'I'm afraid the small events of my life will seem very dull to you, with all the adventure and thrills of empire building; nothing exciting ever happens to *me*. But perhaps it will mean something to you to hear from someone who ...' To everyone's embarrassment Miss Cooper appeared overcome, pulled out a lace-edged handkerchief and blew her nose.

'Mails in those parts must be a bit chancy,' Tilly remarked.

'They depend on the rains, and sometimes on the elephants, you know, who hold up the runners. They always go in pairs – that is the runners – and, of course, there are delays when they're treed by lions, or chased by rhinos. But one generally gets one's letters in the end.'

'I hope they're worth all that, when they do arrive.'

'One never knows. The other day the runners were chased by an elephant and swept away by a flood and all but drowned, and took over a fortnight, and the mail-bag was in shreds and full of mud. All I got was an invitation to dinner in Nairobi from the deputy director of public works, and a bill for some shirts from Ahmed Brothers.'

A distant hoot announced the train's arrival and we found it at rest, with the usual animated crowd getting in and out, greeting friends and extracting mysteriously-shaped bundles. Near the goods shed was a squad of trim askaris standing at ease under the eye of a white officer. They all looked as tall as storks and strong as boxers. The officer was really brick-red, not white, with bare, beefy knees and stiff, scrubbed khaki shorts and tunic buttons gleaming in the sun.

Captain Dorsett was also in uniform. He seemed to grow taller as soon as he put on his hat and tucked his swagger cane under one arm. Looking very grave and stiff he saluted our group of God-speeders and, without another glance at

Miss Cooper, turned smartly on his heel and marched away towards the waiting platoon, with Deslin at his heels. As he strode across the yard he seemed to be transformed before our eyes from an insignificant, hollow, nobble-kneed and rather silly man into a brisk, dashing and formidable warrior. It was almost like watching an insect split its nymphal skin to emerge as a full-blown, strong-winged adult.

He and the other officer stood face to face as stiff as trees and saluted each other. You could see their hands quiver like a plucked string. Captain Dorsett looked taller and bigger than the other officer. His khaki drill uniform was so clean and starched that it shone in the sun, the crease in his shorts was sharp and decisive and his shoes gleamed like brown zircons. Deslin had probably been working on them for a couple of days. After the salute there was a good deal of barking and stamping and slapping of rifle butts, and in due course there was Captain Dorsett in front of the platoon and the other officer walking away, his hands already on his belt to loosen it, relieved of his charge.

An enormous, coal-black sergeant, who looked strong enough to toss an ox over his shoulder, shouted savage-sounding orders and the squad marched away towards the K.A.R. camping-ground, where they would prepare for their long, long march to Archer's Post and beyond, perhaps even to the Abyssinian frontier. They would be thinner by the time they got there and tough as old leather, but still as smart. Captain Dorsett looked tremendously impressive as he strode ahead, the seasoned commander of these hard, brave soldiers, the controller of a well-designed machine that functioned smoothly and tirelessly. One could scarcely believe that this tall, disciplined officer, master of several dozen supermen each twice as strong and bold as any ordinary mortal, had so lately fawned upon a person of such meagre parts as Miss Cooper. He who had been a slave was now the centurion. I wondered if the askaris marching behind him had been seen off from Nairobi by wives and sweethearts with coiled wire bracelets and bead ear-rings even more copious than Miss Cooper's, and if they had noticed the same change. Perhaps some of them had seen their black warriors for the last time. The Northern Frontier was full of perils, and had bleached the bones of many soldiers and hunters in its time.

'I hope that he will remember to take his quinine regularly,' Miss Cooper said, as we walked back to the car. 'Men are so careless about these things. I remember my father, who was a military man just like Captain Dorsett – we are an old army family – was always forgetting his quinine. He had served a lot in India, so I have the Empire in my blood, as you might say, and understand the sacrifices men like Raymond make to build and maintain it. A lot of people nowadays don't understand it, but I do. That's partly why I venture to think he found me sympathetic. It will be a year before any of us will see him again.'

Tears were running down her face, which was embarrassing, but after a few sniffs she brightened up and said: 'Well, I think we have all had a memorable Christmas.' I had had a busy one, and on the way home posted my report of the polo tournament to the editor, Mr Mayer, in Nairobi, satisfied that no one would guess Bamboo's identity.

Chapter 12

MANY wild duck and fat, banded Egyptian geese came that year to the *vleis*, which turned from hard pans into lakes three or four feet deep, blue as delphiniums, ringed by vivid green grass and, beyond that, either by thorn-scrub and the naked-branched erythrina trees, or by regiments of dark green coffee bushes. When the erythrinas shot vermillion flowers from their twisted branches, and the coffee bushes were festooned with tightly clustered, creamy flowers smelling of orange blossom, the blue, green and red, all strong pure colours, set off by brown earth and bark, dazzled the eyes. And on the *vleis* swam, dived and ruffled the sleek wild ducks with their bands of glossy peacock blue and rufus feathers, and the handsome, long-necked, spur-winged or Egyptian geese.

They had no sooner to appear than plans were made to

destroy them, in obedience to the human instinct to kill immediately any creature of a species not his own. I did not question this impulse; everybody wanted to shoot ducks and geese and so did I. They were good eating, but this was really an excuse; it was the sport of killing that appealed. Several duck shoots took place in the district, for everyone had at least one *vlei*, and in the evenings, after tea, I stalked the birds with my ·22 rifle and tried to shoot them on the water, or by the water's edge. The fast swimming ducks jinked about on the water; geese offered targets both larger and quieter, but were more alert than any antelope and apparently able to detect my approach without being able to see me.

My favourite *vlei* was on the far extremity of the farm, where it bordered with the Clewes', and where the land had not yet been brought under cultivation. One or two native shambas were dotted about and herds of goats browsed in the bush, but otherwise it was secluded, and a haunt of reed-buck and duiker. A herd of kongoni had lived there when we first came, but they had vanished, and just over the ridge Harry Clewes had begun to plant coffee. A low spur of bush-clad land jutted into the *vlei*, and provided a means of advancing upon the birds. If I could surprise them in the lee of the spur I could get a shot at twenty or thirty yards, but four times out of five they would detect some sound or movement and be off just as I was raising my rifle. Sometimes I fired at them in the air in sheer exasperation, but the triumph of bringing down a flying duck with a ·22 riffe had so far eluded me. Chegge was my usual companion, but sometimes Njombo took his place. He did not eat duck, nor the flesh of any wild beast or bird, but had the hunter's instinct, and enjoyed outwitting the quarry.

Sometimes we fell in with Kikuyu going to and from the Clewes' farm or returning to their huts near the river. Njombo would greet them with the usual exchanges – where have you come from? where are you going? what is the news? and conclude, as he walked on, with the drawn-out, liquid word *m'wai–ai–ai–ga*, meaning good, all's well, go in peace: the hail and farewell of all Kikuyu conversation. More often we encountered women carrying home heavy loads of firewood or the big, fig-shaped gourds they filled at the stream. They, too, exchanged greetings with Njombo, but with the difference that they neither paused nor halted, but trudged on, as dedicated to their purpose as ants on the march, never hurrying or loitering, the toilers and the makers and sustainers of the African world.

I did not pay particular attention when, one evening, two youngish men walked behind us, talking to Njombo, as far as the *vlei*. The sun was almost touching the horizon when we reached it, the clouds flushing with their sunset anger. A great sadness fell upon the world at this time of day. Everyone was going back to his shelter against the perils of the night, which came down so swiftly and without mercy or compromise. When darkness actually came there was no sadness, and a new life started, for to many creatures nightfall was the dawn, and in huts and houses everything was warm and secure; but this moment of change was a time of nakedness and of a small death. A kind of significance charged the trees and bush and grass as electricity will charge a battery. It was as if some unseen power was sending out a message which our senses were too obtuse to catch, and despaired of us because of our bluntness. A poem in one of my Georgian books, written by J. C. Squire, often came into my head at this hour. It described how, at dusk, the world seemed infinite and lonely, and a small, ugly brick house took on suddenly a great majesty, it became a symbol of courage and endurance, of the 'unshakable dauntlessness of human kind'. Probably it was not a remarkable poem, but it expressed exactly what did happen at dusk, when for a moment a wing-tip of the bird of death touched the cheek of anyone who walked abroad, away from the fireside.

Such evanescent thoughts did not distract me from the hope of shooting a sitting duck. The sun, a great red ball on the horizon, spurted shafts of light across the land to illuminate each tree and bush and clump of grass as by a cosmic searchlight. It would be dark within half an hour. The rays shone into my eyes and gave the birds an advantage, but as I cautiously approached the *vlei*, the red globe sank behind a purple rim and suddenly shadows melted away and the trees and bush went out like stars at dawn. The ducks were dark blobs upon still water, each at the apex of a small vee formed by ripples they created as they swam about, dipping and shaking their heads.

They had not seen me. This was the moment of excitement that tingles in the blood in every hunter, let the quarry be a pigeon or an elephant. I raised the rifle slowly in the lee of a thorn-tree. Here was the movement, however slow and slight, that had so often caused the prey to vanish just as my finger tightened on the trigger. But this time the ducks were betrayed by their concentration on a search for food. At this hour, in fading light, one nearly always fired too high. I aimed well below one of the ducks. There was a quick smack when the bullet grazed the water; the duck spread its wings and struggled to rise but could not, and flapped despairingly while its companions slipped into the air and rose steeply, leaving a circle of ruffled water and sending a melancholy call into the encroaching night.

Njombo gathered up his blanket and dashed towards the *vlei*, but he was forestalled by the two strangers, who loped into the water and splashed and laughed as they waded out. When the water reached to their waists they slipped off their blankets and held them above their heads with one hand while they made for the duck, still flapping in a hopeless effort to rise. I did not wait to see them grab the duck, partly because the quarry's death always saddened me a little, however anxious I had been to bring it about, and partly because I was supposed to be home by dark.

'*M'zuri*,' Njombo said, meaning good, well done, that is satisfactory.

'Those men will bring the duck?'

'Yes, they will bring it immediately.'

'But we don't know them . . .'

Njombo laughed. 'Kikuyu don't eat ducks. They are like hens, and hens are only eaten by women.'

We walked home briskly as the light drained away to leave the bush quiet and watchful, and by the time we reached the house the sky had come to life with stars. Robin was on the veranda pumping up a petrol lamp that hissed at him reproachfully, like a resigned snake. It gave out a hard, white illumination and some heat, and left a ring on every table where it rested, and never worked very well.

'Can you spare ten cents each,' I asked, 'for two boys who retrieved my duck?'

Robin extracted this sum from his pocket, remarking: 'If your mother's dogs were any use at all they could be trained to do it, and earn their keep.' I gave the money to Kigorro, telling him to hand it over to the duck retrievers.

I did not go near the *vlei* again for three or four days. Some geese had settled on a smaller lake closer to the house. I failed to shoot one, however, and decided to inspect again the more distant stretch of water.

'There are no ducks there now,' Njombo said.

'You can't be sure. We'll go and see.'

This time I reached the *vlei* fairly early, to see a flock of ducks feeding on the far side. Right in the middle was a small black hump I took to be a log, but something about its shape prompted me to ask Njombo's opinion.

'Just a log,' he confirmed.

Sometimes, at the water's edge, I found the narrow, pointed footprints of reed-buck and duiker. These *vleis* gave out a sweet, reedy, exciting smell, different from anything else. At night a myriad of frogs croaked continuously, some with a gargling sound, some as if a blunt saw grated on wood. I thought I could detect a sickly, rotten smell mixed with the sweet swampy odour. Perhaps a goat or an ox had been drowned. I looked more closely at the black floating object and decided it was not a log, but that it was too large for a goat and too small for a bullock. Caught up in it, and floating on the surface, was a grey blanket.

'That is a man,' I exclaimed.

'No,' said Njombo.

'I think it is. Don't you see the blanket?'

'That is not a man.'

'Then what is it?'

'Only a log.'

It was no good arguing with Njombo, who kept his eyes away from the object in the water.

'You had better go and see.'

'No.' He shook his head emphatically. I did not know what to do. I remembered the two Kikuyu who had waded out after my duck, but there was absolutely no reason why either of them should have drowned. The water was nowhere deeper than a man's armpits. Now that I thought back, I was almost sure I had heard a splash just as I turned to go home. I had paid no attention, as the men had been laughing and splashing each other in fun.

Njombo was unusually surly and disinclined for conversation. He pointed his chin towards home and said: 'Why do you not shoot one of the geese on the other *vlei*? They are much bigger than these ducks.'

I decided not to tell Robin or Tilly about the floating object. If the man really had drowned while fetching my duck, I thought I should be blamed. I should certainly be cross-questioned, and could not remember whether I had heard a special splash or not. And anyway perhaps Njombo was right. His eyes were keen, and if there was a corpse in the water, why should he deny it? So I did not mention the matter when I got home. Two days later Robin came in to lunch and said: 'There seems to be a corpse in that far *vlei* over on Harry's boundary.'

'What sort of corpse?' asked Tilly.

'A human one. It stinks to high heaven and no one will go near it. Nothing on earth will make them touch a dead body, as you know.'

'But how did it get there?'

'No one knows. And no one knows who it is – was, rather. At least they say they don't. You know what they are.'

'Perhaps we ought to have an inquiry.'

'Well, Mugu says no one on this place is missing, and no one's relatives or friends. I'll send chits over to Harry and Alec and Maggy Nimmo, to ask if anyone of theirs is missing. If not, I don't think there's much we can do.'

None of our neighbours had mislaid a man, nor could anyone be persuaded to wade in and retrieve the disintegrating corpse. Even had Robin managed it single-handed, no one would have touched it, or helped him to bury it, and everyone would have continued to deny all knowledge of its identity.

He sent a message to the local chief, Kupanya, to ask whether he had heard of any missing person. There was no response, and no relative appeared. The man in the *vlei* seemed to have dropped out of existence without so much as a ripple on the surface of the life around him. Considering that every Kikuyu was embedded in a solid matrix of family, that no one ever stood alone, this was peculiar. It was true that death was shunned and dead men's names never mentioned but, all the same, somewhere there must be a family with a gap in it, carrying out ceremonies for the dead. Njombo must have known something, but he would not discuss it.

'Only a stranger,' he repeated. 'I don't know where he came from. I don't know his name.'

There was nothing we could do against this conspiracy of silence, and everyone was busy on the farm. The weeding had clashed with a small picking – both, in Kikuyu opinion, women's jobs – and the men had to be persuaded to take part. Now both men and women were carrying *debes* of red coffee cherries down to the pulping plant by the river. I doubt if it occurred to anyone to send to Fort Hall for the police. All that happened, if you summoned them, was the eventual arrival of a young officer who did not speak Kikuyu, with a couple of stalwarts of some alien, feared and hated tribe, and their chances of gleaning any information were even less than our own. The corpse disintegrated quickly in the water, and when I looked there several weeks later not the least sign of it remained. So the nameless Kikuyu who had perished so strangely while retrieving my duck passed briefly in and out of our lives, and was no more heard or thought of again.

Perhaps it is untrue that he was no more thought of; once or twice, when I passed the *vlei* or stalked ducks on it, a thought did cross my mind, a question, a memory of a lumpy black object and a floating grey blanket. The memory did not disturb me, for people came and went like seasons of rain or drought, like fires that left underfoot a blackened devastation of crisp, powdery grass roots which flushed a vivid green again after the first storm, like the prickly blackjacks you plucked from your clothing after a walk. Only things affecting your own family left a mark on the mind.

Chapter 13

NJOMBO was under strict orders to report at once if any of the ponies was in the least bit off-colour, and refused or only picked at his food. This was because horse-sickness, for which no scientific cure was known, had no other symptoms in its early stages. Every day after breakfast I went to talk to M'zee, and Tilly as a rule inspected Hafid and Fair Play, so although we did not take their temperatures – later on this became a daily routine – Tilly thought that we should immediately spot anything wrong. But one day, when Njombo brought the ponies round after tea, she saw that Hafid lacked his usual spirit, and drooped his head instead of dancing as he normally did.

'Hafid looks sick,' she said to Njombo.

'Yes, memsabu. He did not eat his food.'

'Then why didn't you tell me?'

'He is not very sick, only a little.'

'You know I told you to speak at once, even if he was only a little sick.'

'Yes, memsabu.'

'Then why didn't you?'

Njombo looked sulky and stubborn, and merely said: 'Hafid isn't sick. He's not hungry, that's all.'

Tilly fetched a thermometer and found that his temperature was three degrees above normal. She decided to start the cold water treatment straight away. For although the vets could prescribe no vaccine or drug, a treatment for human fevers invented by a Nairobi doctor had saved the lives of a good many animals.

Dr. Burkitt was the originator of the cure. He had in fact two cures for almost every human ailment, aside from those demanding surgery. One was cold water, the other a pint of blood. The first covered any form of fever, the second everything else, including high blood pressure and liver complaints.

The theory underlying the cold water treatment was simple:

if you brought down the temperature of the body, the germ causing the fever would die. The only thing you had to watch was that the patient did not give up first. Dr Burkitt on the warpath was a famous and a dreaded figure. People with chattering teeth, shivering under mounds of blankets in an attempt to 'sweat it out' – this was the normal treatment for malaria – would have their blankets torn off as by a whirlwind and find themselves crouching in a hip bath, generally in a passageway with a draught, being sponged down with cold water by a frightened spouse or bemused houseboy, and there they would stay until released by a falling thermometer. Sometimes a water-can was brought into play. A friend of Tilly's had a precious baby who contracted pneumonia, ran a temperature of 106, turned blue and lay *in extremis* between blankets and hot-water bottles. Dr Burkitt arrived in a mule buggy, having come ten miles through mud too deep even for his hardened T-model Ford. When she saw who the doctor was she moaned and ran from the room, abandoning her last hope. The doctor threw off all the blankets, remarked fiercely in his Irish brogue about the stuffiness of the house and shouted for a wickerwork basket. In this he put the naked baby, slung it to a beam on the veranda and organized a chain of shamba-boys with *debes* of water and a fruit spray. In an hour the baby had revived, by evening it was out of danger and in two days quite well again.

Once his temperature fell, the patient was permitted coverings. There was a story that on one occasion Dr Burkitt was called to a woman seriously ill with malaria on a farm so drought stricken that no cold water could be had. Dr Burkitt stripped off all her clothes, put her in the back of his car and drove furiously for Nairobi. At intervals he stopped to take her temperature; when it began to fall, he took off his coat and wrapped it round her. As they proceeded her temperature continued to fall and he continued to divest himself of his clothing, and the story ran that when they reached Nairobi she was dressed as Dr Burkitt and he sat naked at the wheel.

Dr Burkitt became a legend in his lifetime and many stories of this kind used to circulate. Some of them have been collected in a brief, lively memorial called *Under the Sun* by his latter-day partner, Dr Gregory. During the malaria season Dr Burkitt had patients all over Nairobi in cold baths, under wet sheets, being sprayed with watering-cans or sponged, while he hurried from case to case checking temperatures. The more rebellious patients posted guards, and when the doctor's car was seen approaching they would leap from the warm bed into which they had retreated to crouch in the bath. Dr Burkitt never suspected such duplicity. 'This is a terrible bad case!' he would exclaim, shaking his head over the thermometer. But those who stuck it out were generally cured in twenty-four hours.

The other hazard you faced if you called in Dr Burkitt was to find your arm bound and punctured and your blood flowing into a vessel held by Assumption, his Goanese assistant. 'Too fat, too fat!' the doctor would cry accusingly to ladies over-fond of elevenses, whether his patients or not. 'Heatstroke, that's what it'll be — heatstroke. I should be taking a pint of your blood!' If he saw a man in need of the treatment he would pursue him relentlessly. One such was Major Gailey, a heavy, choleric individual fond of his food and drink, but determined to keep his blood in his own veins. One day a patient in hospital needed a blood transfusion (this was before the days of blood banks) and a donor had to be found. Dr Burkitt hurried straight to the firm of Gailey and Roberts and recounted with all his Irish eloquence the plight of the man dying in hospital for lack of a fellow creature generous enough to give his blood. Major Gailey had no alternative, and was displeased some weeks later to receive a bill for two guineas for his humanitarian act. 'Ah, but it did ye a world of good,' was all the change he got from Dr Burkitt.

Once broken in, however, some of the doctor's patients took to regular bleedings in the eighteenth century manner. One such was Mr Greswolde Williams, who came to value the treatment so highly that, when on holiday, he demanded it from an English doctor. At first the doctor indignantly refused; when he was at last persuaded there was such a to-do with blood counts, cardiac tests, hospitals and second opinions that in later years, when air travel came in, Mr Greswolde Williams, who had retired to England, used to fly to Nairobi to be bled.

'Burkitt just looks at the whites of my eyes and I'm bled in five minutes,' he said.

Dr Burkitt was delighted when Randall Swift consulted him about a mastoid growth, and took a skull down from the wall. 'Now look here, it's years since I did this operation,' he said. 'You see this bit of bone here? I must take that away with a hammer and chisel; if I touch this nerve here the whole of one side of your face will drop down, do you understand that now?' Randall said that he did. 'And then again, it's very near the brain and if I touch it just a little here you'll be dead, do you understand that now?' Randall looked round for a way of escape but could see none; he returned from hospital intact and cured.

Surgery was Dr Burkitt's pleasure as well as his trade. When Dr Gregory met him in London, in answer to an advertisement, Burkitt proposed a visit to a theatre after their business talk. The young man readily agreed, only to find himself at St Mark's Hospital for Diseases of the Rectum, watching a distinguished surgeon perform. In all he did, Dr Burkitt was equally single-minded. Immensely busy, he would still devote many hours a week to reading the Bible, in whose literal truth he was a firm believer, and every Sunday morning, unless called to a patient, he would give an exposition of his views on the Scriptures at a hired hall to an audience of seldom more than a dozen, and often four or five. But he was not discouraged, holding that to glorify God is the chief end of man.

When he was called to farms Dr Burkitt would often prescribe for animals as well as men, and after his cold-water treatment had saved the lives of several ponies it became the accepted, and indeed the only, way to fight horse-sickness. Everything depended on catching the fever in its early stages. As soon as his temperature was revealed, poor Hafid stood shivering in the open, dripping and dejected, while water squeezed from Tilly's and my bath sponges trickled down his back and flanks. Tilly stayed up all night; had she left, the sponging would have stopped at once and everyone gone to bed. The little group, illuminated by a couple of safari lamps under the starlight, looked like devotees of some pagan cult rendering homage to Hafid with arms up-raised, lamp-light gleaming on bare, wet, coppery limbs and silence prevailing save for the clink of buckets and the squelch of feet on wet ground. When I awoke soon after six o'clock I found the spongers just knocking off. They had kept it up all night and now Hafid's temperature was almost down to normal and he was nibbling at a bran mash. Njombo and his helpers had retired, stiff and silent, to get some sleep. The morning was bright, and at seven the work-gong sounded its high metallic note through a limpid air quavering with the calls of birds. Hafid was alive and, as we hoped, saved, and despite Tilly's tiredness she looked satisfied.

But after breakfast we found that Fair Play had a temperature and that Hafid's had risen by half a point. Two cold water teams at once were bound to tax everyone. Shamba-boys were drafted in as spongers and both ponies now stood dripping under a small tree near the stables. It was not big enough to cast its shade on both animals and emergency measures had to be taken. Luckily we had some sisal-poles, half a dozen women were dispatched to cut grass and in a remarkably short time a shelter had been erected to protect the ponies from sunshine, while allowing them to be cooled by the light breeze.

Hafid had grown so listless that he did not seem to care what happened to him, and would not touch any food. Probably he had been running a temperature for twenty-four hours before we took action. Njombo was in disgrace. He had seemed so fond of the ponies, and so well seized of the need to treat them immediately they showed the least sign of sickness, that we had never thought he would let us down.

All day long the sponging continued, and all the next night too. Robin and I took over in the afternoon while Tilly slept. The spongers worked in four-hour shifts, and we took the ponies' temperatures every hour. Hafid's fell a little but then it stuck, and despite fits of shivering it would not go back to normal. His knees grew weak, his breathing shallower. Tilly stayed up all night again and gave him several drenches of brandy with beaten eggs. In the morning he was still alive, but only just.

'I don't think his heart will stand any more sponging,' Tilly said.

'Burkitt never worries about that.'

'He's down on the ground, too weak to stand.'

We sat over breakfast during a pause in the sponging, to await the arrival of the water-cart. I often thought that breakfast was the best time of day. The sun was bringing everything to life. Dappled lizards were darting about on a low wall half smothered in bougainvillea and in passion-fruit vine. Later they became torpid, and dozed under stones. Sunbirds fluttered round montbretias and plumbagoes in the herbaceous border, wagtails hopped about on the lawn and a grey fly-catcher with white rims round his eyes, just as if he wore spectacles, chirped from a thorn-tree. Sinbad was basking in a patch of sunlight, an epitome of peace and satisfaction; grapefruit shone like lanterns from a dark-leaved bush; golden shower blossoms trembled from a veranda post and threw shadows on white concrete; a scent of wood smoke and geranium and moist earth and coffee hung on the air. The toast was hot, the marmalade dark and chunky, there was fresh paw-paw or home-grown grapefruit to start the meal. On a clear morning we could see the outline of Mount Kenya against an azure sky across green ridges, but more often clouds had already gathered round its peak. It did not look like a mountain at this distance, but like a shape that had been cut out and pasted in the sky.

Even breakfast could not be enjoyable with death so near. Hafid was fighting for his life; he shivered all over and took shuddering breaths. Each one needed an effort of will which wholly preoccupied him, he paid no attention even to Tilly when she stroked his neck, although normally he always gave a little toss of his head when she patted him. His Arab blood showed in a head finer and prouder than Fair Play's, more bony and alert. But now his coat was rough, his nostrils bloodshot and his ribs went out and in like a bellows. There was a sort of grating in his lungs as he drew in air and his neck was stretched out and propped on a bundle of grass. It was no good going on sponging him. Tilly was stroking his ears.

'I'm afraid he's a goner,' she said.

Robin, with his head on one side, could only look distressed.

'That fool Njombo. If only he'd said ...'

'Well, it's too late now.'

'More brandy?'

Tilly shook her head. Hafid was shuddering more with every breath. It seemed appalling that we could do nothing now in his extremity to help him, we who must seem to him providers of food and shelter who now denied him the life he did not want to lose.

'There must be *something* we can do ...'

But there was not. His breaths grew shallower and even more laboured and some white froth came out of his nostrils and ran on to the ground. The grating in his throat grew worse. Then he drew a longer, quavering breath, almost a sigh, and his bloodshot eye rolled round as if to look at Tilly with some message of despair. He shuddered all over and ceased to breathe, and a lot more white froth came out of his mouth and nostrils. Tilly got up, gave his neck a final pat and blew her nose. Njombo was standing in silence a little way off. With a lot of shouting and creaking and clanking of chains, the water-cart arrived.

Chapter 14

ONE night thieves broke into the Clewes' office, opened the safe with a key and stole all the money, which included a large sum drawn to pay an Indian contractor for a new store. Harry held an inquiry, and a young police officer summoned from Fort Hall held another, but no amount of questioning produced any information of use. A theft of such importance was bound to come to the ears of chief Kupanya, who was told by the inspector that he must find the culprit, or at any rate tell the police where to look. The weak point of this procedure was, of course, that Kupanya would throw suspicion on anyone he had a grudge against, while blackmailing the real criminal for goats. All the police could do was to probe any suggestion of Kupanya's with a care which they hoped, as a rule vainly, would enable them to detect such double-dealing. The truth was that among the Kikuyu double-dealing was children's stuff; it was treble and quadruple dealing the authorities were up against, and even higher powers of deception than that.

The police got nowhere and retired to Fort Hall, but Harry continued his inquiries with relentless vigour, threatening everyone with terrible penalties if they refused to talk, offering rewards and inflicting mass fines. He was like a dowser walking with a twig over the surface of Kikuyu life; now and again the twig gave a nervous twitch, and in due course it pointed its accusing end at Harry's trusted headman, Kamau.

Robin and Tilly were not at all surprised. Kamau had worked for us once as a rudimentary sort of clerk, having learned to read and write at the local Mission; he had been inefficient, untrustworthy and conceited, Robin said. I had rather liked him; he had asked questions about life in England and other matters which did not normally interest the Kikuyu; he had the quality of curiosity, and some queer, muddled ideas about the world outside Thika, instead of the usual indifference. But there was no doubt he had been a bad clerk of dubious honesty. He could always talk himself out of any trouble, and find excuses for the things he had failed to do. After we left for the war, Alec had dismissed him because of some *fitina* – a useful word meaning feud, fuss or quarrel – with other and more trusted Kikuyu, and suspicions about the pilfering of tools. He had gone to Nairobi and wormed his way into a semi-clerical job at one of the many military establishments, to emerge at the end much fatter and more prosperous, with a pair of spectacles and a smattering of English. Harry Clewes had taken him on and soon promoted him to headman, so now he was more prosperous than ever, oily to Europeans and hectoring to the Kikuyu.

It may have been that we were unjust to Kamau, and unconsciously resented his success in raising himself above the general level, at least materially – in his character he did not appear to have done so. He was no longer a loyal, faithful servant who accepted without question the authority of Europeans; he had become a harbinger and so, indirectly, a threat. Perhaps a subconscious realization of this lay behind our distrust of Kamau. On the other hand, the Kikuyu did not like him either. Almost alone among our group of farmers, save for the Judds, Harry found it difficult to get enough labour, and few of his people stayed for any length of time. It may have been that Harry was too strict for them, too concerned with brisk efficiency, but it was probably even more the behaviour of Kamau. Prosperity had puffed up his conceit and plated his manner with arrogance. He had three wives, one of them a daughter of Kupanya, which put him in a strong position to get labour, but did not enable him to hold it. No one could understand why Harry kept on Kamau, still less trusted him. But as Kamau was Harry's headman, Kamau was perfect, or nearly so, just as Harry's ponies were faster and better than anyone else's, his coffee more prolific, his maize crop heavier, his wife more desirable and his twins brighter and stronger. Robin said sourly that it always rained more across the river and that all the antestia bugs, a beetle pest of coffee, had retreated after a good talking-to, their faces red with shame.

The only thing that surprised us about the present episode was that Kamau had not been caught out before. It was generally believed that he had been pilfering from Harry ever since he became headman, and had large flocks and herds in the reserve. Harry kept a small herd of cattle that he was grading up with a superior bull, to produce beef for the Nairobi market, but his intentions were defeated by the death of all the calves. This was not a good cattle district, but even so it seemed strange that no calf ever survived. When the dead bodies were produced for inspection, they always turned out to be wizened little creatures, and Alec said that Kamau was building up a splendid herd in the reserve, based on Harry's calves abducted at birth and replaced by deceased native changelings.

Despite all this, in the matter of the burgled safe, Harry was unable to secure any solid evidence against Kamau, who was caught in nothing more substantial than a web of rumour and suspicion. This infuriated Harry, who detested half-truths and evasions, and became more determined than ever to root out the truth.

'The police cost this country hundreds of thousands a year and they're no more use than a pain in the guts,' he fulminated. 'What's the good of telling me they suspect the fellow when they can't nab him? They make the law the laughing stock of the reserve.'

'It's more the fault of the law,' Robin said. British justice, he added, was made for one set of circumstances, for one way of living, and did not apply to the Kikuyu any more than cricket, morning-coats, monogamy and roast beef on Sundays. The whole idea of laws of evidence, and of assuming innocence when everyone knew a man was guilty, made no sense to them, and they were not going to get themselves mixed up in anything so absurd and dangerous.

'Our law was made by people who play games,' Alec Wilson agreed, 'and it's only understood by games players. You have two sides, each one takes it in turn to bat, let's say, and there are certain very strict laws. It doesn't matter how clever you are, or how determined, you can't win unless you stick to the rules. When the game's over the umpire says who has won and that's the end of it.'

'The players argue sometimes,' Robin pointed out.

'They argue, but only about the way the umpire's interpreted the rules; they don't argue about the rules themselves. They don't say a batsman *ought* to have his leg in front of the wicket, or that a man who's caught should be allowed to go on batting. But the natives don't play games, and so they don't think about rules, they think about who's really guilty, and if it's safe to accuse him or if he'll bewitch you. In this case Kamau married one of Kupanya's daughters, so everything depends on the relationship with his father-in-law. If they're on good terms he's nothing to fear, but if he's fallen behind with his goats or anything, then he may have to watch his step. No one likes him.'

Apart from Alec, most of our news on matters of this kind came from Njombo, who liked a gossip while we exercised the ponies or rode down to the post. But on the subject of the burglary he was uninformative.

'Why should Kamau steal shillings from bwana *pesi-pesi*?' he said. This was Harry's native name, and meant hurry-up. 'I expect it was a stranger who has gone far away, perhaps to Uganda.'

'Why to Uganda?'

'I have heard that everyone there is a thief.'

We were passing near the dead man's *vlei*, as I called it to myself, and I asked Njombo once again if he had ever discovered the drowned person's identity. His response was as blank as before.

'I don't know. How should I? It was not my *shauri*.'

'But ...' I did not add what I could only half express, the doubts I still had as to whether anyone could cease to be with less fuss than if he had been a pigeon. Nor was there anything to link that accident with the wholly unconnected burglary. Yet I had linked them, no doubt by a simple coincidence, in conversation with Njombo. Something had upset him, and he did not speak for the rest of our ride.

Harry Clewes did not give up, and at last a search unearthed a hoard of new coins from the thatch of a hut belonging to one of Kamau's wives. That these were some part of the loot he had no doubt; new coins were seldom seen in circulation, their passage from hand to greasy hand soon rubbed off their shine, but, of course, there was no way to prove it, and Kamau had a plausible story about a brother who had done a deal in goats, and even produced a brother (as he said) to swear to it. But Harry had Kamau up in front of his labour force, recited the case against him, judged him guilty and sentenced him, illegally of course, to twenty-five strokes. Kamau was then dismissed with ignominy, and left Clewes' with two wives, many children and goats and various household goods. His third wife was looking after his shamba in the reserve. That night there was a dance and feast among the Clewes' Kikuyu, and rejoicing all round. There was no doubt that everyone was glad to get rid of Kamau, and Alec said there was no doubt about his guilt either.

'Then why didn't the boys tell the police, if they wanted him sacked?' Tilly asked.

'Oh, well – fear of witchcraft, passing the buck, family

connections. And Kamau's got plenty of goats, he's rich.'

'Richer than ever, since he's got away with most of the money.'

'Yes; I believe he's going to start a shop in the reserve.'

'How *do* you know all these things, Alec . . .'

I saw Robin glance at her with a slight shake of the head; Tilly looked owlish and began to talk about the pair of silky-fleeced Angora goats that had arrived as a present from Hilary. He had bought them, he wrote, from a shepherd with eyes like garnets, wearing a homespun cape of purple, in a valley carpeted with wild flowers in a remote province of Turkey. In fact, Tilly suspected, he had probably ordered them from Dalgety's in London, but she called them Mustard and Cress, short for Mustafa and Cressida. Mustard had a magnificent white beard that gave him the look of a venerable prophet, and both had made themselves at home in a pen on the lawn. Robin feared that the Kikuyu would steal them, but Tilly proposed to spread the story that they were the spirits of two particularly potent ancestors and could turn into leopards or snakes if they so desired. Robin said she had cribbed this idea from his own family history. One of his forebears, who had commanded a garrison in Calcutta, had been accustomed to inspect the sepoys every morning on the ramparts. He had died suddenly of a stroke. One morning he had paraded the troops, the next he was dead; but exactly at the hour of his inspections, a large white cat had walked with dignity down the lines of waiting soldiers. The officer in command, acting on an impulse he could never afterwards explain, gave the order to present arms. Every sepoy thereafter believed the General's spirit to have entered into the white cat, which received a punctilious salute wherever it appeared on the ramparts.

The downfall of Kamau ended the matter of the Clewes' burglary for us, but not for the Kikuyu. For us, events occurred because things fell out that way, probably by accident. A man drowned in a *vlei*, our best pruner vanished without a word and never returned to collect his pay, Kigorro's wife had a dead baby, Mugu's son was afflicted by the dreadful elephantiasis that rotted away both distorted feet. All these events were for us isolated happenings that were dealt with and then more or less forgotten. For the Kikuyu they were part of the net of life in which no one thread was isolated or finite. Everything flowed from something else, just as all springs and streamlets ultimately join a single river, and nothing was ever concluded: a debt could not be paid without liberating a spirit which would in turn command other lives, an infant was a re-creation of his ancestor, and the lightest action would roll like an echo among the hills and back again, as the sun travels through the darkness only to return next morning. There was no beginning and no end.

So with the burglary affair. Harry got a new and better headman, and we did not think again of Kamau. We heard later that he had started his shop and was doing well. The Kikuyu still bought their food and household needs like pots, hoes and ornaments at markets that had been held under certain trees ever since memory ran, but for novelties like paraffin, matches, safari lamps, soap and blankets they would venture into a shop, arriving with their shillings tucked into a leather pouch hanging on a chain, and their cents strung together on loops of string. They would hesitate for hours over a comb or a single box of matches that could have yielded little profit to a shopkeeper, but Kamau seemed to thrive, probably by lending money at exorbitant rates of interest. Later he started a small maize grinding mill, and later still we heard that he had gone to Nairobi. Probably he bought, or otherwise acquired, a plot of land and built a house of sorts on it; letting off rooms was the quickest and easiest way to make money. His wives stayed in the reserve to cultivate his land. Now and then, one of them would plod the forty miles or so to Nairobi carrying a load of produce on her back for his sustenance, and return with goods for the shop, which was in charge of a relative. In this way Kamau saved the transport charges.

All this I did not learn until much later, when men who had been young and vigorous had become old and wizened, when feuds that would once have gone on for generations had been lost in the confusion of new and fiercer quarrels, and when men no longer stood on their own feet but, as Njombo put it,

161

were carried along like twigs cast into a river. Although it is out of sequence I had best conclude the story now, for I never did hear it until we had all left Thika and Njombo, by then a sort of elder statesman, recalled it, and told me what had caused the duck-retriever's death and, for Kamau, a downfall that set his feet upon the path of riches.

Kimotho was the name of the duck-retriever. Njombo, who had so emphatically sworn the man to be an unknown stranger, was in fact his brother-in-law. And this Kimotho had been involved in a profound dispute with Kamau. Three things lay at the heart of all Kikuyu quarrels: land, goats, and women; often all three were intertwined. In this case Kimotho, whose father was a poor man and a tenant, wished to marry a girl called Wanjiko, one of the innumerable daughters of Kupanya: for this portly chief, after a most successful war, had fifteen wives. Wanjiko had already borne a child, and Kimotho claimed to be its father. The *kiama*, the local court of elders, accepted this claim but also imposed a fine, on top of the bride-price. And so Kimotho and his needy family found themselves deeply in debt to the powerful Kupanya.

Kimotho rashly borrowed goats from Kamau – no doubt he had no alternative. Then Kamau foreclosed on the debt and, when Kimotho's family could not pay, claimed the girl Wanjiko instead. Probably this is an over-simplification, but it was how I understood the story Njombo told many years later. Kamau was hand in glove with Kupanya, who no doubt had the local *kiama* under his thumb.

So Kimotho lost his betrothed, and would have lost the baby also had his family not spirited it away to some distant part of the reserve. He was understandably bitter, although he had no leg to stand on in Kikuyu law. A debt was a debt, and must be paid. Since Kimotho could not meet it, Kamau secured the prize and took Wanjiko as his third wife. The idea of consulting Wanjiko's wishes never entered anyone's head. I thought she might have preferred Kimotho, who evidently wanted her badly, in preference to a man who already had two wives. When I suggested this to Njombo he roared with laughter and looked at me with incredulity.

'Kimotho was a poor man,' he said, 'and Kamau a rich one.

He gave her ear-rings and bangles. Whoever heard of a girl who would praise a pauper when a rich man offered goats?'

Kimotho had to accept the judgement openly, but in his heart he rejected it. With no land and no wife, but a load of debt, he had little to lose. There was only one course open to him. That he took it, and had recourse to a sorcerer, could be inferred from the events that followed. Disasters began to overtake the rich Kamau. A baby died from choking, his second wife had a miscarriage, a cow slipped her calf and queer sounds were heard at night, as of spirits scratching on the thatch of his huts. Kamau's wives took fright. But Kamau himself did not say anything. He brought no case against Kimotho, but was heard to remark that troubles came like locusts, and ate up your substance, and left everything bare, but that grass and crops always grew again afterwards. This was interpreted to mean that the trouble caused by Kimotho would vanish in the same way.

One day Kimotho, without apparent reason, disappeared into the waters of the *vlei*. No one saw him actually go under. There was a splash, a ripple and then silence. The man who was with him, knowing of the feud between Kimotho and Kamau, saw the ripples widen with incredulous eyes, felt his stomach shrink (he later said) into a ball, and saw a great black bird fly away from the lake and make for Mount Kenya. He turned and fled. Njombo saw him go, saw the empty water with the widening ripples and turned his back. Did he see the black bird? He would not say. Neither man thought of going to pull out Kimotho. A European would have assumed that he had tripped on a submerged obstacle, fallen and lost his head. But they would not have known why he did not thrash about or call for help, and they would not have seen the black bird fly away towards Mount Kenya.

Njombo did not mention his experience to any living soul, and shut his mind even to the name of Kimotho. There was no one who could be sued for blood money by Kimotho's father. Everyone knew it was sorcery, and for this reason nothing was said. Kimotho dropped out of life as he had dropped to the bottom of the water. Kamau was treated with more deference than ever, and everything seemed to lie at his feet, until Wanjiko, the girl who had caused all the trouble, now his third wife, ran away.

Women very seldom did this. If a woman's husband ill-treated her beyond endurance, or if he could not give her a child, she had a right to return to her father, but it was seldom exercised. Kamau seemed to have treated Wanjiko well; that is to say, he gave her a shamba and expected her to cultivate it, he gave her the goatskin aprons to which she was entitled, and he – or someone – had given her another child. It was said that he often beat her, but that was not a matrimonial offence. She did not run back to her father, but to a young man who had worked for an Indian stonemason on the Clewes' farm and had evidently cheated Kamau behind his back. Everyone considered that for this she deserved all the beatings Kamau had ever given her or ever would, and more.

Kamau, his pride offended, then made a mistake: he fell out with Kupanya, his father-in-law, over the return of the bride-price he had paid for Wanjiko. In revenge, the chief threatened to reveal to the authorities various tax evasions in which Kamau had indulged for some years. And so Kamau, instead of recovering the bride-price, found himself obliged to pay more goats to Kupanya, which amounted to blackmail.

This rankled deeply, and he cast round for a way out. To employ sorcery against so powerful a man as Kupanya would be foolhardy. He had to pay the goats: but why should this impoverish him? The wealth of his employer was bottomless; as soon as the safe was empty, more shillings came to fill it from an inexhaustible source in Nairobi. To steal them would be quite easy. With them he would buy goats to pay Kupanya, and no one would be any the worse off. If police askaris came they would find out nothing and Europeans, he knew, were helpless without them; white men left everything to the police and did not safeguard their property with charms, with curses or by means of ordeals by which a thief could be revealed.

Kamau was right about the police but wrong, in this instance, about Harry Clewes, who upset the plan by taking a line of his own. This humiliation embittered Kamau, but he still had most of the money, which had left immediately for the reserve in the load of maize on the back of his senior wife.

After he had settled with Kupanya, the balance was ample to stock a little store, and so for him the episode ended happily. The store prospered, and in time Kamau joined a relative in Nairobi who had started a *hoteli*, that is an eating-house, with a brothel and a gambling parlour attached.

Kamau prospered, and in time his wealth attracted the attentions of those who were beginning to take account of politics. These men were better educated than Kamau; they were mostly school teachers, but they badly needed money, and Kamau thought it provident to contribute to their funds and sometimes to arrange for meetings to be held in his *hoteli*. He soon mastered the art of making speeches, conjuring up for his audience the vision of a shining world where everyone would be rich and fat and no one debt-encumbered and hungry, and the Europeans who ordered everyone about with contemptuous hearts would be humbled. With these speeches he stirred up discontent that lay like sediment in the bottom of a barrel, bitter and strong, but quiescent, until a long arm thrust into it and fingers stirred it and the particles rose in bubbles which exploded all over the surface, and changed the nature of the brew. Kamau's own business expanded until he owned several *hotelis*, and his wives continued to cultivate his land in the reserve.

All this Njombo told me many years later when he heard, one day, that Kamau was dead. Kamau was not old, but died in an accident to his car. 'And yet he was a rich man,' Njombo said, shaking his head at the queer ways of God. 'A rich man, with a motor-car, and yet a lorry killed him like a chicken. He had four wives, and many shambas, and in Nairobi a house, *hotelis*, places for prostitutes. Much wealth, and he was killed like a chicken. We must put our faith in God.'

Even Alec had known nothing of all this at the time it was going on. Kamau's triumph over Kimotho, his quarrel with Kupanya, the affair of Wanjiko, all that had led up to the burgling of Harry Clewes' safe had been as hidden from us as events taking place on the dark side of the moon. Alec's knowledge, superior to our own but still fitful and shallow, of the closed Kikuyu world, was a fact I accepted without question. Once I rode over to Alec's with a chit and saw sitting on the steps of the veranda a girl who attracted my attention because, instead of goatskins stained with fat and ochre, she wore a fairly clean cotton cloth knotted over one shoulder, and because her head, instead of being shaved like that of a Kikuyu girl, had a crop of woolly black curls. I thought she was probably not a Kikuyu, but a girl of some other tribe, although she had the usual beads in her ears. She replied to my 'jambo' in a high, soft, liquid voice as melodious as a bird's. One of the shortcomings of the Kikuyu, in my view, was the fact that one could not talk to girls or women; they knew no Swahili, and the girls only giggled and moved their shoulders coyly if you addressed them in rudimentary Kikuyu. I thought this girl might be more profitable.

'Is bwana dungbeetle here?' This was the name by which Alec was known to the Kikuyu.

'No.'

'Where is he?'

'I don't know.'

'On the shamba?'

'Perhaps.'

This seemed no better than my usual experience, except that the girl did not giggle, but looked at me with large, dark eyes like an antelope's and had a hint of insolence in her manner. Perhaps not insolence, I though, but shyness, or strangeness, and I asked her where she lived. She pointed with her chin towards the kitchen quarters.

'Over there.'

'Is your father one of bwana dungbeetle's boys?'

'No. My father is not here.'

She looked at me gravely, fingering a white cowrie necklace between her fingers. She did not look as if she did shamba work.

'I am bwana dungbeetle's woman,' she said.

At the time the implications of her reply did not come home to me; I merely thought it odd to have a woman, everyone else had men in the house. But this was evidently a superior woman, with cleaner clothes than usual, although I did not think her manners very good. She made no effort to help me find Alec, and seemed absorbed in picking her nose.

'Will you give this note to the bwana?'

She took it in a languid hand with dirty fingernails, without moving from her seat on the steps. Behind her a morning glory glowed freshly in the shadow of the eaves, its tendrils clasped loosely round the supporting poles, and its intense blue trumpets open to to show their paler veins within. I thought for a moment she was like the morning glory, decorative and useless, clinging to a post and quite self-confident, graceful and empty-headed, beautiful and yet with all the beauty on the surface, to be seen in a single glance. Although I did not question her presence, I did not mention it to Tilly, but told her I had left the chit with a boy. It was a small, unimportant lie and I had no idea why I told it. Some time later, I overheard Tilly say to Robin: 'Alec really ought to marry. He's stingy enough already and he'll grow worse as he gets older.'

'He's quite comfortable with his present arrangement,' Robin observed.

'Yes, I know, but *that* won't get him very far. And one would think the smell of red ochre . . .'

'Now, Tilly. *Chacun à son goût,* I suppose. After all, look at Lord Auchinleck.'

'Why should I look at him?'

'The one who was Governor of the Punjab in the eighteenth century. He used to send all his thirteen Indian wives out for exercise on elephants on the Maidan in Calcutta every morning.'

'Poor Alec! All he could manage would be one, on a mule. And not a wife exactly either.'

'Perhaps Lord Auchinleck's were not exactly wives. It's difficult to know the definition.'

This had never struck me before, but when I looked up the word in the dictionary I found that Robin was right. It could mean simply a woman, especially one engaged in selling something; the mistress of a household; the landlady of an inn; the female of a pair of lower animals; the Willow Red Underwing moth; or a woman joined to a man by marriage. And marriage seemed merely to involve a ceremony – any kind would do, like dancing on the sands, as the owl and the pussycat had done when they married with the pig's nose-ring. The Kikuyu were just as married as Robin and Tilly, although they had only exchanged beer and goats and had a feast, with no religious service, no dressing-up and no ring. So I supposed that Alec was married, in a doubtful sort of way, to this rather silly, uninteresting girl, though I never said anything to Alec about it, or even to Njombo, for I thought it was a subject he would not like to discuss.

Chapter 15

EVERY year Robin and Tilly talked about a holiday together, perhaps to the coast, but four or five years passed before they actually took one. A polo team was going from Makuyu to play in Zanzibar. Neither Robin nor Tilly was a particularly good player, but several of the star performers had to withdraw, and they managed to get themselves included in the team. They took Fair Play and Hafid's successor, a mare called White Lady, but not M'zee or myself. I was to be discarded at Ulu, a station about fifty miles down the line from Nairobi, to stay with friends.

When these friends, the Joyces, had ridden across the plains, a distance of sixty or seventy miles, to spend a weekend with us at Thika, and ridden back on Tuesday, they had completed their annual holiday. They rode everywhere because, although they had a half share in 50,000 acres of plain and bush, they could not afford to buy any petrol. They had the land but no capital, and the land, instead of producing income, was like a huge ravening beast that gobbled up every cent they could earn or borrow. There was nothing on it except bush and long grass, and above all there was very little water. Before it could support cattle, a number of expensive boreholes had to be sunk, and fewer than half of these turned out to be worth while. When they had enough boreholes, they had to start a herd. They bought native cattle, but even these cost about £5 a head and a great many were needed. So for many years they had no money in their pockets, and Frank Joyce complained that his whole budget for the year had been upset by breaking his watch glass, and having to pay a shilling for a new one in Nairobi.

Frank Joyce, who was Irish, was the best-looking man I had ever seen, and the gayest. He and two other young men had gone into partnership, before the war, to make a fortune out of ostriches. Plenty of ostriches inhabited the plains and it had seemed a simple matter to collect some eggs and hatch them, rear the chicks and sell their feathers for large sums. Like many apparently simple projects, this did not work as they had hoped. Not only did the ostriches themselves object, if necessary to the extent of dying, but the introduction of motoring in Europe put ostrich feather trimmings in woman's hats out of fashion and the market collapsed.

Two partners out of the three then sought jobs to bring in money, pound by pound, for investment in the ranch, while the third stayed at Kilima Kiu (as it was called) to keep things ticking over. They traded in cattle, worked as road foremen for the P.W.D., and as labour recruiters. Frank Joyce found a use for some, at least, of the ostrich feathers. The young men of North Nyanza prized them as head-dresses, and he used them as bait to recruit labour for the company that was building a railway line to carry the soda dug out of Lake Magadi. Every recruit got a blanket, a cooking-pot and two or three feathers, and these gave Frank an edge over rival recruiters and earned a little money for the ranch.

The war destroyed one of the partners, equipped the other with two wives and gave Frank a stiff leg. Each of the survivors built a small, square house on a flank of the bush-clad, brindled range of hills that gave the ranch its name, meaning hill of thirst. These hills had formed a no-man's-land between the Masai on the plains below and the Kamba people in the jagged hills to the north and eastwards. Because of a lack of water no one dwelt there, or ever had, but in the rainy season pools formed among the rocks and buffalo would move in, with herds of eland and impala and waterbuck, to join the species needing very little moisture, like reed buck and klipspringers, who stayed there all the year round. The partners, F. O'B.

Wilson and Frank Joyce, waged war on lions because they killed cattle, and on buffaloes because they carried rinderpest, and gradually these animals were shot out or withdrew. This dry country was much favoured by game birds like sand-grouse and guinea-fowl, and with these and the buck the two families never had to buy meat. They had their own milk and butter, they irrigated small vegetable gardens with the bath water, they ground their own wheat, they bartered coffee with their friends and scarcely any money had to change hands to keep them enjoyably fed. Shirts and trousers cost a few shillings at the Indian *dukas*, firewood was there for the cutting and, although a man could not, like Goldsmith's parson, be passing rich on forty pounds a year, he could live on it without going cold and hungry, which was more than could be said for most parts of the world.

A *syce* with a spare pony was waiting to meet me at Ulu and we rode about seven miles across a plain very different from the country I was used to at Thika. It was far more open and everything looked twice as big. The plains, speckled by thorn-scrub, went on forever and everything lay in immense, long, brilliant bands – the tawny savannah, the heat-blurred horizon, lines of marbled hills, and then frothy banks of cumulus that filled the sky with majestic shapes and soft colour. The only mark scratched by humans on this great flank of Africa was a double track cut by the wheels of wagons, that a single year's growth would erase if wagons ceased to creak along it behind the little humped oxen with their patient long faces, their scarred hides and their small shuffling feet.

The apparent flatness was deceptive and our track led imperceptibly uphill. The hills grew closer and larger, and beyond them arose other, steeper hills. We rode towards Machakos, where the first caravans, the foot caravans, had rested after their savage march from the coast across two hundred miles of scorching desert, and where the slavers had camped to stock up for the last, costly stage to the markets of Mombasa and Zanzibar. To many, these hills had been the gates of salvation, but to many more a shutter that had forever fallen on the last gleam of hope. In the distance blue and beautiful, closer at hand they were mottled in red and umber, in rust and burnt sienna. Among them dwelt the Wakamba, a tribe related to the Kikuyu and yet quite separate from them, more warlike, less tortuous and deep but just as intelligent, and with a certain creative element the Kikuyu lacked. For some reason no one could explain they had an inborn talent for machinery, although they had never seen any before, and wherever engines had to be looked after, there would a M'Kamba be, tending it like a shepherd his flock. But their passion was for cattle, and they were adventurous hunters, roving far afield with poisoned arrows to shoot elephants and rhinos and trap beasts for their hides.

The small square bungalow of the Joyces, surrounded by a wide veranda, stood on a shoulder of the hills with a view towards the Masai plains that stretched to the invisible Tana river. In front was a curious conical hill just like a pimple, a very large pimple, on the face of the plain. A rectangular patch of bush had been shaved off its base to make a field of about three hundred acres, and there wheat was being cut with an ancient ox-drawn reaper, and gangs of Wakamba were binding the grain into sheaves. The Joyces were excited because this was their first crop of wheat, and whether to spend the proceeds on a new dam, a borehole, on fencing for paddocks or pipelines for water, on an Ayrshire bull, on Masai sheep or on a tractor, was the main topic of conversation. Mrs Joyce, who came from Maryland and was called Mary Early, wanted a guest-house, but this clearly had a low priority.

At Kilima Kiu, Frank left early on his pony and would be out until two or three o'clock riding about the ranch to inspect cattle herded beside distant sand-rivers, where holes were dug for water to seep into, or to set a day's task for Wakamba making a dam in a fold of the hills, or to examine the carcase of a calf perhaps killed by hyenas, or to put cattle through a dip. The partners kept on the ranch many cattle which belonged to their Wakamba labourers and herdsmen, and at intervals these, as well as their own, had to be branded and counted, inoculated against rinderpest and pleuro-pneumonia, and generally supervised.

Sometimes I went out early with Frank and spent all the morning cantering after him or waiting while he dismounted to examine a sick beast, set a plough, or mark out a line for a gang of bush-clearers. This manless country had no paths or tracks and I was amazed that Frank never lost his way, for in places the bush was thick and you could see no landmarks. There were no rivers, only dry, sandy gullies that turned into brown torrents in the rains. Frank had, I think, made two dams, and sometimes, in the evening, he would shoot a brace of duck on one of them. Mary Early had taught her cook to make southern dishes, and for the first time I had maize-flour scones. For although maize-flour was the staple food of Africans, the British stuck firmly to wheat, even when this had to be imported and cost three or four times as much. Africans were not the only ones to be conservative about food.

The northern boundary of Kilima Kiu marched with the Kamba reserve, and one day we rode into the hills to see a chief about some stolen cattle. The Wakamba were always on the alert for opportunities to steal from Kilima Kiu. That was why one of the partners had to inspect every carcase said to have been killed by hyenas or lions, and to count the beasts every week when they went through the dip. Despite these precautions, cattle sometimes disappeared and then a long *shauri* with the local chief developed. The chief was supposed to find the culprit and return the beasts, but sometimes he or his relatives were involved in a theft themselves.

The chief had sent word to say that he had accused a certain man of having stolen five beasts from Kilima Kiu, and Frank was going up to find out how the case stood. Before the war, a district officer at Machakos had made use of a Kamba ordeal. They had an object called a *kiputu* on which they took an oath. The *kiputu* was charged with such a deadly potency that, if a man lied, he was sure to die before the next moon. The Wakamba believed in this so implicitly, Frank said, that a guilty man would refuse to take the oath, and so a thief scarcely ever evaded justice under Kamba law. Under its British substitute, they always denied their guilt because they had no cause to fear a supernatural sanction, and so, unless they were caught red-handed, there was no way of convicting them.

Frank had suggested to the chief that the *kiputu* should be used, and I was anxious to see it. Frank had never seen one either. A *kiputu* was such a sacred, deadly object that it must never be touched by anyone but its appointed keeper, except during the ceremony. Frank said he thought it might be part of a meteorite, an object considered to be sacred because it fell from the sky in a blaze of light.

The Kamba hills were even steeper than our Kikuyu ones, and our ponies had to scramble up like mountain-goats. The chief's homestead was perched on a ridge and he himself was waiting for us under a tree, flanked by several elders and dressed in a red blanket and a hat with a badge. He was a brisk, upright man who had been a sergeant in the K.A.R and had a strict manner, and a monkey-like, intelligent face. While Frank talked to him I rested by the sweating ponies and looked down at the immense view, so steep and vast as to be alarming. The hills had a frenzied, tumbled look as if they had been churned up by some colossal beater while in a molten state and had then solidified suddenly, just as they were, without any pattern or order. The valleys seemed to be singing quietly to themselves in the heat. Patches of forest clung to the hilltops but most of the trees had been felled to leave bare scrub broken by big, smooth boulders. I felt sorry for the women, who had to scratch about for firewood and also to walk down these great hillsides, a drop of fifteen hundred or two thousand feet, to dig for water in the sand-rivers. Springs ran freely in the rains, but in the dry season they might have four or five miles to go for water, and that hard climb back with a heavy gourd or pot.

'This young man is going to take the oath,' Frank said. 'At least he says he's ready to. The chief thinks he'll refuse at the last moment. We shall see.'

Under a nearby tree several oldish men were squatting on their haunches near a small heap of stones. I could see nothing else at first, until I noticed an untidy sort of parcel wrapped in the peeled bark of twigs. It was quite small, and had a loop by which it could evidently be carried, and looked like the horn of a redbuck filled with dark earth.

'That doesn't look very dangerous,' I said, and stepped

173

forward to get a closer look, but one of the old men waved me back. I could now see that it was resting on stones.

'They think it's so powerful that if it touches the ground, it will blast the crops,' Frank said. 'In fact it isn't allowed out in the planting season.' Yet it looked dirty and neglected, as if anyone could have made it by wrapping strips of bark round an old horn.

There was a lot of talk among the Wakamba gathered under the tree and at last Frank grew impatient, as Europeans always did at native ceremonies. Probably the Wakamba would have spun the matter out for a day at least. One of the onlookers, a younger man, came forward and stood on top of the small heap of stones. He had on ear-rings and several ornaments and charms, and a grey blanket, and stood as impassively as a statue, grasping a twig in one hand. Apparently this had to be taken from a certain kind of shrub. The bush, which looked so uniform to us, was composed of many species and each one had a separate Kikamba name, with separate properties and uses in magic and in daily life.

The squatting elder now addressed a string of questions to the man standing on the heap of stones, who was clearly the accused. Questions and answers droned on in the heat and the flies buzzed round us, tormenting the ponies, who kept shaking their heads. At last the chief gave an order, gentle but firm. The accused man lifted his twig and hesitated. His face was wooden and quite blank as if he did not see his surroundings. There was a pause in which the tension could be felt: now was the moment when, if he was guilty, he must confess, or bring down disaster upon himself, or upon his family. Man could be cheated, but spirits, never.

Everyone watched him closely. He bent down, twig in hand, and lightly touched the *kiputu* on its separate bed of stones. Silence persisted, and he did this three times, saying something in Kikamba each time. No doubt he was affirming his innocence. At the third stroke there was a sort of 'aaah-aaah-aaah' from the onlookers as if to record their witness of the act, and the man stepped down stiffly from the stones. A small boy appeared tugging a goat on a string. The goat would no doubt be killed and eaten, a payment to the guardian of the *kiputu*, which would then be carried away and hidden in a secret place. No one knew where a *kiputu* was kept, and to touch one by mistake would be fatal.

'Was everything correctly done?' Frank inquired.

'Yes, it was correct,' the chief said, and I suspected that he was either disappointed, or not really convinced of the man's innocence.

'Then you still have to find the thief.'

'Perhaps he has gone to Kitui.'

'In that case you must send after him.'

'How can I fetch him if he has gone away? Perhaps if you send to the D.C. at Kitui . . .'

'You had better find him,' Frank said, 'or I will refuse to let your people hang their hives in my trees.'

The chief laughed heartily, and so did Frank; he was nearly always laughing, and he gave the chief a handful of cigarettes. 'Can you order bees where to settle?' the chief inquired. 'And plant honey in a shamba? Trees belong to God, and bees are his cattle.'

Any ceremony such as this with the *kiputu* had to be carried out exactly right. If the least detail of the procedure was incorrectly followed, if for instance someone faced in the wrong direction, said the wrong words or struck the *kiputu* with the wrong kind of twig, the curse could not work. Frank had therefore to trust the chief to see that everything was exactly in order. If for any reason, the chief had not wanted the culprit to be found, which was always possible – he might, for instance, be one of the family – he could always deceive a European. This was the reason why district officers at Machakos had given up relying on the *kiputu*. It worked all right so long as the chiefs and elders wanted it to, but if they did not, guilty men could strike it with twigs until the stolen cattle died of old age before they came to any harm. So we returned none the wiser, but we enjoyed the ride and Frank thought that if the man was really guilty, he would not try to steal a second time.

'Though, of course, someone else will,' he added. These frequent thefts naturally infuriated him, and yet he could see the Wakamba point of view. For centuries they and the Masai had proved their manhood and blooded their spears on each other; to them cattle raiding was a sport, a gamble, and the salt of life. Now all this had been extinguished by the white man's peace. One of Frank's herdsmen had shaken his head and said sadly: 'Bwana, I am ashamed. I am married, I have a son nearly fit for circumcision, and I have not yet killed a Masai warrior.' Frank had no doubt killed German warriors, and could understand.

Missionaries had made life even emptier by banning many of the Kamba dances. It was said that a previous Governor, on a visit to Kitui with his ladies, had been greeted by a posse of naked Wakamba performing an erotic dance that had left nothing whatever to the imagination, and the officials had been told to support the missionaries' ban on such displays. So nothing much was left to the Kamba men – who, like the Kikuyu, left the cultivation of their land to their women – save to sit about and drink beer, and steal cattle, when they could, from the European ranchers. Some joined the police and the K.A.R., but this meant leaving home, mingling with alien tribesmen and eating strange food, and did not have a universal appeal.

At Kilima Kiu you seldom went out for a ride or walk without encountering wild animals. Once I watched two reedbuck playing on the hill behind the house, less than a hundred yards from the stables. With outstretched neck, the buck bounded after the doe, and then at some unseen signal he whipped round and fled in his turn, the smaller doe after him. They leapt with the grace and freedom of a fountain, their slender feet and ankles precise as pistons among the scrub and boulders. I had my rifle with me and waited for the offer of a shot, but did not want the opportunity, they were too graceful in the honey-coloured light of early morning that smiled on the grasses, with birds twittering in every thorn-tree. I was glad when some warning on the wind halted their game. They stood for an instant frozen by alarm and then, with a shrill sharp whistle, bounded for shelter and vanished into the bush. I did not go after them.

But Frank wanted them shot. They ravaged his crops, and

jumped the fence into his vegetable garden, and plagued Mary Early's roses. The graceful buck were enemies of ranchers and farmers. This country had belonged neither to the black man nor the white, but to the wild animals, and now they were being dispossessed. They were being driven back; but the empty wilderness waiting to receive them seemed limitless, and no one foresaw that in less than forty years scarcely any would be left and that, like grain between grindstones, they would find no salvation.

Chapter 16

WE always had breakfast on the wide veranda, a mild sun streaming in, with hot scones on the table and dark honey provided by wild bees. Outside a pony waited for Frank and a M'kamba called Kioko waited for me. He was a middle-aged man in a blanket with a snuff-horn round his neck, charms worn as armlets and a hunting-knife tucked into a leather belt set with beads. Normally he herded cattle but at heart, like most Wakamba, he was a hunter, and Frank had put me in his charge. The more buck I shot the better both were pleased, and even when I failed to shoot any I enjoyed walking about the plains and hillsides, never knowing what we should come upon next.

So after breakfast we set off, Kioko leading the way. He walked with long strides, following a predetermined direction through thorn-scrub and scattered trees. The place was full of birds. This was a haunt of glossy starlings, the gayest of creatures, as far removed from the starling of the north as a peacock from a crow. With his purplish-blue wings folded he shone all over like lapis lazuli, his breast the colour of ripe strawberries, and when he flew a sea-green tinge appeared, banded with white. Even more splendid were the rollers we often came upon in pairs. In flight they looked like sapphires tossed in the air, and when they perched you could see their puffed-out breasts of lilac and their greenish necks and tails. I had been told they smelt like curry powder, but this I was never able to confirm.

So on these walks there was always something to see. The acacias had tiny balls of sweet-smelling blossom, yellow or white. Canary-coloured weavers fussed and twittered in the trees they had selected for their feverish nesting, which seemed to go on all the year round. Sometimes we would almost tread upon a duiker, lying so close that it waited until we were a yard away before bolting for the bush, its head laid back and neck outstretched and feet flying. Hawks and buzzards were little specks high overhead, an infinity of ants kept up their ceaseless questing in the grasses. It was a scene of restless, unremitting activity devoted to the purpose of keeping alive. Later in the day the pace would slacken and everything would idle in a torpid heat.

There was a daily rhythm among all creatures inhabiting these hills and plains, from eagles to beetles, from buffaloes to mice. The venturing forth in a cold white dawn, the search for food as the long light spread, the browsing and scurrying and fluttering about, the flash of brown and blue in dappled sunlight; then a falling tempo and the period of suspension, of tail-twitching sleep, of drowsing in branches; then the gradual renewal of life, like sap creeping up the bark or a breeze awaking leaves: the evening parade and questing, less purposeful than that of early morning, more haphazard; and at last night and the slumber of one set of living creatures while another came to life to fill lungs and bellies under the stars.

After about an hour's walk we halted on the edge of a gully for the ceremony of testing the wind. A pinch of earth, a few grass seeds was sufficient. A wind blew fairly across the plains, but as the day went on it turned treacherous. Gusts were the enemy. After his test, Kioko led me across a shallow gully and we clambered up the far side. I tried to tread in his footsteps and to avoid getting caught up in spiky branches that snapped back and tore at my clothes. Once or twice we halted while Kioko listened with his head slightly on one side. I could hear crickets simmering, but nothing else. It was getting hot now and the birds had fallen silent. In crowded countries

you can always hear a distant sound if you listen long enough:
a dog's bark perhaps, a tractor's chug or a train's whistle. But
here there was nothing. Almost I could seem to hear the heat
haze twitching on a blurred horizon. A foot slipping on a stone
cracked the air. Yet there could be eyes watching us from a few
feet away without our knowledge.

With a slow movement Kioko raised his arm and pointed
through the bush to our right. I moved the rifle cautiously,
but he very faintly shook his head: so it was not a herd of
impala or of grantii. I watched for several minutes before the
faintest motion caught my eye. Then there sprang into existence a shape that had been there all the time: a little steinbuck
under a tree. Its neck drooped and it was dozing, ignorant of
danger in the heat of the day. I did not want to shoot a steinbuck, and anyway it was a doe. We moved on, leaving it in
peace. A guinea-fowl scuttled out of the way followed by a
flock of eight or nine striped chicks. She cheeped as she ran,
and dived into the bush with the agitated balls of fluff behind
her. Complete silence supervened: she and the chicks were
squatting motionless as stones in the panicled grasses. To
everything that lived, we were the enemy. Our passage cut a
swathe of menace through their peace, we carried death in our
smell like poison. Every living creature fled or froze into fear-
struck immobility. Only hawks and buzzards high overhead
paid us no attention, searching at all times with their skinflint
eyes for mice and snakes and small, defenceless things that had
ventured out of hiding.

We advanced slowly towards a hummock crowned with
bush, an old degenerated termite heap. Kioko crawled up on
hands and knees, then waved me towards him. He had seen
something he thought I should shoot. With the rifle in one
hand, trying not to get out of breath, I crept up the slope until
I lay at Kioko's side. He did not need to point now. About fifty
yards away, below us in the open, was a grantii buck, dead
and stretched out on his side, and over him crouched a lioness,
as I thought, chewing a flank, in a sphinx-like posture, with a
twitching tail.

I edged the rifle very slowly to my shoulder and brought
the sights together on the easy yellow target. I had never shot

at big game before and was not, indeed, supposed to do so; at all costs I must not bungle the shot through over-excitement. I aimed with all the concentration of which I was capable, low down and just behind the shoulder.

The rifle went off with its sharp crack, I heard the smack of the bullet and the creature gave a convulsive leap, rolled over and lay there kicking. I stood up and fired into it again. cleanness of the shot, a small victory. But if I had known it was not a lioness after all but a cheetah. This robbed the event of its splendour, but all the same I had never shot a cheetah and ran eagerly towards it where it lay limply stretched out, muscles twitching and blood on its handsome black and yellow coat. I never shot an animal without feeling sorry afterwards and somehow poorer, yet there was a feeling of pleasure at the cleanness of the shot, a small victory. But if I had known it was a cheetah perhaps I would not have fired, for cheetahs were quite harmless and I already had the skin given me by Alan. Especially I should not have shot it had I known it was a female cheetah. Kioko knelt down beside it, ran his hand over its velvety flank and said:

'There are cubs. Look, it has milk.'

This was dreadful, and destroyed all the pleasure of the hunt. Now the helpless blind cubs would mew themselves to death in some shelter under the rocks.

'Perhaps we can find them,' I suggested.

'Eeeh! These *chuis* go a long way to hunt meat.'

'Perhaps if we looked for the male, he would show us. Perhaps he is close by.'

'We can look,' Kioko said, without any confidence. And so for a while we searched among the grass and scrub, and in a shallow gully, but I knew it was a hopeless quest.

'There are grantii over there,' Kioko said, pointing towards the plain. 'Are we to look for them?'

'Perhaps they have taken fright from the shot.'

'Perhaps. Very well, I will skin this *chui*.'

This he did deftly, and my spirits revived. It was not as good a skin as Alan's but now I should have something to write about to Alan. I was always trying to think of excuses to write to him and never could. My life had little in it of interest to an aspiring young hunter. Even the shooting of a cheetah would not seem at all remarkable, but perhaps I could tell him that I would now have a second skin. And I could ask him for directions as to how to cure it. This was an inspiration: he would have to reply. On second thoughts I doubted it; he would be away somewhere, on an exciting safari with the rich and great, too busy to give advice on taxidermy. Still, it was worth a try.

We left the cheetah to the vultures, and the cubs to their slow protesting end, and walked home through the heat of the day, slipping on tough grass clumps and weaving a way through patches of thorn. Kioko carried the cheetah's skin slung on to a stick he had cut from the bush.

'It is bad there is no meat,' he said. 'Why did you not go on and shoot a buck? A *chui* is no good, men cannot eat the flesh, like a hyena. A hyena eats others but it cannot be eaten, like a man with many cattle who invites no one to the feast.'

'Have you many cattle, Kioko?'

'Eee-eee!' Kioko reacted as if stung by bees. 'How should I have cattle? Where is my wealth? My cattle are the wild castor oil bushes, my wife goes to milk them in the bush.'

Before the days of Europeans, Kioko added, parties of young men went out into the bush for several weeks to trap elephants with poisoned stakes and to hunt them with spears; they sold the tusks to Arab and Swahili traders for beads and wire, which in turn could be transformed into wives and cattle. This was how a poor man got his start. Now that hunting was forbidden, Kioko said, how was a man like him to gather up a herd of cattle? Nowadays everything needed shillings; did shillings grow in the bush like wild aloes, could you hunt them with a spear like elephants?

I felt so moved by Kioko's poverty that I very nearly gave him the cheetah skin, but not quite. I only had five shillings, for tips; perhaps when Tilly came I could convince her of Kioko's need. But when I asked Frank why Kioko should be so poor he roared with laughter and said he had fifteen or twenty head of cattle in the reserve, as well as some at Kilima Kiu, and two wives with several shambas; and as for ivory hunting, that still went on, although illicitly, and no longer in large parties, because by law elephants could only be shot on payment of a licence fee. This was to raise revenue, not because of any concern for the elephants.

Kioko, Frank added, claimed to be a skilled cattle-doctor, and Frank had tested some of his remedies, but the only useful one had been a cure for inflammation of the eyes. Kioko had taken the leaves of a certain shrub, chewed them, and spread the pulp over the beast's eyes, and in two or three days the inflammation had gone. Also the sap of a kind of euphorbia did help, he thought, to heal sores. Otherwise Kioko's remedies were magical. For instance, when a cow with a sore udder kicked her calf, the treatment was to give her the droppings of a python, and for a cow who persistently kicked her milker he had recommended a drench containing the ashes of a nightjar. Frank supposed that the nightjar's tranquillity – these birds will squat like stones upon the path until you all but tread on them – was thought to pass into the cow, just as the Wakamba would rub a new beehive with mutton fat, put into it a certain kind of torpid lizard, and enjoin the bees to be as peaceable as the sheep and the lizard. It was seldom, however, that the bees listened to his advice.

The Wakamba robbed hives at night, when cold partially numbed their inhabitants, who were smoked out with certain kinds of shrub. Many of the trees we passed had beehives in them, hanging from branches or wedged into forks, for the Wakamba treasured honey next to cattle, and would collect from hives fifteen or twenty miles from their homes. Wild honey was full of grubs, and these they relished so highly that women were not allowed to eat them. Most of the honey itself went to make beer. The Wakamba were tremendous beer drinkers, their honey mead strong, and drunkenness the worst curse of the tribe. Honey beer was said to make people much more quarrelsome than millet beer, which had a soporific effect. Perhaps the bees' aggressiveness somehow got into the honey, and thence into the beer.

Kioko and I discussed such matters as we tramped about bush and plain on this and on succeeding days, and he told me a good deal about the habits of wild animals, some of it accurate, some based on superstition and legend. For instance, he said, you could always tell a klipspringer from a reedbuck, whose females looked much alike, by the fact that when disturbed a klipspringer would bolt up, and a reedbuck down, the hill. As an example of the second class he mentioned a belief that if you were charged by a buffalo, it meant your wife had a lover. Frank's comment on this was that no sensible man would go after these beasts during race week, when the country must be full of charging buffaloes.

The Wakamba had many animal tales meant for children and for telling round the fire at night, and as I was a child, Kioko entertained me with some of them; but I soon forgot them, as few had a point, according to our ideas. A European fairy story must be grappled here and there to reality, so that you can imagine the strange incidents happening to you. All sorts of magical things may occur up the beanstalk, but Jack must be a real boy; when the pied piper leads away the children, his motive is a human one; underneath the fantasy lies a foundation of logic.

With African tales, this did not seem to be so. Things happened without apparent rhyme or reason, they carried no moral, although ingenious they were generally unpleasant, and sometimes they ended in mid-air. The hare was often the hero because he outwitted everyone else, mainly by glibness of tongue. The fool was the hyena, a gullible, greedy, cringing creature who could be tricked even by the cock. Animals paid each other frequent visits, usually with fatal results. When the hyena, for instance, visited the cock, he was told by the cock's wife that she had cut off her husband's head, and that the head had gone out by itself to drink beer. But really the cock was hiding in the hut. After a while the cock emerged, complete with head, repeated the story to the hyena, who swallowed it whole, and the two sat down together to drink beer.

This happened several times, and each time Kioko told the tale in full: how the cock's wife informed the hyena that she had cut off her husband's head, and that the head had gone out by itself to drink beer, how the cock came out of hiding to repeat the same story and the hyena believed it; how they sat down together and drank beer. At last the time came for the cock to visit the hyena. 'Cut off my head,' the hyena instructed his wife, 'and tell the cock it has gone out to drink beer.' She obeyed him, and of course that was the end of the hyena. When the cock arrived he beat the hyena's wife severely for having killed her husband, and then took her home as his reward.

Another little tale that I remember, perhaps because it was more logical than most, concerned the hen and the guinea-fowl. In olden days these two were sisters, and shared everything. One evening the guinea-hen was cold, and asked her sister to fetch fire from a Kamba village. The hen entered a hut and warmed herself by the fire all night. At dawn the shivering guinea-hen went to look for her sister, who climbed on to the hut's roof and cried out that no fire was to be found in the village. On the following morning it was the same, and for several mornings after, until at last the cheated guinea-hen flew away to hide in the bush, and the friendship between the two birds ended.

The Wakamba, unlike the Kikuyu, loved meat of any kind and would even eat it maggoty and rotten, but only according to a strict protocol depending on the age-grade to which a man had attained. They had five grades of elder, and each grade was entitled to a certain portion of a slaughtered bullock. Members of the lowest grade ate the shin, and of the highest, the head and tongue. Women, of course, had the bottom rating, and could eat only the stomach and the worst of the shin.

A man's grade was not determined wholly by seniority. For each step he took up the hierarchy he must pay a fee of one bull, so a poor man never did work his way to the top. Nor could a man attain the highest grade of all without passing through an arduous ceremony called the third circumcision, or the circumcision of the men. No M'kamba would talk about this nor, I believe, had any European seen it, but a Swedish anthropologist had unearthed the details and published them, and the book was at Kilima Kiu. The unfortunate candidates had, for several days, to endure the most rigorous and degrading tests of hardihood and obedience. They ran the gauntlet of initiates armed with sticks, were forced to eat filth and practise in public sexual obscenities, at night a sort of bull-roarer made from hollow sticks frightened them out of their

184

wits, and whatever devices their tormentors could invent had to be meekly accepted. Then for several days they lived a life of pure savagery, released from all the normal rules governing human behaviour. Anyone who came their way they could beat, rape or even kill, without being called upon to account for their actions. But after they had passed through all this, and paid the initiation fees, they became full and respected members of the tribe. Although these rites were, in European opinion, revolting and barbaric, through them fortitude and self-discipline grew; and years later, at an American university, the rites of initiation into their Greek-letter fraternities struck me as a reflection, if a pale one, of this same masculine need.

In European eyes, the lives of Africans appeared simple, carefree and in harmony with nature, and Africans themselves child-like in their spontaneous, often naïve responses. But when you looked a little way beneath the surface you saw that Africans lived like so many Gullivers, bound by innumerable threads of custom, and allowed so little room for manoeuvre that the individual personality was cabined and confined. Their behaviour, and especially their relations with each other, re-called the complexity of some highly sophisticated, mannered society such as the court of Versailles in the eighteenth century. While people drank from calabashes, dressed in skins or blankets, relieved themselves in the bush and had created scarcely any art, they used special forms of address for each class of relative, a mother-in-law was so respectfully treated that even her name could not be mentioned, ritual purification had to follow a hundred small, daily actions and a complex system of fines and penalties existed to cover every small or great transgression. My own fears of dropping social bricks often embarrassed me, but for the young of the Wakamba and Kikuyu matters must, I thought, be infinitely worse, especially as they had not only the disapproval of their elders to reckon with, but all the malevolent, cantankerous and unruly powers of the spirit world.

On the evening of the day I shot the cheetah, a houseboy came to say that Kioko wanted to see me. He was standing near the kitchen with a basket in his hands.

'I have something here to please you,' he said. 'A *toto*

herding goats has brought them and will sell them for five shillings.' He pulled aside some grass; inside lay two small, bedraggled objects the size of kittens. I touched them and they were warm, but lay quite still and silent, paying no attention when I stroked their fur.

'They are nearly dead,' Kioko said, 'but if you give them milk perhaps they will recover. The *toto* found them in the grass and would have killed them, but God helped us, he took them to his father, who brought them here.' It was much more likely that Kioko, scenting a reward, had gone back to look for the cheetah cubs, but that did not matter. He got his five shillings, we found a baby's bottle and the cubs were offered warm milk and brandy. They were so weak that they would not suck, but I managed to squeeze a little milk into their mouths. Their eyes were closed and they had black markings on their blunt, blind faces. A little strengthened by the milk, they made faint noises like mewings. They spent the night beside the kitchen stove, and when I hurried in first thing next morning, one of them was dead. But the other was mewing for food. This time it took the teat and held on so strongly I had to tug at the bottle to cut short the feed. It had made up its mind to live, and the danger then became that I might overfeed it. Its rough yellow coat grew glossy and its little tummy round as a balloon. The houseboys laughed at it, thinking us absurd to fuss over a small, wild creature that would be useless to everyone if it grew up, and meanwhile was wasting good, fresh milk; but they humoured us, and did not wish it harm.

The survivor was a male, and in two or three days his eyes began to come ungummed. After that he soon grew active and tried to wriggle out of his box. The question of a name was freely discussed. Nothing fitted him completely, and in the end I decided on Rupert. This had always seemed to me a romantic sort of name, perhaps because of Prince Rupert, Rupert of Hentzau and Rupert Brooke. The Joyces had a box made for him in which he could travel to Thika.

The return of Tilly and Robin from Zanzibar was now imminent: and, while I was looking forward to showing off Rupert, I did not want to leave Kilima Kiu. Life there was more free and exciting than at Thika, with ponies to ride over the great tawny plains, with Kioko to take me out after the different kinds of buck, with the feeling that you could walk or ride as far as you could go without coming on another human being, and with the beauty of the blue distant mountains, of the bush-clad hill behind the house with its ravines and silence and a view from its crest broken only by the blue of distance, of early mornings when a mist lay like an enormous white lake over the plains, of the freshness of dew and serenading birds, of the evening sadness of long shadows, of white sand-rivers and a red flare of aloes among the rocks. All these things, and the warmth and gaiety of the household, the sun-filled veranda and the hot scones and Frank's laugh, I wished I could take home with me, and I now understood why Thika with its neat rows of coffee and its neighbours, one or two of whom were making tennis courts, was sometimes likened by Tilly to Welwyn Garden City.

A train came from the coast three times a week and reached Ulu early in the morning. Tilly and Robin were to ride from the station, and we did not expect them much before eight o'clock. But soon after seven we heard a sudden clatter of hooves on the short hill leading to the house from the dairy, and saw a pony approaching at a smart gallop with a figure bent over the reins. Mary Early darted on to the veranda, the houseboy put down his broom and ran out also in time to see the pony, dark with sweat, pant to a halt, and a khaki-clad figure clasping a saddlebag leap from its back and take the veranda steps two at a time. It was Tilly, flushed and breathless, her hair dishevelled, her eyes bright, spurred on, we feared, by news of some tremendous disaster.

'Quick, Mary Early, quick,' she cried. 'Water, a *debe* of water instantly, tell the boy to run for it; I may be just in time!'

'Oh, my dear Tilly, whatever's wrong?' Mary Early cried in deep agitation. 'Is it Robin, has he —'

'Water first, quickly, and then I'll explain. In a *debe*, there's not a moment to lose.'

Tilly was peering into the saddlebag, and thrust in a hand. 'They were alive and kicking in the train and we've galloped

187

most of the way; they *should* be all right if we hurry . . .'

The houseboy came running with a tin of water, spilling it over the veranda as he sped towards Tilly, who delved into the saddlebag, pulled out something mottled and writhing and hurled it into the water with a splash.

'For mercy's sake *tell* me what the matter is!' her hostess cried.

'Lobsters. Fresh yesterday.'

Tilly peered anxiously into the *debe*. 'Two of them are all right, they're kicking, but the third's sunk. It *may* revive. I thought they'd be a treat, Mary Early; I don't suppose you often get lobsters here; I'd forgotten how good they are. But, of course, they have to be alive. I brought them up in a *debe* in the train, but had to take them out at Ulu and hope for the best, and came as fast as I could go.'

Of the three lobsters, one had perished. Tilly thought she heard it draw its last breath as she came up the steps of the veranda; but the other two were much enjoyed.

Chapter 17

COUSIN HILARY had once remarked that just as there are two kinds of bird, migrants and residents, so there are two kinds of people, questers and squatters. Robin and Tilly, he had added, and especially Tilly, were questers. Something always beckoned from just over the hill. They saw this something as a fortune, but it was not; what they really wanted was to plant seeds, sometimes literally, sometimes in a general sense: seeds of change, of enterprise, of improvement. They had the itch to alter things and then to move on. They wanted money too, of course, but not for its own sake; they thought of it only in terms of what it would buy. This might be a new span of oxen or a trip to England with no fettering economies, but it was never cash in the bank. The great point about money was to convert it as quickly as possible into something you could use or enjoy.

At Thika the house was built, the garden made, the coffee coming back into bearing. This, of course, was only a beginning. The garden was raw, the lawn coarse and stringy, every year ten or fifteen acres of new coffee had to be planted and at least ten years were needed to bring into use all the suitable land. Gradually, year by year, tumbledown grass sheds were to be replaced by permanent stone ones, new machinery for treating the coffee was to be installed, roads had to be made about the plantations, paddocks fenced for cattle, windbreaks and shade trees established, irrigation put in for the seedlings – there was no end to the things wanted, as and when money could be found. That was part of the trouble. To bring the plantation up to its full capacity would take perhaps twenty years, and this seemed an eternity to Tilly and Robin.

Three or four years after our return to Thika, the questing instinct began to reassert itself. Thika, it was true, still had some way to go before it became really suburban. In the township, cars sank almost out of sight in the rains. Log bridges on the track leading along our ridge were still washed away by floods, coffee shambas were only clearings in the bush, and people could get a good day's shooting by driving down to the plains. There were no hospitals or schools or policemen nearer than Fort Hall, and no shops, other than a few Indian *dukas*, nearer than Nairobi. Still, there were changes. The Clewes had made a tennis court, the trains took three hours instead of five to reach Nairobi, a young parson was living at the Blue Posts until the Chaplaincy Fund could run to a mud-and-wattle vicarage, and the hole in which a camel had drowned on the main road had been filled in by the P.W.D. And so, like a touch of spring in temperate countries, the questing instinct was in the air.

There was still plenty of virgin land, undeveloped and un-occupied, to be had for very little money. Tilly and Robin did not actually look for another farm, but they could not help hearing about splendid opportunities, most of which turned out to be illusory. I do not remember how they first heard about the land at Njoro. Tilly went to look at it, and gave a report, on her return, that was rather off-hand. The farm had good, rich forest soil but was covered with dense forest that would need a fortune to clear. There was no labour; the nearest reserve was that of the Masai, who never stooped to farm work. No doubt Kikuyu would come, attracted by the prospect of shambas, but the altitude might be too high for maize, and certainly was for coffee. The crops that seemed most likely to thrive had no market; large wild beasts from the forest would trample the shambas; potentialities for sheep and cattle were unknown. On the other hand, the climate was perfect, the views superb. From all this it was plain that Tilly had lost her heart to this stretch of land on the western wall of the Rift Valley, but refused to admit that she had been seduced.

'If it's so attractive,' Robin inquired, 'why does the owner want to sell?'

'He took up a lease before the war, when the Government couldn't get anyone to go there; he got five thousand acres for a song and now he wants to sell most of it.'

'I daresay it would cost three or four pounds an acre to clear,' Robin suggested.

'One could get in squatters to do it gradually, and, of course, Kavirondo gangs on contract.'

'There'd be no return for years. I'm afraid Playfair ...'

'No, the old pincher, I don't suppose he'd help. We should have to sell up here.'

'Seems a pity, when it's just coming into bearing.'

'That might be the best time to sell. Before it all gets die-back, or thrips attack it, or it's wiped out by *hemelyia*.' (This was a fungus everyone was frightened of, for it had destroyed all the coffee in Ceylon.)

I could see the questing instinct stirring in both my parents, as in birds before a migration. I did not want to quest at all. Like all children I was conservative in habit and attached to my home, and could not bear to think of leaving it. Tilly assured me that the idea was most unlikely to materialize, but added that it would be fun to go and see the land when we could get away.

We did not manage this for some time, because the coffee picking, pruning and planting seasons were always overlapping, Robin was designing a better, cheaper way to hull coffee – that is, to remove the dried husk wrapped around the twin beans – and Tilly was planting geraniums. It was believed that a Frenchman was about to build a factory to distil, by secret processes, essential oils for the scent industry of Grasse, and numbers of farmers were planting not only geraniums but eucalyptus, bergamot, mint and lavender in order to get in on the ground floor. She was also making goats' milk cheeses from the produce of Cress, who had produced an enchanting white kid, and she had laid in a supply of native wives for Mustard, who treated them with profound contempt but was not above the practice of concubinage. I had my work cut out to keep up with my polo articles, look after Rupert and do some of the lessons Tilly set for me.

My career as a polo correspondent was complicated, because of the need to attend as many tournaments as possible without revealing my reason for doing so. Bamboo's identity was still a secret, and one of my greatest pleasures was to hear people speculate as to who he might be. Another problem was to get my reports to the post without anyone noticing their address. A most satisfactory flow of ten-shilling postal orders resulted, and these, too, I had to cash when no one was looking. I was often surprised that Tilly did not wonder where I got the money to buy so many conjuring tricks and poetry books, but it did not seem to cross her mind.

Polo tournaments held at Makuyu were easy to cover, but those farther afield presented more difficulty. A Makuyu team generally went, and somehow or other I had to attach myself to it. If Robin or Tilly played this was comparatively simple, but if they did not, I had to pretend an irresistible urge to stay with the Beatties, from whom I had an open invitation. This led to the belief that Barbara and I were the closest of friends. As our mutual dislike, strong from the start, strengthened with time, my visits were painful, and I could not afford an open quarrel for fear I should not be asked again. Only a dread of cutting myself off forever from Will Goldstone and the Poetry Bookshop kept me faithful to my task.

The Beatties had more wolf-hounds than ever, and larger ones, bounding all over the house, and for each polo tournament some extra diversion was arranged. Once it was a pig-sticking competition, another time a gymkhana organized by

Commander Strudwick, when we all had to leap in and out of rings of flames. A grass-fire started despite the various precautions, and the entire population of the district, black and white, with all the competitors, gathered in posses directed by the Colonel and the Commander to beat it out with sticks and branches before it swept into the forests of Mount Kenya to destroy thousands of pounds' worth of timber. Barbara played sentimental tunes on a gramophone all day long and told me that a rich baronet with an aeroplane was imploring her to elope in it to South Africa. I always hoped I might see Alan on these visits, but he was making headway as a hunter and was generally away with a rich safari in some remote, exciting region to which I longed to go, but feared I never should.

The catalogues of Will Goldstone and the Poetry Bookshop would have mocked me had I received my ten shillings only when there was a polo tournament to report. My aim was to have an article in the *Standard* every week. Readers therefore found themselves confronted by accounts of international polo contests in America, historical essays ranging back to Tibet in 600 B.C., reminders of classic matches at Hurlingham and instruction on what to look for in a polo pony, and how to train it in the arts of the game. Fortunately I had struck a rich seam in a magazine called the *Polo Monthly* to which I subscribed, and hoped that my readers did not. There was nearly always something in it I could re-shape into an article, such as a series of do's and don'ts for players, and hints on how to build a riding school.

Bamboo became so well-known an authority on polo that an Indian Army major wrote: 'I hope you don't think me presumptuous, but I think I've enjoyed your articles more than anything else since I've been out here,' and a Colonel entreated my advice on how to set about buying two good ponies. Flattering as these communications were, they imprisoned me within my false identity and obliged me, in framing replies designed to strike a note of bluff, man-to-man camaraderie as between one old player and another, bleakly to sign myself 'Bamboo'. At the same time I received a less flattering letter from the editor, instructing me to confine myself more to original and local matters with less about history and Hurlingham.

A great deal of everybody's time, and especially mine, was now take up by Rupert. From the first he was a strong cub and had a good appetite. After a while he started to swallow bits of raw meat, and to explore the house in a tentative manner. He was just like a kitten – which, of course, he was, since cheetahs are related to cats, but possess also certain dog-like features, notably about the feet, which are shaped for galloping and do not have retractable claws. Rupert attached himself closely to me and, after a period in a box, he was allowed to sleep on my bed. I think he was naturally clean, and much easier to house-train than a puppy. But he was worse than a puppy for chewing things. He demolished not only shoes, Tilly's knitting and a mosquito-boot, but gnawed table legs and cushions and ate a valuable book on trees and shrubs that had been left on a chair. Like most children brought up in places with servants, I was extremely untidy and left things lying about. Rupert taught me several sharp lessons; I had to start putting things away, and Tilly remarked that every household ought to have a cheetah, if only to instil the rudiments of tidiness into the young.

When he was small Rupert passed the day in a pen on the lawn with various bones and toys, but when he grew larger he was allowed his freedom and spent a good deal of time chasing birds. To begin with he rollicked with the dachshunds, but when he grew bigger and rolled them over roughly they wisely refused any further dealings, and would lie motionless gazing at him with a look of obstinate entreaty if he invited them to play. Should he refuse to take no for an answer, they would snarl and give a warning snap. This was always enough to quell Rupert. He was not an aggressive type, but rather humble. The only thing he could not resist was an object in motion. Anything that ran had to be chased. When he grew larger, and his spots darkened and became plainer, native strangers would sometimes mistake him for a leopard and take to precipitate flight. Then he would be after them with a few tremendous bounds, and his speed was prodigious. He meant no harm, but to see a hunting animal hurling itself in your direction was, of course, alarming, especially to children. At such times there would be roars from anyone present of 'Stand still! Stand still!' and if the stranger had the sense to obey orders, Rupert would halt dead in his tracks – he could stop the fastest rush almost miraculously – give the half-paralysed *toto* or adult a look of disappointment, and trot away.

To watch Rupert move was always a delight. His spotted skin became supple and soft as chamois leather and the sinews beneath it like wires, there was no fat on his body and one could see the muscles rippling just under the skin like ears of corn when a wind passes over them. For his size his haunches were immensely powerful and his legs were loosely jointed to his body. He had a tremendous stride, but when he galloped you could not see how his legs moved, he was just a yellow projectile hurtling through the air. Cheetahs are faster than race horses, faster than greyhounds, and, like these, they are designed for speed: streamlined, hard and beautiful. When he was half-grown Rupert had a yellow mane down the ridge of his spine from his broad, flat head to his long, tufted tail. As he grew this disappeared, leaving him short-haired and velvety all over. From quite an early age he had a loud purr, and would rub his hard little head against my knees just like a cat, rumbling with affection. I often wondered what natural advantages a purr could bring to cheetahs or lions: how it helped them to survive, or to live more efficiently; perhaps there were evolutionary luxuries, as it were, and this was one of them. Rupert purred a great deal, and had an affectionate nature. I do not remember his ever showing ill-temper towards a human being.

From an early age he made great friends with Mustard and Cress. When they had first arrived the two goats had roamed at will about the garden and explored the house, but they had proved so destructive that Tilly had reluctantly confined them to a paddock. Rupert did his best to make playmates of them, but they were much too dignified to run away from a half-grown cheetah, and Mustard gave him a prod with his horns whenever he made a spring, provoking Rupert into a little squeal of protest. After that Rupert was fascinated by the goats, and spent a lot of time in their company. Mustard unbent sufficiently to make short rushes with a lowered head and pretend to drive Rupert away, while Rupert skipped about just out of reach and then made tremendous bounds across the paddock after an imaginary prey, fetching up short by the wire, spinning round and leaping towards Mustard, who butted at him all over again. Cress was more aloof, gazing into space, when he approached, with the air of a scholar intent on some esoteric calculation.

Rupert's favourite occupation was to come out for a ride. At first, his sudden movements had upset the ponies and they never quite got used to him; for his part he paid them no attention, and never tried to make friends. But as soon as he heard the jingle of a bit and the click of hooves he would dash out of the house and make short rushes of anticipation on the lawn, chasing a wagtail or even a butterfly. Then he would lope along at my side for a while, M'zee showing by the prick of his ears that he knew the creature was there, and was not going to give him any encouragement. Once away from the plantation, Rupert would be off in a yellow flash into the grass and bush to see what he could find: usually a flock of goats, who did not behave so disdainfully as Mustard and Cress but took to their heels, bleating frantically and crowding together. The small goatherd would squeal and fly too, throwing his stick in Rupert's direction in a desperate effort to perform his duty, and make headlong for his home. Cries and shouts from the women would summon an older youth to round up the goats, shaking his stick at Rupert, who by that time was lying down in the grass watching the confusion he had created with, I always felt, a sardonic pleasure. I was afraid that one day he would pounce upon a straggler and demolish it, and these rides were nerve-racking experiences, but Rupert enjoyed them so much that I could not leave him behind.

This was also very hard to do. The only method was to shut him in a loose box, where he fretted and sulked. Like all pets, Rupert was a responsibility. I could not take him with me to report polo tournaments, and it was always an anxiety to leave him behind. On these occasions, Njombo looked after him. He trusted Njombo, whom I believed to be fond of him, and would stroke and pat his head and make him purr. At the same time Njombo was naturally not as devoted to him as I was, and at night returned to his hut, some distance away, leaving Rupert alone in a loose box which anyone could enter. I got a padlock and impressed on Njombo the need to fasten the stable door in case any of the Kikuyu tried to poison him, but I could not be sure this was done, and in any case a padlock could be easily broken.

Although he never actually harmed the goats, Rupert soon discovered the joys of chasing duikers and steinbuck. He was off like a rocket as soon as the buck bounded from his form, and generally sprang before it had gone twenty or thirty yards. He did not bite it in the back of the neck as a lion does, but knocked it sideways with a kind of bump and then sprang and ripped its throat open. The buck died instantly and cleanly, but my feelings were torn between sympathy for Rupert, who so much enjoyed the hunt it was his very nature to indulge in, and for the buck, who did not have much chance of escape, and looked so pathetic when they were bedraggled and bloody. Now and again, however, by jinking about among the shambas and doubling back in its tracks, a clever buck managed to elude Rupert, and then he had no desire to go on chasing it, and no hunter's cunning. A short, lightning rush and it was all over – either he brought the prey down or he missed it, and if he missed it he did not fret or search, but waited for the next opportunity. Of course, he was not hungry, and might have behaved differently if he had been. He hunted on sight alone, and I never saw him cast round for a scent.

My principal fear was that one day Rupert might be mistaken for a leopard and speared, or that he would be poisoned. The Kikuyu did not like wild animals of any kind, even when they knew them to be harmless like Rupert. Anything wild was, in their opinion, better dead, whether a bird or an elephant. And a cheetah skin, although nothing like so valuable as a leopard, would fetch a few shillings. It was unlikely that any of the Kikuyu living on our land would venture to harm him, but people in the reserve might well be less inhibited. I seldom let Rupert out of my sight, but when we went away always felt a niggling anxiety. I was devoted to him, even more perhaps than to M'zee, and determined to keep him with me for the rest of his life, or of mine: no one seemed to know the normal life-span of a cheetah.

Chapter 18

ALTHOUGH Rupert was absolutely without ferocity or malice, and no more dangerous to mankind than a cat, some of our European neighbours distrusted him almost as much as the Kikuyu did. Miss Cooper, for instance, was fond of saying that although he might seem harmless enough, no animal knew its own strength. One day he might turn nasty, and then where would we be? For her part she would not bring the twins over while there was a wild animal in the house, and if she had been Tilly, she would have thought more of other people's safety and less of unsuitable pets. Everything was Captain Dorsett now, with Miss Cooper. She corresponded with him in his distant frontier deserts, and they had planned a meeting in Nairobi when he next came on leave. This would not be for a year, so the courtship could not be of the whirlwind variety. He was after the Havash, she said, and having many adventures, but Alec remarked that he would never be in such danger as when he had visited the Clewes.

'I'm afraid I don't find Mr Wilson's remarks amusing,' she said. 'Perhaps there is something wrong with my sense of humour, though I've always been told that it's one of my strong points. Certainly Captain Dorsett never found any shortcomings, and he's very fond of a joke. I'm afraid I find people boring when they can't see a joke. He told me some quaint tales about some of his native bearers and orderlies, I can tell you. Some people found him quiet, but he expanded with me. In fact as a companion he's a great deal more entertaining than many people who fancy themselves as wits.'

'I hope you will be very happy,' I said politely. We had all gone over to tea with the Clewes in order that Robin should admire a splendid new machine to deal with coffee. Harry had imported from Scotland. Tilly was being shown Betty's roses and, as usual, I was left with the twins and Miss Cooper. The twins were splashing in a miniature swimming pool Harry had made for them, so it boiled down to Miss Cooper.

'I'm sure I don't know what you mean,' Miss Cooper replied archly. She was the only person I had met who bridled, a fascinating accomplishment. 'There's no understanding between Captain Dorsett and me, if that's what you're thinking of : we're just friends. Of course, I won't deny that he finds me attractive. And I think I can say that we are congenial companions. We have many tastes in common, and when he returns from the frontier and we see more of each other, well, there's no saying ... You see, I am making you a confidante. You are rather young, I know, but then you're growing up and one day you will understand what we feel for each other. And now, you mustn't betray my confidences. There is so much gossip and scandal in this country, it is most unpleasant. I never gossip myself. It is very ill-bred. And I have other things to think about. But others, I'm afraid, are not so restrained.'

I had no wish to be a confidante of Miss Cooper's and, in any case, her interest in Captain Dorsett hardly seemed a confidential matter, so I changed the conversation to birds. Surprisingly, Miss Cooper was interested in birds and quite good at knowing their names. She had a collection of eggs to which I had contributed. It was difficult to find nests, because one never knew which time of year to look for them; some species nested at one time of year and some at another. However, Miss Cooper was not in the mood for birds and after a while she reverted to the characters, relationships and goings-on of her employers, a topic that never staled.

'Mr Clewes is such an energetic man,' she said. 'I must admit that I admire energy and enterprise in a man. As my father used to say, take care of the seconds, and the hours will take care of themselves. Of course, he's sometimes a little insensitive to other people's feelings. There's no need, I always say, to get your way by bullying. I always use more subtle means. All the same, I do like a man who knows his own mind and has a decisive manner. There's no doubt about who wears the trousers in this family – and the right partner, I say. Mrs Clewes means well, I'm sure, but she's such a scatterbrain. I do like to see a household run with method and order. Sometimes I'm quite sorry for Mr Clewes, he has to do so much for both of them.'

'Vicky's trying to push Simon under,' I remarked.

'Simon can look after himself; I never believe in molly-coddling my children. I think I can say that my children are properly trained to stand on their own feet. One thing I will say for Mrs Clewes, she's a good mother. But there are certain things going on in this household that are not at all what I'm accustomed to. I'm a woman of the world, of course, and nothing if not broad-minded, but marriage vows are marriage vows, in my opinion. In this country they are taken a great deal too lightly. What sort of example does that set to the natives, I ask you? Of course one expects a man to have a certain licence, but when a woman marries she should put temptation behind her. You're too young to understand all this, but I hope that when you grow up you will not have been influenced by the lax attitude one meets in this country. I know that if *I* ever marry, I shall keep my vows. 'Forsaking all others' – they are beautiful words. There is not enough forsaking done in this country. That is one of the things that Captain Dorsett and I agree upon. We discuss everything, you see. There are no barriers between us. I mean, no *mental* barriers. In his last letter he –'

Tilly and Betty fortunately appeared at this moment to release me; her talk was hypnotizing, and there never seemed a chance to break away. Her hints were wasted, for I had heard plenty of talk about the Clewes. Harry was said to have taken up with the wife of a German farmer up-country, and Betty to be consoling herself with one of the playboy pseudo-settlers who had appeared after the war, dressed in bright silk shirts, richly coloured corduroy trousers and wide-brimmed hats, driving box-body cars with rifle racks inside, and lions' claws as mascots on the bonnet. They congregated mostly in Nairobi at Muthaiga club, or in the so-called Happy Valley on the slopes of the Aberdares, where Lady Idina presided at a house named Clouds. Everyone called her simply Lady Idina because her surname changed so often it was impossible to keep up. Now and again, at polo tournaments perhaps, she flitted through the periphery of my life like some gorgeous bird of paradise, brilliant in green or plum-coloured corduroys, a gay silk shirt, pearls and pendant ear-rings, slim as a wood-wasp, the clarity of her complexion and the candour of her fine eyes evidently freshened by the all-night parties and gallons of gin on which she and her circle so manifestly thrived.

It was one of the post-war playboys who was paying court to Betty Clewes. While Tilly disapproved, in theory, of the breed, she took at once to Philip individually, because he was amusing and provided laughs. Her idea of purgatory, had she formulated one, would have been to spend it in the company of someone like Miss Cooper, who tramped through life with heavy boots and no humour. Robin simply referred to him as the lounge lizard, a phrase of the times. Betty was generally thought to have had provocation, because Harry had made the first move and often disappeared to stay with his German friends. 'After all, it's only tit-for-tat,' Tilly remarked one day. Robin looked thoughtful, and added : 'Or tit-for-tit, perhaps?'

It had been decided that, to save the petrol, all three of us were to ride to Njoro to look at the bit of land Tilly coveted, and so Rupert became a problem. Njombo was to come with us, and we could not leave Rupert on the farm in charge of Kikuyu whose authority he would not accept. Even the obliging Alec would not take on a cheetah who might fret and refuse food, or get poisoned or trapped. If you are a wild animal everyone is against you, however innocent your intentions, and only the protection of your master stands between you and death. And Rupert had no guile or cunning, only trust in human beings. It seemed extraordinary that this seed of love for humans could lie dormant for so long, never called upon normally, but ready to grow and flower when a twist of circumstance gave it the opportunity. In nature, men were always enemies, yet Rupert loved being stroked and fondled, and after a few moments would start up his loud purr as suddenly as an engine when you press the self-starter, and then make one of his unheralded bounds.

Our difficulty was solved by the Beatties, who stayed a night with us on the way back from Nairobi and offered to take him for the fortnight we expected to be away. They already had a tame oryx and a buffalo calf the Colonel hoped to rear, to see if it would mate with his cows, and they said Alan

200

would be at home and could look after Rupert. Tilly and I took him up by car. He enjoyed motoring, and displayed a lively interest in everything we passed, but we did not enjoy it at all because there was nothing to stop him jumping out of the car whenever he saw anything chaseable. Between the roof, supported on posts, and the low wooden sides was a gap deep enough for a dozen cheetahs to jump through. Tarpaulin blinds, attached to the roof, could be unrolled in wet weather, and we tried enclosing him in these, but he merely jumped on to the front seat, dragging Njombo with him. Our drive left in its wake a trail of craned necks and looks of amazement, for people mistook Rupert for a leopard as we jolted by. We passed innumerable herds of goats, which seemed to be depastured mainly on the road, all of which Rupert wished to chase, and he and Njombo appeared to be engaged in a bout of all-in wrestling for most of the journey.

It was after dark when we arrived. Something had gone wrong with the lights, so we travelled with a safari lamp tied to the radiator. All sorts of living creatures scuttled out of the way and naturally excited Rupert, who twitched and fidgeted, but cheetahs hunt by day and luckily he did not feel impelled to launch a pursuit. Nightjars squatted in the car's path until the very last moment and rose from underneath the wheels in a soft, silent, voluptuous explosion of feather and flight. Each time you thought the tyres would hit them but each time they judged their moment to within a fraction of an inch. Hares spurted away from the light's faint and drunken lurching, squatted until we caught up with them, and then repeated their manoeuvre. Why hares always got the best of other creatures in native tales I could never understand. They did not seem at all intelligent. I only heard one African suggestion: 'Look at the hare: it's mouth moves all the time: it is always talking: what a lot it must know to talk like that!'

The darkness of this track through grass and bush was mysterious with half-glimpses, half-shadows, half-movements, glint of eyes, alive with secret activity that shut out man. Nowhere was a light, a fire, twinkle of company to be seen. Once we saw a low, long form glide across the jerky beam with snout outstretched and the motion of a heavy, furry tail. It must have been an aardvark, a beast seldom seen by night, and never by day, that could dig a wide, deep tunnel in an hour, and all to search for ants : strange that so big a creature should live on such specks of nourishment, which it fielded with its long, darting tongue. I often wondered why these ant bears should make so many tunnels in roads and paths, and learnt that this was not coincidence. On a road, the soil became impacted, enabling those faint sounds created by life proceeding in the earth to travel more easily. The aardvark sought out roads to listen for the sound of tunnelling ants, and when he picked it up, he dug for them with his grab-like claws.

We received a boisterous welcome from the wolf-hounds and a more subdued one from the Beatties, and a meal awaited Rupert in his quarters. He was put into the polo school, whose wire-netting walls would protect him from the pack. It was unlike the Beatties to be subdued, but they had reason. They had all grown fond of Commander Strudwick, who had become engaged to a nurse at the cottage hospital and had bought some land where he proposed to set up in married life; already he had planted his first vines, and bought a flock of native sheep. Every Sunday he drove his betrothed to this future farm, where they would picnic and inspect the progress being made in putting up stables and farm sheds which, following the local custom, preceded the house. His land thrust up into the forest and was bounded on each side by a river already stocked with trout, it possessed tall cedars and stored fertility, and game like bushbuck and forest francolin, in fact everything that Commander Strudwick wanted; and his nurse also was perfection in his eyes. She had taken with delight to riding, and learned to cast so well that she had caught a four-pound trout the previous Sunday.

On their way back to Nyeri they had to cross several bush-clad gullies. There had been rain, and in one of these gullies the wheels of Commander Strudwick's car sank into a large hole. It was necessary to put on chains. The Commander and his nurse got out of the car and, as they were inspecting the scene, there was a crash in the bush surrounding them and there emerged on to the road above a rhino with a lowered horn, in an attitude of anger and menace. He stood for a moment with his huge feet like tree trunks planted in the road and then launched himself down the hill and at them like a mighty cannonball.

There was no time for thought and cunning, only for the first action that instinct prompted. Commander Strudwick's instinct was to seize his jacket, which he had thrown across the radiator, and run towards the rhino holding it like a bull-fighter's cloak, and with the same intention, while he shouted at his companion to get behind the car. As the rhino rocketed towards him, he threw the coat at its lowered head and jumped for his life. No doubt his intention was to blind the rhino for the moment, in the hope that it would dash into the bush and vent its anger on the jacket. And this, indeed, is what it might well have done, had it not been an embittered rhino. It threw off the jacket, whipped round and went straight for the Commander. Its horn caught him in the back and sent him flying, and it turned again and gored him to death. Satisfied, it trotted off without glancing again at the car and the nurse, who was struggling to extract an unloaded rifle. And so Commander Strudwick was buried next day on the site of the house he would never build, under the peak of Mount Kenya.

Alan, instead of attending the funeral, had searched all day with trackers for the rhino and managed to locate him towards evening, and to exact revenge. The rhino proved to have an excuse for his ill-temper in the shape of a festering sore, full of maggots, on his haunch, caused by a bullet. Whoever had hit him and let him go was the true culprit. Colonel Beattie told us the story in front of an open fire of spitting cedar logs while Barbara, dressed in black corduroy trousers and a scarlet shirt, played dance-tunes on an old gramophone muffled by stockings thrust into its maw, and Mrs Beattie told Tilly about a wake held for her great-grandfather. 'They finished off every drop of whisky in County Cork, people said; it was a beautiful party.' Tilly was examining the gums of one of the hounds. 'Looks a bit yellow,' she remarked. 'Who's yellow?' roared the Colonel. 'I won't have that said in my house!' 'The gums,' Tilly said loudly. He was getting a bit deaf. 'Huns? Yellow my arse! You should have been at Deauville Wood. The Hun's no gentleman, but he's got guts, and that's more than can be said for some of these poodle-fakers we've got out here who call themselves officials. This fellow in the *boma* at Nyeri . . .' 'Stephen Portcullis took me up in his Tiger Moth last week,' Barbara said. 'He's teaching me to fly, then we're going down to South Africa. It's easier than driving a car, except just when you're landing. We missed a couple of buffalo just the other day by six inches coming down on the Amboni. Stephen's got marvellous hands. If you've good hands on a horse you make a first-rate pilot.'

I tried to edge away towards my father, who was smoking a cigar and paying no attention to any of the Beatties, each in full cry after his respective hare. If Alan had shot the rhino that had killed Commander Strudwick he could not be on safari, unless he had left that day, but I could not bring myself to ask his whereabouts. 'What have you got there?' Tilly asked, eyeing my drink. 'Lime juice and water.' I tried not to betray by a jerk of the muscles the snapping taste of the gin Barbara had added. 'Then you tie it up in muslin soaked in brandy and boil it for two days,' Mrs Beattie was saying. 'I used to have a little aunt who lived in County Kerry,' Tilly recalled. 'She kept her coffin in the attic and after tea we were allowed to see it, tiny it was, but so, of course, was she.' Colonel Beattie had got on to Nagas, fakirs and shooting black buck in Nepal. 'Actually South Africa's a blind, we're going to fly to Aden and buy camels and explore the Hadramaut,' Barbara whispered dramatically into my ear. Robin took out his cigar and murmured reflectively: 'I don't suppose the soil is acid enough for vines. Or it may be too acid, I can't exactly remember – one or the other, anyway.' 'Damn it,' shouted Colonel Beattie, 'we'll all be dead sooner or later and *then* we shall look bloody fools!'

A houseboy in a rather dirty *kanzu* came in with a plate of roasted nuts. He was followed by Alan, who stood in the doorway looking round with a smile I took to be sardonic, although as he was in shadow I could scarcely see whether he wore a smile or a scowl. But he looked dark with mystery and promise, and was standing (or so I imagined) like an antelope poised for flight. However, he moved forward into the lamplight and helped himself to a drink. He caught my eye, grinned and raised his glass.

'I've just seen Rupert,' he said. 'He's eaten half a sheep. You must find him almost as expensive to keep as a pack of wolf-hounds.'

'Sometimes he doesn't eat for two days.'

'He looks very fit.'

'Touch wood. I believe they get worms ... Thank you for the skin.'

'Glad you got it. You wrote, you know.'

'Well, yes ...'

'Sorry I didn't answer, but I've been away a lot.'

'Will you go on with it?'

'Safari work? You bet I will, if I can get it. Pays a lot better than sheep or cattle. More fun, too.'

'Yes, I expect so ...'

There was a pause, while Alan sipped his drink and I gulped mine, hoping that the unfamiliar dash of gin would generate inspiration. I thought of many things to say but none of them seemed likely to interest Alan. Yet everyone else was chattering like a house on fire.

'Did you have a good trip?' Alan at last politely inquired.

'Yes, thank you. The road was quite dry.'

'Good ...'

'I hear you shot that rhino.'

'Rather late in the day.'

'Awfully bad luck, running into it like that. I mean for Commander Strudwick.'

'Yes, rotten luck.'

After that we both gave up and Alan walked off to talk to the others, leaving me to black despair. It was bitterly unfair that Barbara should be able to talk the hind leg off a donkey in any company and I should be about as entertaining as a hibernating mole. Try as I would, I could do nothing to put things right. The more I searched for subjects the more they vanished, like motes in a beam of sunshine when you put out your hand. So abysmal was my dullness that I did not think I should ever be able to face Alan again. The gin, instead of making me loquacious, had given me a singing in the ears.

The call of a bugle, loud and peremptory, sounded through the living-room. Alan laughed at Robin's startled face. 'Don't you know the family custom? Bugle calls from reveille to the last post and a lot of odd ones in between. This is the bath-and-change.' The Colonel had all the military bugle calls on a record, and had trained a houseboy to put on the appropriate section at different times of day. The record was very scratched and the sounds that issued from it more like caterwauls than a military summons. In my bath I heard the distant and lugubrious refrain 'Ashes to ashes and dust to dust', the Dead March in Saul and then the Indian love lyric beginning 'Less than the dust beneath thy chariot whee-eels'. Everyone but me talked all through dinner.

Next morning I was up early to say good-bye to Rupert, who came bounding out of his cage as if in great relief to see himself still among friends. A ride had been discouraged because of the game he might chase, and I was afraid he would have to spend a lot of time in his cage on account of the wolf-hounds. But Alan came up and admired Rupert, and said that he would take him out for daily rides and let him pursue the buck on the plain.

'He can feed himself then,' Alan pointed out. 'It'll be much cheaper.'

'You don't think he'll go off and never come back?'

'Not he. He knows when he's well off. It's funny, but if a wild animal's allowed its freedom it very seldom goes off for good. If it's caged, that's different.'

We discussed this for a bit, and then the Beatties' oryx, and then went on to unsolved mysteries like the spotted lion and the Nandi bear. Suddenly I discovered we had been talking for at least fifteen minutes without any difficulty at all. So the sadness of my parting with Rupert was lightened, especially as I knew how much he would enjoy the chance to hunt on the plains, and that he had found a friend in Alan.

Chapter 19

THE Aberdare mountain range has three main peaks: Kinangop, Sattima and Kipipiri. Sattima, in the middle, is the highest. Our plan was to ride a shoulder of Kinangop, following one of the many streams to its source in the moorlands, and then proceeding down the other side through forest and plateau – down and over the wall of the Rift and into the valley where the bluest of lakes, Naivasha, lay with the jagged stumps of old volcanoes around it. We did not want to take porters and make a safari of it and, after reconnaissance, Robin and Tilly decided that a Scotch cart with oxen could proceed some way along a track winding upwards through the forest, made by cattle being driven to the uplands either for pasture in dry seasons or, more probably, for concealment after theft.

Fair Play and M'zee, of course, were coming, and White Lady, who had replaced Hafid. We had only three ponies, but Harry Clewes offered us a mount for Njombo from his well-stocked stable. Tilly disliked accepting this, but could think of no alternative but a mule of the Nimmos' which bit.

'It'll do him good,' Harry said. 'And, of course, you'll look after him, Tilly. Ride him on the snaffle, see the *syce* rubs him down at night and keep a good look-out for saddle-galls.' I knew that Tilly's toes were curling up in her riding-boots, but she thanked Harry mildly and took charge of the pony, an ageing, hard-mouthed half-Somali kept for odd jobs like fetching the mail.

The country got greener as we climbed upwards, and wilder, with fewer shambas and more bush. Open stretches of pasture, mostly sites of old shambas, were velveted with dwarf white clover that would have delighted any English dairy cow, but the native Zebu did not thrive on this close, rich sward. Goatbells tinkled from the aromatic bush, the yellow candle-blooms of *cassia* glowed like gorse, black wattle stood in feathery clumps on hillsides, the air grew crisp and heady and soon we came to thick, waist-high bracken that smelt like English

woods, and the big mauve blooms of the *vernonia*. Maidenhair
ferns hung over mossy stones along the banks of rivers whose
water was pure and limpid as a peal of bells.

About midday the track petered out and we followed the
imprint of cart wheels in spring turf. They crossed another
stream and then the forest began. Suddenly the warmth of
sunshine faded from our backs. Our world became cool,
gloomy and quiet save for the chink of bits and creaking of
leather, and the ponies' feet squelching in leaf-mould. We had
to watch for hanging lianas and low projecting branches fallen
from tall black trees that let through only pinpricks of sunlight. The oxen must have had a hard passage. The drivers
had been using their pangas on the undergrowth to hack a way
through. How the cart had jolted over some of the fallen, rotting trunks it was hard to say.

All forests are alarming, and so was this. The stillness is a
mask for sounds one knows to be inimical, it is not an absence
of sound. Now and again a large bird flapped and squawked
in unseen treetops, or foliage broke into unheralded commotion as a troop of monkeys took flight. Branches creaked
without apparent reason, even the butterflies that drifted past
looked sinister in all the vivid and barbaric glory of their
markings. One felt the presence of malevolent spirits.

Then came bamboos: at first in isolated clusters, then in
larger masses and finally they ousted altogether the smooth-
boled and dark-foliaged trees. Overhead their feathery
branches met like the tracery of a medieval cloister, and you
seemed to be advancing towards some hidden mystery along
an endless green nave. Sometimes a fallen branch cracked
with a bang that cannot have been loud, but seemed so in
this queer underwater silence, with everything heavy and
damp and deprived of sunlight. For the bamboos spent their
lives mainly in cloud and Scotch mist and were sodden with
moisture. When my knee touched a trunk or branch, a little
shower bath of cold moisture was released and trickled down
my neck. The ponies did not like it at all. They squelched
uphill warily, with disapproving slithers, their ears pricked.
It was hard work, for we were climbing towards the crest of the
shoulder, although we could tell this only by our laboured

breathing. Elephants were about, the ponies could no doubt smell something strange and alarming. M'zee picked his way round a large heap of elephant droppings with his neck arched, snorting in protest.

'Those are fresh,' said Njombo. He did not sound at all pleased.

'No, no,' Tilly contradicted. 'They are yesterday's.'

'No, memsabu, those were made this morning.'

'Perhaps last night. The elephants will be far away by now.'

Robin loaded the heavy rifle and carried it across his saddle, where it frequently knocked against tree trunks and got in the way.

'That gun's more dangerous than a whole herd of elephants,' Tilly remarked.

'Hush!' said Robin with authority: and on the right we heard a heavy crashing among the bamboos. The ponies stood stock still and quivered. The crashing grew nearer, and there were loud cracks from the splitting of trodden bamboos.

'Monkeys,' Tilly said firmly in a low voice.

'Monkeys my foot,' Robin hissed.

'*Tembo*, bwana,' Njombo affirmed.

'Monkeys,' Tilly said again, but in a whisper.

'Go on, go on,' urged Njombo.

'Be quiet,' Robin ordered. 'Don't move.'

It was weird to hear the cracks and crashes coming closer and to wonder whether we were being hunted, and what we should do if we were. In this thick forest the ponies would have no chance to outstrip elephants, they would certainly panic and fall. It was a question whether they were not going to panic immediately and give us all away. A bridle jingled as Fair Play shook his head. Robin rubbed the pony's taut neck with a soothing hand. The thumping of my heart seemed as heavy as a foot on the stair.

'I think they are going past us,' Robin said in a very low voice. Although the crashes were not receding, neither did their volume seem to be swelling, and after we had listened for a few moments more, our lungs scarcely moving, it did indeed seem apparent that the crashes were pursuing a path parallel to our own.

'They don't know we're here,' Robin murmured. Suddenly the ponies displayed an anxiety to be gone that nearly undid us. We had to rein them in, despite the jingling of the bits, and pray hard for deliverance, for elephants have wonderful hearing. Once or twice we heard a noise like a distant kettle boiling magnified a score of times, running up and down a sort of scale.

'Tummies rumbling,' Robin softly explained. This was a good thing, it showed they were feeding and not in a state of tension. Gradually the crashes receded to our right.

'I think it's safe to go on,' Robin said.

'That was a near thing.'

'It would have been tricky if they'd got our wind,' Robin admitted.

The ponies continued to be nervous and, despite their tiredness, went on seeing phantoms among the bamboos and snorting or halting to stand as still as rocks. The light was dim as in a cathedral, and tinged with green. With thin, pale bamboos arching and interlocking overhead the ecclesiastical illusion was deepened. And then the bamboos ended as suddenly as they had begun, and we were out on to open moorland. The sun shone down through an air rarefied by an altitude of over nine thousand feet. We felt invigorated, but the going was bad. Grass grew in thick, coarse tumps, and in between the soil was wet and slippery. After a while we got off and walked to rest the ponies, and found difficulty in standing upright. All around were clumps of giant heather, taller than a man, but no trees, and although it was mid-afternoon, everything was wet and cold.

The cart had done marvels to get through the bamboos. Soon after we emerged on to the moorland we came upon it outspanned by a little stream. The drivers looked miserable, huddled under their blankets, and the oxen were gazing with dispirited expressions at the coarse grass and giant heather, scarcely attempting to graze. Njombo and the drivers crouched over a fire kindled from branches of the heather and exchanged snuff.

'This is a dreadful place,' Njombo said. 'Elephants in the forest, cold everywhere, savage beasts – bad for men, bad for oxen. Why did bwana not go by motor-car?'

'He lacks shillings for the petrol,' I explained.

'Eee-eee-eee!' The sceptical content of Njombo's long-drawn-out ejaculation was plain enough. 'What good are shillings if we are killed by elephants or buffaloes, or by the fierce *marozi* that lives with spirits in this bad bush?'

I had not heard the word *marozi* before, and asked Njombo what it meant. A kind of lion, he said, but spotted like a hyena; it lived only in the mountains and attacked people who slept there. Our view was of moor, bog, crag and rock, and strange animals could well be lurking in the shadows.

Robin unpacked the shotgun and led us forth to seek something for the pot. The rough going and the altitude soon made us pant and puff. The solitude was absolute, and as the sun declined a mist came down and lay in wisps and wreaths about the rocks and clumps of heather.

'We'd better not go far from camp,' Tilly said. 'We might – there, look!'

Running game-birds were ahead, but not the little partridge-like speckled birds we were used to. These were twice the size and splendidly handsome, black rather than brown and with a crest falling over their beaks like a plume – the mountain francolin. They rose with a loud whirr, showing wide white bands on their wings, and Robin's shot sent one plopping heavily into matted grass so tough it would cut your finger, rather than break, if you tugged at a stalk. There was plenty of spoor about – bushbuck, duiker, the great cow-like eland, buffalo, many kinds of bird, and a feline creature too small for a leopard, perhaps a serval cat. To spell out from marks in the mud beside a stream, and round water-pools, what had passed that way, how long ago, whether male or female, whether loitering or in haste, all that was fascinating. I was a rank amateur and could read only the barest facts; Njombo was far more expert, but even he was not a tracker as the Dorobo people were, and many of the Wakamba. A good tracker could even estimate the weight of an elephant's tusks.

After dark we huddled round the camp fire, muffled in sweaters and blankets, hoping it would not rain. The giant heather brushwood and tindery rotted logs gave out a peaty, pungent smell and smouldered rather than burnt. The mists had gone; the stars looked close enough to touch, the Milky Way arched the heavens like a vast and incandescent plume of frozen smoke. Out of the dark came many wild noises: the sharp cough of a bushbuck, the screech of hyraxes, the guttural cry of owls and many calls and whispers I could not identify.

Robin and Tilly talked of what they would do when they sold the Thika farm. Now that the matter had been openly broached, neither would be content to stay: it was as if the spirit of the farm had already been discarded, whether or no they found a buyer. It made me sad to hear them talk in this way. I had a small room with an eastern window, a writing-desk, skins on the floor. These could be moved perhaps, but not the garden, the roughcast walls I picked at with my fingers, the orange grove by the river, the graves of birds, chameleons, cats. But Tilly's heart was set on the new forest land and Robin's mind had already travelled farther, down to Tanganyika where unpeopled wastes of bush and veld could be had for a song. For him, a fortune must be quick and spectacular; if it had to be plodded for, he lost interest.

We went to bed early, rolled in sleeping-bags, and in the morning broke a thin crust of ice on the water in our enamel basin. The first light was shining through a mist and making everything pearl-grey and opalescent. I looked out over a fleecy, nacreous sea from which heaths and boulders reared up like black ships marooned in a silent ocean. Everything was dripping wet, each cobweb loaded with moisture. In a few yards I was soaked to the skin, but I had to see what was astir in the mist and in a very short space of time I came upon three bushbuck, each hair of their heavy pelts tipped with a bead of dew, then several tiny dik-dik and a large, black creature that might have been a forest hog. I wandered farther than I had intended and, when I turned back, found that all the crevasses and ravines and shoulders of the landscape looked alike. To miss a button of a tent in the spreading moorlands was all too easy. The very thought of being lost arouses a hot instinct of panic that makes your blood pound, your ears sing and your reason scatter. I pushed through the grass tufts as fast as I was able and, scrambling over a rocky rise, saw just below me, perhaps at thirty paces, a long-horned rhino facing me with a calf at her side.

There was only one thing to do and that was to stand absolutely motionless. The rhino was black and rounded like a tick, and looked as if she had grown out of the rocks like a lobelia or the stump of an old tree. She belonged here and I did not, and it gave her a monumental dignity and self-possession. When she lowered her horn I took a breath and wondered which way to run. But she did not mean to threaten. Perhaps she did not see me clearly, with her poor rhino sight, and had only heard something to alarm her. She wheeled, and with surprising light-footedness trotted away over the rise, with the child at her side like a fat porker. I waited thankfully to let her out of earshot and then started down the hill, praying angrily for safety. I might indeed have missed the camp if I had not heard a shot and turned in that direction. It was Robin once more after francolin. Tilly was angry because I had gone off alone, so I did not mention my adventure, but the sight of the rhino standing so blackly and squarely with her calf against a background of heaths and pale tufted grasses stayed with me a long time. And the smell of bacon and the sting of hot tea were better than ever.

After breakfast we left the ox-cart and its drivers to go home, and rode on across the ragged moorland, squelching through bogs that were the birthplace of the rivers we knew far below. There had been a path here once, Njombo said, used by bands of Masai warriors to descend on the Kikuyu herds. The Masai must have had a hard task to drive cattle back over the mountain and through the bamboos, but the Kikuyu did not follow and harry them. We took our direction from the sun, and from Robin's compass that lived in a little leather case, from which he extracted it at intervals to study its quivering needle. Tilly said it never seemed to know its own mind and put her faith in the sun, until we found ourselves riding through clammy white cloud that made our voices hollow, and threw us back entirely on the compass.

'It's rather odd,' Robin said. 'According to the compass, we should be going back the way we came.'

We plodded dubiously on through the mist, passing the

213

queer, tall, phallic shapes of giant groundsel, which suggested an altitude of well over ten thousand feet. Sunbirds quivered around the clustering florets of the groundsel and, whenever the patchy cloud rolled back, we saw buzzards and kites, but no other living creatures. It was disappointing to enjoy no view, only a certain bleak grandeur, and a feeling of approaching the roof of the world. The ponies kept on stumbling and sometimes shied anxiously at a looming rock or bush, or at a movement in the grass. Everything was muffled and dank, and we began to worry about our direction.

'Can a compass go wrong?' Tilly inquired. Robin said: 'Not wrong exactly, but of course it can be distracted – magnetic rocks, and so on.'

'It sounds a horribly misleading instrument.'

'It's a jolly good one. It belonged to my father, and took him right across the Himalayas.'

'Perhaps the Himalayas haven't got as many magnetic rocks as the humble Aberdares. If we have to spend a night up here without blankets we shall freeze to death.'

'If we push on till all these little trickles go the other way, we shall be all right.'

Njombo took a robust view. '*Kwenda, tu,*' he said, which means roughly: 'Just go ahead.' He added that Kikuyu women used to carry loads of millet and beans along this route to trade with the Masai at Naivasha, when the two tribes were at peace. That anyone could hump a fifty- and sixty-pound load over this terrain, at this altitude, made us feel effete and unadventurous. All the Kikuyu men ever carried was a spear.

Robin noticed a trickle of water dripping from a rock. 'Look,' he exclaimed. 'It's going away from us – we've crossed the watershed.' Encouraged, we urged the ponies on, but seemed to be going uphill instead of down. So broken was the country you could not tell which way the land fell, but we must have started to descend, for after a while we noticed no more giant groundsel, and later still came to the first clumps of bamboo. We halted near them to rest the ponies and eat our sandwiches; it was three o'clock. The journey had taken far longer than we had expected. We had hoped to reach Naivasha before dark, but clearly we should be lucky if we got through the belt of forest we knew to lie between the moorland and the plateau below. Somewhere on the edge of this forest a family called Duncan was thought to dwell. If our calculations were correct, we should pass across their farm, or near it, to reach Naivasha, and it looked as if, although they did not know it, they would have to put us up for the night.

It was dark in the forest, and damp, and slippery, and cold, and tangled, and we were all weary, ponies and riders alike. M'zee was drooping his head and making little effort to control his feet, and I kept pitching forward on his neck and only just staying in the saddle. We all thought longingly of fires, dry clothes and hot baths, and anxiously of leopards. The journey seemed endless, the darkness fell swiftly and we believed we should have to spend a cold, hungry, stiff, alarming night huddled together with the ponies in a forest full of unseen savage beasts. And then suddenly the trees were no longer overhead and we came to a fence, with a picket gate.

'Civilization, thank God,' Robin said. We filed through the gate, Robin still with the heavy rifle in his hand. A light gleamed ahead. It was wonderfully comforting, this little yellow eye that spelt humanity, winking in a hostile blackness seeming to stretch unbroken to the edge of the world. Our depression fell away, we advanced happily towards the friendly welcome we anticipated from these marooned islanders in a sea of wilderness. Abruptly, the light winked out, and when we reached the hut from whose mouth it had shone we saw that a hurdle had been thrust across the doorway to block our entry. Even Njombo's Kikuyu summons went unanswered, save for muffled whisperings from inside.

'They don't seem very welcoming,' Robin said.

We proceeded towards the dim shapes of squatting buildings ahead and saw at last a lantern moving in the dark. Robin hailed it; the light halted; in its little pool of illumination we saw the glint of metal. Robin's voice protested: 'Hey, don't point that thing at me,' and a thick Scots answer came: 'And who may ye be, coming armed to a Christian home at this time o' the night?'

A brief disarmament conference followed. Our host explained that, owing to stock thefts, he had threatened to shoot the next uninvited person who set foot on his land. So we were lucky: although stock thieves did not normally arrive on horseback, we supposed. Mr Duncan was a stocky, bushy-haired, barrel-chested man with thick eyebrows, very blue, clear eyes and only one arm, as resourceful as two of most people's. He lived in a log cabin, and we could see at once what career he had followed before he had settled on the Kinangop. The unglazed windows were round, several ships in bottles stood on tables and a ship's wheel hung on one wall. While Tilly and Robin enjoyed the whisky they had been hoping for, I got home-made wine brewed from loquats, which I found sickly; however, we thawed gratefully by a log fire smelling deliciously of cedar.

Mrs Duncan was large, motherly and vague, with a habit of leaving sentences unfinished and a half-smile that suggested a pleasing set of thoughts kept to herself. She apologized for our accommodation, but certainly need not have done so; the guest-house, a smaller cabin, was clean and weatherproof, the packing-case furniture neatly covered with cotton prints and the floor with skins. Later on there appeared two stalwart sons who spoke little while their father grew loquacious, once he had decided we were not stock thieves or Government officials, whom he disliked about equally. There was no part of the world he had not visited, and of all that he had seen he preferred this mountain-side under the forest, four or five hundred miles from the sea.

Next morning I could understand why. The house was like a little ship anchored on an inmmense sea of plain and bush that fell away, in the farthest distance, to form the escarpment of the Rift Valley. Mr Duncan had built a look-out in a tall cedar and, on a clear day, you could just discern a blue, hazy smudge across the sky that marked the mountains on the far side of the great valley. The forest, like a thick fur pelt clothing a mighty crouching beast, came right to the fence marking off the garden, and was scoured with great ravines. Below lay a plateau, pale in the early sunshine, with dark tongues of cedar forest cutting into it, no sight or sound of man, wild game still in abundance, and many cold streams. It was bleak but magnificent, and Mr Duncan's thoughts could sail forever across the vast mountain moorlands and plain laced with trees while his body remained secure in his anchored cabin, with the fresh smell of cedar in his nostrils and the call of birds in his ears.

A stream ran past the house and the bush had been cleared from its banks, leaving only tall cedar and podocarpus trees. The morning mists and high rainfall kept moist and dark earth that was full of leaf-mould from forest untouched not for centuries, but millennia. Frosts often rimed the grass-blades and laid a thin skin of ice on puddles and water-butts. In this shaded, cool and sheltered spot, warmed in daytime by a genial sun, Mrs Duncan grew daffodils as well as violets, narcissi, hyacinths and jonquils – even snowdrops and crocuses came up, if a little hesitantly. We were amazed to see a sheet of yellow quiver under the trees, and sunshine distil through the parchment-thin trumpets of daffodils an essence of gold, to find the purity of temperate spring recreated here in the wilderness. The smell of damp violets lying under sappy leaves was so fresh and sweet it left one disarmed, and the stark, harsh, mindless and magnificent beauties of Africa appeared by contrast alien, armoured and remote from our hearts as the stars. The Duncans' garden with its gentle violets, the bright daffodils drooping their heads a little as if in thought, the slender, delicate jonquils and narcissi drenching the air with sweetness, all these were soft and confiding, made to delight and not to challenge.

The sunlight was subdued and dappled by trees, and the garden alive with birds. Even these birds were of a gentler kind than usual: a golden oriole fluted by the stream and a pair of dark-red firebirds darted about. Tilly was overwhelmed with pleasure and excitement, she had never imagined that such a garden could exist in Africa. Mrs Duncan was reso-lutely modest. She had just put the bulbs in and up they had come, but it was early days yet; no one could be sure they would survive.

'It's the hard winters they'll be missing,' she said. 'The frosts here never bite into the ground.' But Mr Duncan said there was not so much difference between the Kinangop and the Western Isles, except for the details of nine thousand feet and a little variation in the length of days, which would perhaps puzzle the bulbs. And they had many enemies such as moles, termites, and moulds.

'It's wrong, really, to make that sort of garden on the Kinangop,' Tilly reflected as we rode away after a breakfast of porridge, home-baked scones, home-churned butter and wild honey, in the bird-bright freshness of a new day. 'One shouldn't use nostalgia as a principle of gardening; and I'm sure Hilary would say it was a kind of *trompe l'oeil*. Down with exotics: up with the indigenous. But I must say, right or wrong, it was very pleasant. Mrs Duncan may be a sentimentalist, but she's pulled it off.'

'She makes excellent scones,' said Robin.

Chapter 20

FOR several hours' journey we saw no sign of the great valley ahead, and then quite suddenly it lay before us and we were silenced, although we had known what to expect. Below us the ground tumbled away for perhaps three thousand feet and there lay the gigantic trough, stretching on each hand into the blueness of distance and simmering in the heat haze.

The clouds, I think, struck us most, the clouds rolling ponderously in never-ending processions across an illimitable sky, each casting a purple shadow on the valley's floor, so that another procession was taking place far below. They were not just white, they had many different shades of violet and grey and mauve, and were solid-looking, as if you could have scooped them up with a spoon. And although the sky was always full of these massive, gravid clouds, they never crossed the path of the sun. Far, far below lay speckly pimples that were the cones of extinct volcanoes like Longonot and Suswa, or smaller lumps of jagged lava thrown out by them, and a couple of lakes that winked up at us like hard, blue eyes. But nothing could be seen of the works of man, no roads, no roofs, no cities. Men did exist down there, even a railway, but its single line, constructed with so much effort and danger, was a tiny thread invisible in so great a cloth of plain and mountain that you felt a single twitch of the bony shoulders underneath would dispose, in an instant, of such trivial little scratches.

To scramble down this enormous precipice looked impossible; yet, as we advanced, a track of sorts opened up before us, winding in and out of crevices and round boulders; we knew that the Duncans sent butter to Naivasha along this route, and sometimes drove bacon pigs to board a train. As our ponies picked their way down, the heat came up to meet us, and soon we could scarcely recall the mountain coldness. We could smell the heat as well as feel it: a dry, punching smell of dust and the silver-leafed *leleshwa* shrub, of leather and pony, of rock and cattle dung and thorn. Blue and orange lizards scuttled under stones, quartz glinted in the coarse red soil, beetles worked amid the tufty brittle grasses; we were back among the red-barked acacias with their tight-balled florets and hanging beehive logs, amid the stunted bare thorns loved by ants, and here and there the near-black, thrusting fingers of the thick-fleshed candelabra euphorbia. We had come back to the yellow weavers and their frenzied nest building, the mongoose with his ringed bushy tail jinking among grass-tufts, the dipping flight of the ungainly crested hoopoes, the ever-circling buzzards and kites, the white-banded crows flapping, the waggle-tailed gazelle, the velvet-coated, sad-eyed, mild-mannered giraffe gazing over the umbrella-thorns and loping off with the motion of a rolling ship, and as silently.

Contrasted with so much natural magnificence the works of man, represented by a straggle of Indian shops whose grubby little verandas were crowded with ragged, sweating customers and treadle sewing machines, by a single dusty, pot-holed street lined with squat buildings made of corrugated iron whose roofs shone like puddles in the sun, by Naivasha station, a shed or two near the twin steel ribbons and some whitewashed stones – the works of man were not impressive. After refreshment at the inn, and a rest for the ponies, we rode on beside a reed-fringed lake shore. The westering sun shone into our eyes and turned the bark of the acacias a rich red-gold. The reeds were alive with birds, and ducks flighted over the passive water with their sad cries. Small islands jutted from the lake and we saw the pig-like snouts and small pink ears of hippos floating in their coils of rubbery fat.

We were to stay with a couple Robin had known years ago in the Transvaal; German in origin, they had settled in Tanganyika, and everything they had owned there had been confiscated by the victorious British during the war. Afterwards they had come to Naivasha to make a new start. Walter painted pictures, but not for a living, and was said to be going in for Persian lambs. This put Tilly against him because the lambs were slaughtered at birth, but Robin argued that this was kinder than to kill them later, when they had tasted the sweets of life.

We reached their house as the sun's rays were thrusting rapiers of light into every tuft, hillock and crevice of bark. The homestead stood back from the lake on a rocky outcrop, without a garden or anything to mark it off from its sursoundings, even a fence. Grass grew right up to the walls of the rondavels, which were of different colours – one a pinkish dove-grey, one pale blue, a third sea-green and ochre. A square hut with an open side stood in the middle, commanding a tremendous view over the lake and the distant mountains. It all looked foreign, perhaps because it was designed to blend into the landscape instead of to defy it with a neat garden, English flowers and a lawn. It did not look cosy.

As we climbed a short hill to the house, we rounded a corner to see a black-maned lion crouching in the bush just in front of us, snarling viciously. The ponies saw it too and, tired as they were, shied violently. Tilly was in the lead, and called urgently for the rifle, which had been thrust into a bucket holder strapped to Njombo's saddle. Several minutes of confusion, in which only the lion remained calm, ended by Robin calling out: 'It's a spoof!' And it was indeed a stuffed beast, realistically arranged.

'Someone might get thrown and break his neck,' Tilly said, angrily. 'I think that a rotten sort of joke.'

'Well, it did take us in,' Robin replied appreciatively. He had more taste than she for practical jokes. Later, we found others. A stuffed cobra was curled up in the garden privy in such a position as to be seen only when you sat down, and

Walter had enjoyed the spectacle of guests bolting in all sorts of undignified conditions, shouting for a gun. There was a mechanical nightingale that sang outside the window, an imitation spider sitting on a cake of soap, a cigarette box that played a tune and cushions that made rude noises. Walter never failed to be amused at these things, although at other times he appeared melancholy. He was tall and thin with deep-set, rather pleading eyes, a large nose and a slow, deliberate manner of speaking. He played the piccolo with skill, and he, his wife and sister-in-law, who lived with them, performed as a trio.

Kate, his wife, was charged with so much vitality one almost expected to feel the crackle of sparks when she touched you. She had two children, both away at school – where I should have been, she implied, smiling at Tilly. 'But then, I expect you cannot spare her, she is so much help to you in the house.'

'I wouldn't exactly say that,' Tilly replied. 'I teach her myself.'

'You were a teacher, yes? You have diplomas probably? That is a fine thing: how diplomas would be useful, for a woman with a family! But no one thought of such things when I was young. My father had so much land, more than from here to Naivasha, so many servants, so many workpeople – his daughters had no need of diplomas. They would have rich, handsome husbands instead. Now all that has gone, gone ... Now we must think only of the future, yes? Our future in this great land. Walter has many plans to make a fortune: he has always plans. He has big thoughts, big like his pictures, you see ...'

We did see, indeed; the living-room was painted all over with murals, enormous animals and people filled the scene. His theme was the Creation in an African setting; God was represented by a huge clenched fist in the centre of the ceiling with beams of light shooting from it, and on the walls animals were standing as if newly formed, birds stretching their wings in the branches of erythrina and acacia trees, and a black Adam, dressed like a Masai, was flexing his muscles on one side of the door, gazing at a full-breasted naked Eve on the other. They had lost no time, for the dusky Eve was already clutching a baby. The figures were angular and, to my mind, crude and distorted, but I was only used to illustrated magazines with reproductions of Academy portraits, so I was in no position to judge. Luckily the colours were dark and smudgy, otherwise the room would have seemed even more restless and nerve-jangling than it did already. Walter had used only such paints as he already had on the farm for coating wagons and corrugated iron, together with pigments he had ground experimentally from local rocks and clays.

'It is all created out of Africa,' he said, 'the pigments, the models, the ideas. One day I will paint a companion piece to have in it the gods of Africa – it is our God, our legend of Creation, I have painted there. African gods rule by fear, not by love, they are deformed and distorted, and in native legends of Creation man came first from God's knee, or from his stomach or his anus. He did not come out innocent, like Adam and Eve, but already old and steeped in sin and full of tricks. Most of all, you see, they admire trickery.'

'They should do well in the City,' Robin said, recalling old wounds.

'But in the City, tricks can succeed only when for every rogue there are a hundred innocents. If all are rogues, you see, there is a stalemate. I think that is what has happened to African society.'

Walter was full of theories about everything, and Tilly found this trying; she liked things to stay on a more practical plane. But Robin enjoyed these conversations and he liked Walter. After dinner – excellent and very large – Walter took Robin off to his office rondavel until after midnight, leaving the ladies to themselves. Kate's sister Freda was reserved, and preoccupied with dressmaking; both women made their own clothes, and Tilly thought they did the cooking, too, but would not admit it, because they pretended to be richer and grander than they had become. The houseboy wore a red-and-gold braid Zanzibar waistcoat, but his lack of skill and air of bewilderment suggested that he was a shamba-boy drafted in for the occasion. What the family lived on was a mystery. The Persian lambs were only a project, so far. Meanwhile Walter had a field of sunflowers, a magnet for seed-eating birds

222

'This is a place of many birds,' Kate remarked. 'Next year, Walter will find a way to prevent them eating the sunflowers.'

'It's hard to prevent birds from doing what they want to, when their minds are made up,' Tilly pointed out.

'To everything, there is an antidote.'

'Walter is very clever,' Freda put in. 'And he works so hard! He has a son to work for, you see.'

'Yes, Walter is going to make a future for his son,' Kate agreed. 'He must have a position to inherit, just as Walter had. Now that has gone, and it must be a new future in a new Africa.'

'Walter will succeed,' said his sister-in-law firmly.

I left them adulating Walter, and sought my camp bed on the veranda of the guests' rondavel. A half-moon, bright as a sodom-apple, was making a path on the lake's quiet and silent waters, and islands rose up like dark monsters crouching on a silvery bed. Distant hills were sharp against a sky pulsing with stars, and the reeds made a black line across the white shore. I longed to go down and swim in the warm, still water, and watch the hippos lumbering out to graze, glistening in the moonlight. The lonely, heart-piercing call of a fish-eagle disturbed the night and was answered by a fainter cry. Ducks and many water-fowl were moving on the water and feeding in the reeds. Always at night, when the earth and its creatures were secretly at work, you felt that a message of immense importance was waiting to be understood, that all would be made clear if only you could hear words just out of earshot and grasp truths you were too dull to see. I felt muffled by layers of sensual obtuseness, like a hippo in its fat: a prisoner of bluntness. Half with the idea of trying to strip off some of the layers, I decided to walk down to the lake, but had only gone a little distance when Kate overtook me.

'You should be sleeping,' she said. 'At your age it is easy to sleep. Perhaps your dinner was too big and rich?'

'No, I just wanted to see the lake.'

'It is too far, the lake, for midnight prowls. But I will come with you for a little stroll.'

The last thing I wanted was to stroll with Kate, or with

223

anyone else, so I said that after all I was tired and we turned back for the rondavels, Kate talking all the way.

'How beautiful it is by this lake shore! Never have I seen before such beauty, but you know, it is dangerous, like some delicious drink perhaps, with a little drop of poison in the bottom. Oh, I do not mean the animals, or the natives, it is something else that steals away your wits. And a woman, she must never give her heart to anything except her man. Everything she must give up for him, all her friends, her thoughts, nothing can be held back. He is like a hungry tiger. You will learn one day, how they are jealous unless they have the last little scrap of meat. How old are you, child?'

'Nearly sixteen.'

'In many countries you would be already married, with a child yourself perhaps. Well! You should stay as long as you can in this half-way house we build for our children, where we keep life outside the windows and truth beyond the door.'

Kate alarmed and fascinated me, like a snake with handsome markings. She said embarrassing things, in fact there was something about her presence in itself I found embarrassing, almost as if she were naked: something not held back as it was among all the other people I knew. She seemed almost to vibrate with a desire to impart and share: I thought of someone with an unquenched thirst. Also I was afraid she was going to take an interest in me as an individual, and I was not used to this. She asked too many questions.

'You have a lover yet, someone to whom your thoughts turn whenever they can? I do not mean a man to sleep with, you are a virgin still, I can tell: I mean this fine prince we carry in our hearts until he awakes us, and we see that his coat of brocade and velvet is only sacking after all. Some handsome young farmer with his brown legs and English gentleness? But you are too shy to let him understand your feelings and you talk only of stupid things when you are with him, horses and dogs and wild beasts – always animals, it is extraordinary how you English are obsessed by animals, if they are wild you try to kill them, but if they are tame you will let yourselves be killed to save the life of one of them. Am I right, is he like that?'

She was laughing at me now, but there was something predatory about even that, although I supposed she meant it kindly. She added: 'You know, your secrets will be safe with me, I do not babble.'

'I haven't any secrets.'

Kate laughed again, and I could see how attractive she might be to anyone who could overcome their alarm, or did not feel it; her eyes were magnificent, the clear sepia iris marked with bracken-coloured flecks and a great depth in them, her features clear and decisive. I thought of Betty Clewes, her exact opposite in every way, fluttery where Kate was firm, soft, silly, muddled and kind where Kate was hard, intelligent and deep.

'There, you have locked it all away in the drawer of your mind and swallowed the key; wild horses wouldn't drag it from you, is that right? Never mind; to grow up is painful, there is so much hurt. Have you ever watched a dragonfly breaking from its hard, ugly case into the light and air? It clings to the reed trembling, naked and soft, exhausted by the breaking and cracking of the shell, and the wind and sun hurt its delicate folded wings. But soon it will become a dragonfly and eat other insects and fly locked together with its mate. It is greed that drives us all. Well, then, tell me something of your life, your friends. One I know, that is Harry Clewes, who comes here sometimes, but his wife he has never brought. She is congenial, is she, a friend of your remarkable mother?'

Then it came to me that she must be the German woman with whom Harry was said to be having an affair. I was dismayed at my own denseness in not tumbling to this before, and looked at her with a new interest. She was two-faced as well as alarming, and I felt an involuntary spasm of respect for Harry, as for those people who caress cobras without getting hurt. And all she wanted was to pump me about Betty.

'She's all right,' I said cautiously. 'She talks a lot, but not *about* anything, and dithers rather. She's no good at riding, but does embroidery. Not awfully well, though. She's got twins.'

'Yes, you make her very clear, she is the pure feminine. There are men who find the pure feminine boring, as anything can be that is not mixed – honey for instance, or spring water, they are good for you but there is no taste. Such women are like burrs, they will stand everything and in the end they will still be there, they triumph by just being meek. And Harry Clewes, do you see him?'

'Oh, yes, he's a close neighbour. He does very well.'

'Does very well ... What does that mean exactly?'

I found it impossible to sum people up as adults did, in a sentence, and when I tried I only echoed opinions I had overheard. I knew I was echoing Robin when I said: 'Everything he does turns out successful. If lucky stars really worked, he'd have been born under one. And he's rather pleased with himself. Tilly thinks he ...' I shut up in time, before I called him a bounder – whatever that might mean, I never really understood it – thinking myself a fool to let her entice these second hand opinions from me. But she was like a magnet pointed at a heap of pins, and seemed able to read my thoughts.

'You think I'm too curious. You must try to forgive me, and remember that I have a daughter of my own about your age, so you see I understand a little the feelings of the nymph that will soon become a dragonfly. And then we are lonely here in the bush, for us it is a big event to have such visitors. So you must think of me as a friend.'

'Thank you very much.'

Kate laughed and said: 'You reply as if I had offered you a second helping. You take after your father; he likes ideas because he is afraid of people. Walter is devoted to him, they are such good friends. Here is a man, says Walter, that I can trust ... But now it is time for bed, and beauty-sleep. Sleep well, my child.'

When she had gone I felt a sense of relief. She was unpredictable, and I thought that she might jump from affection to hatred as easily as one jumped across a ditch, and take too little trouble to conceal either emotion.

We rode away after an enormous breakfast, much affectionate leave-taking and many invitations to return.

'The loyal little woman act was laid on pretty thick last night, considering,' Tilly remarked. 'Do all German women really think their men are wonderful, or is it simply a conven-

226

tion, like women wearing hats in church and men removing them?'

'It's just Teutonic,' Robin said. 'And of course, most enjoyable.'

'It doesn't seem to go very deep. Walter's either got no eyes in his head, or no spirit. What were you two talking about all night?'

'As a matter of fact, it was rather interesting. He's a knowledgeable fellow, studied geology among other things, and just before they interned him in Tanganyika, he was on the verge of some remarkable finds.'

'Oh, dear,' Tilly said.

'What do you mean, oh, dear?' Robin asked crossly. 'Everyone's always known that Tanganyika's stiff with minerals. The Germans did a lot of prospecting and if it hadn't been for the war, they'd have opened up big lead and copper mines. Diamonds too, I shouldn't wonder. Walter knows a good bit about all that. He was a director of a company that had some valuable concessions. Then the war came and it went phut, but the minerals are still there all right.'

'And Walter wants to form a company to dig them up.'

'Actually he's formed the company, with very influential backing from Johannesburg, and got a concession out of the Tanganyika Government; and they've got some extremely promising experimental assays.'

'And he can get you in on the ground floor.'

'He thinks he might,' Robin corrected. 'All the shares have been snapped up, but he thinks he knows someone who might be willing to sell a small parcel at a very small profit. Of course I couldn't afford more than a few, but it does sound like a wonderful opportunity.'

'It sounds like a wonderful way to drop money you haven't got.'

'Why do you throw cold water on everything?' Robin asked reproachfully. 'I'm only trying to do the best I can for us all. It's perfectly open and above-board. You don't think Walter's a crook, do you?'

'Not a crook, but not a very good man of business either.'

'I don't see what right you have to say that. It wasn't his

227

fault he was a German and lost everything in the war. And now he's getting on his feet again very well. I think he's on to a winner with those Persian lambs.'

'He's not on to it *yet*.'

'I wish you were a little more Germanic,' Robin said sadly, 'and thought everything I said was wonderful.'

Chapter 21

WE rode round the western side of Lake Naivasha, under the lee of the Mau escarpment, to the next lake, Elmenteita, which was opaque with soda and rimmed by a beach of dazzling white. A cleft hill like a molar tooth, standing by the northern shore, was reflected in the hard blue water with a solid clarity. Flamingoes in their gossiping millions were like a rim of blood-stained ice round the lake's margin. On our left rose the forested escarpment, on our right the mountain called Eburru still flickering with volcanic life in the shape of steam jets whose vapours formed permanent clouds over the summits.

There was game in plenty. A herd of waterbuck loped from a gully and stood among the flat-topped thorns with their heads laid back and the white showing on their chins, as large as donkeys. Striped tommies and their graceful elder brothers, the grantii, were everywhere, and the lolloping kongoni and cantering zebra. These wild animals were wiser than the men intent on replacing them by domestic flocks and herds, for they never overstrained the land's capacity to feed them, as cattle did; they never trod down the grasses and churned the ground to pulp and scarred the earth with gullies where they filed to water. Nor did they quarrel among themselves. Zebras never ousted kongoni, nor did lions multiply so as to obliterate antelopes, nor buffaloes interfere with giraffe. They lived in harmony with their surroundings.

We passed a few herds of native cattle, fat on the sparse, dry pastures that suited their taste, so long as they could find water every two or three days. That was the trouble. We crossed only one stream, most welcome to the ponies who drank and splashed and tried to lie down and roll in its cool water. On banks lined by acacias we admired the brilliant green and sapphire plumage of the malachite kingfisher and saw a great variety of other birds, from drab stonechats and babblers and coarse long-tailed mouse-birds to bright-feathered swallows, and glossy ungainly whydahs, a marsh harrier with a stony yellow eye and wicked head biding his time on the branch of a dead tree, and the neat grey blacksmith plovers with their dark-ringed eyes, their slender legs and their high-pitched, monotonous call like the light, continuous tapping of a hammer on anvil.

That night we stayed with a junior manager of a ranch called Soysambu, in a wooden bungalow on a rocky bluff over-looking Lake Elmenteita. His young wife was struggling to make a garden in the light-grey, volcanic ash that served for soil, and blew away in choking clouds once the anchoring grasses had been skimmed off. Only a little water-furrow taken from a cattle-trough kept her plants alive and they looked exhausted by the struggle, and were constantly eaten by ter-mites and scorched by sun. Yet she was determined, and had planted round the house trees that she watered constantly. It was a battle between her will and the ancient apathy of soil and climate. For the moment, with the water-furrow, perhaps she would triumph, and indeed a vase of limp roses in our guest-hut spelt victory, but, in the long run, one felt the odds were on the valley.

For his part the young manager was struggling to establish flocks and herds despite disease, Masai stock thieves and pre-dators, especially hyenas which preyed on newborn calves. The cattle were confined in thorn-scrub *bomas* every night but, even so, a few nights before a lion had jumped the fence and killed two beasts. The manager had poisoned their carcases but only hyenas and jackals had suffered, and vultures whose painful ends no one regretted. The need for poison worried the manager whose boss, he said, would never allow it if he knew, but would expect him to sit up all night in a tree, over a kill, to shoot the lion.

His boss was Lord Delamere, who sometimes appeared

with hair flowing almost to his shoulders, a huge sun helmet that gave him the look of a mushroom, and a dirty old cardigan, and turned the place upside down. His first manager, an austere Scots shepherd called Sammy McCall, had carried a letter of resignation in a pocket of the tweed waistcoat he always wore, and presented it once every three months or so for about ten years. But now Delamere was mellowing, or perhaps merely deflecting more of his energy into politics. A twice-broken neck and a leg mauled by a lion were nothing, but war service among the Masai and prolonged malaria had left him with a strained heart, and he had given up a favourite pre-war amusement, which had been to buy a sack of oranges, distribute them to everyone he could find in the cow-town (as he called it) of Nakuru, and then direct an assault on the hotel of which he was the proprietor until every pane of window-glass had been smashed.

On the fifth day of our ride we left Lake Nakuru on our right and started to climb out of the valley. The landscape changed completely in a mile or two. Behind us lay thorn-scrub and *leleshawa*, dust-devils and heat, the jagged relics of volcanoes, flamingo-red lakes; now our ponies pushed through tall red-oat grass, signifying soil fertility, under spreading umbrella thorns and straggle-branched olives, where tongues of cedar forest thrust down to meet the plain. The air grew cooler and fresher, a scent of jasmine surprised us, we heard a chatter of monkeys and the grating squawk of turaco. A few shambas, little clearings full of charred tree stumps like blackened teeth, showed where pioneer Kikuyu squatters, introduced by their employers, were beginning to cultivate on virgin land. The forest thickened as we climbed, and cedar trees began to appear. A few miles farther up, a trace marked the boundary of the forest reserve. Above that, close-packed trees stretched in wave upon wave over the crest of the mountains and down to lap upon the sun-drenched Masai plains the other side.

In all this country, until a few years ago, there had lain no human habitations, nor any tracks or roads. Now a number of farms had been demarcated for settlement and it was on one of these we were to stay with Trevor Sheen, a genial and hospitable Irish adventurer with white hair and a complexion the colour of mahogany who never gave his age, but must have been well into the fifties. He had reached the country before the railway had been built, and for his first job had conducted a caravan of donkeys from Mombasa to supply the surveyors who were mapping its route. All the donkeys died from tsetse-fly and he tried again with camels, more successfully until they reached the highlands and died of wet, discouragement and broken legs.

Trevor Sheen was said to have begun life as a strong man in a circus and to have got his start in India as an opium smuggler. In Africa he had scratched a living as a transport contractor, a cattle trader, an ivory poacher, a labour recruiter, and never settled down until, still a bachelor, he had bought the leasehold of a few thousand acres of bush and forest at Njoro, built himself a cedar-log shack and taken off his first crop. Either he was flush with money and a host to all in sight, or he was stony broke, but his charming weather-beaten smile always won him credit, especially as he spoke fluent Hindustani to the Indians. Another tale was that he had travelled to England on a single second-class railway ticket from Elburgon, two stations up the line, to Nakuru.

When Robin asked him what he was going in for at Njoro he answered: 'Wheat and overdrafts.' His ideas were as generous as his hospitality, and he had marked out a thousand acres, as near as he could guess, engaged a mob of lusty, naked men from Kavirondo and set them to work with picks and pangas, hired oxen, ploughs and harrows, to break the land. With prodigious effort the thousand acres were drilled with an Australian wheat, and Trevor watched his enormous field turn green as an English lawn, then gradually yellow, and at last become a golden sea rippled by the wind, beautiful as well as enriching. He reckoned his crop to be worth ten thousand pounds.

Wheat had many enemies, above all rust, a fungus which could, and often did, wipe out an entire crop. It was a gamble, and this was no doubt why it appealed to Trevor. Before the war Delamere, the wheat pioneer, had ploughed a three-mile furrow on the plain and put in 1,200 acres, and rust had demolished every blade. So Trevor awoke each morning riddled with anxiety, and hurried out to ride along the margins of his field looking for streaks of yellow on the leaves, or of black on the stems. He even prayed for the safety of the wheat and felt, he said, like one of those Crusaders who undertook to found a monastery if God would deliver him from shipwreck on the voyage home.

God, luck or the seasons were on his side: the wheat turned and filled the ear unrusted. Nothing seemed to stand between Trevor and a fortune. He hired bags, machinery and oxen, and even arranged for the railway to provide a special train to take his wheat to Nairobi. We heard the story with mounting suspense, for it was plain that something, somehow, had gone wrong. If Trevor had made ten thousand pounds we should be living on champagne; as it was, he had to shoot buck on the plains for his dinner.

'What was it?' Tilly asked. 'Rust at the last moment? An invasion of zebra?'

'A spark from the Uganda Railway. My God, what a blaze! And a roar like a thousand trains going through a tunnel. I never harvested a bag.'

Stunned, we sat in silence for a few moments, like mourners. He had been within a week of harvest. 'At least the overdraft has done well,' he added, tilting his white-shocked head to one side and roaring with laughter. 'Take my tip, and never borrow *small* sums. If you go in deep enough the bank's got to keep you afloat, can't afford not to. Then you're all right.'

'Yes, but how?' Robin asked enviously.

'You've got to pick your manager. The best of all was J. C. Shaw.'

This Mr Shaw had opened a branch of the Standard Bank of South Africa in Eldoret in 1912. It had been a simple process: he had arrived in an ox cart with a heavy safe which he had pushed out at the back on to a wagon track that traversed the bare, brown plateau. As it was too heavy to move, a mud hut had been built round it with two rooms, one for the safe and one for Mr Shaw. The town then consisted of a few little stores and was called Sixty-four, after the survey number of the farm on which it stood. Sixty-four served a sparse community of Afrikaners who had arrived together – men, women, children, babies, predikants and household goods – from Bethel in the Transvaal, and trekked in their semi-covered wagons up the roadless, forested escarpment to a promised land devoid of boundary-marks or inhabitants, black or white, called the Uasin Gishu.

Mr Shaw was not an early riser, and sometimes his first customers would arrive to find him splashing in a hip bath behind the counter; later in the day he would put on his dressing-gown and proceed to a shack next door called Eddie's bar, to refresh himself before conducting business. This consisted mainly of advancing money on the security of a span of oxen, a growing crop, a capacity for work and a lot of faith in the future. For these Boers worked hard; they built their own houses with their own hands, and they harvested their first crops of wheat with sickles, tying the bundles with straw because they lacked twine. A good man, it was said, could tie 1,100 bundles a day.

These Uasin Gishu Afrikaners made their own shoes and wagon reins from the hides of antelopes, and harrows from the boughs of trees, and the women boiled fat and moulded their own candles, so they did not have to buy paraffin. They shot tens of thousands of zebras, and sold the hides. In fact they lived off the country as much as any African, but with more forethought, and the cash they could not do without they earned by hiring out their skill with wagons and teams. In order to secure a title to his land, each farmer had to prove to the Government his ownership of £500 worth of assets. Wagons, teams and household goods counted as assets, and the District Commissioner, a Mr Corbett, instructed every applicant to bring these to Sixty-four for him to see. A span of oxen, drawing a wagon loaded with furniture, was driven past his office with much cracking of whips, and the owner's name called out – to be checked against a register. Mr Cloete, Mr Retief, Mr Engelbrecht, Mr Roos, Mr van der Merwe ... past went the wagon and its assets time and time again until Mr Corbett, growing tired of gazing at the same double bed, plough, cupboards and personal belongings, called a halt for the wearied oxen to rest. Now a railway line was advancing towards Eldoret, as Sixty-four had become, both Mr Shaw and Mr Corbett had retired, and the place would soon be civilized.

Trevor Sheen said that of all the regions he had seen in Africa, the best was this one he had chosen, on the heights above Njoro. To hear him talk, the Elysian fields paled beside it. Here was perfection of climate, fertility, prospects, neighbours – even to opals in the Njoro River. I could see Robin, who had been lukewarm, turn the corner at this. But he tried to fix his mind on the objections.

'There's no local labour,' he remarked.

'Once the word gets round, there'll be no holding them back. If you fancy Kikuyu, they'll come to your whistle; if you prefer Kavs they're even easier; if you want Nandi, Lumbwa, Wakamba, you've only got to send word.'

'But there's no one actually *here*. And the clearing's awfully heavy.'

'Ah, what you'll need are charcoal burners. They'll clear it for you in no time and pay you for the privilege.'

'They won't dig up the stumps.'

'You'd be surprised how easily a good gang will clear them out with a team of oxen and the right tackle. And then you'll see some soil! Rich loam twenty feet deep, forest mould that's lain undisturbed since the Creation, fat as butter; crops that'll make your eyes pop out of your head!'

'But no one has ever actually *planted* anything?'

'Look at the red-oat grass, look at the big trees! And no horse-sickness, no east coast fever, no diseases, everything thrives ...'

'It sounds like paradise,' Tilly said.

'It is, but with more lively company. You won't find many saints here.'

Robin tried to be hard-headed about weak markets, high costs and the low price of maize, but I could see he was excited, and that Tilly had made up her mind. By the evening's end they had cleared five hundred acres, reaped record crops, established a herd of pedigree cattle, imported a race-horse and brood-mares, bred hundreds of Angora goats and blackface sheep, discovered a deposit of opals and toured Europe in a

Rolls-Royce on the proceeds. Trevor was all for starting off the very next day to recruit labour.

'You shouldn't wait, or you'll miss a planting season,' he advised.

'We haven't actually bought it yet,' Tilly pointed out.

'Not only that, but we haven't sold the coffee farm,' Robin added.

'Oh, that won't present any difficulties,' Trevor said. 'I'll go down to Nairobi myself and find you a buyer.'

'With the cash,' Robin stipulated.

'In that case I'd better go to Mombasa, and get him as he steps off the ship.'

Next day we rode up to see the land. A rough track led steeply uphill to the edge of the forest reserve, which formed the whole of one long boundary. Above us, if we came to live here, would be nothing but untouched and only partially explored native forest, and beyond that the Masai plains running into Tanganyika. Even Tilly could not accuse it of suburbanism.

The true mountain forest, mainly of cedars – really junipers – mixed with olives, here met and mingled with the tall acacias of the foothills. All grew side by side among red-oat grass interspersed with open glades in which, Trevor told us, buffaloes and waterbuck came out to graze. As we climbed closer to the forest boundary our wet, slippery track twisted to the right between two flat-topped thorns that met in an arch overhead. In a cleared space stood a small, square, naked bungalow made of cedar posts, mud and wire-netting, with a corrugated iron roof. We approached to find that it lacked doors, windows, floor or ceiling, and was stacked to the roof with bags of maize. No one seemed to know who these belonged to, but afterwards we learned that they were Trevor's; he had been buying maize from Kikuyu squatters who had no legal right to be there, and storing it in a house he did not own, so he had kept his mouth shut.

The veranda, which was just big enough to take two chairs, commanded a view over treetops to the whole panorama of the great valley, the winking lake, the gentle slopes of the extinct volcano Menengai, the tawny plains of Rongai and a hazy distance enveloping Lake Baringo and, far beyond, the deserts of Suk and Turkana. The air was cool and crisp, and smelt of dew and juniper. We were nearly eight thousand feet above sea-level, nights would be cold, the days never oppressive.

'Not too bad?' Trevor inquired, laughing.

'You'd better start for the coast tomorrow,' Tilly said, 'to find our Thika buyer.'

We stayed two days at Trevor's, looking at the land and picking out a site for a future house. This was on a hillock in a glade just below the forest boundary. From it you could see over a grove of flat-topped thorns to the blue and purple valley below and, beyond, the dark line of the Aberdares. In the early mornings and late evenings, the boles of the acacias turned a pure red-gold, and their brilliant green umbrella-tops looked as if they were supported by innumerable golden pillars, like some fabulous temple of the east. Reedbuck picked their way in pairs among the tree trunks and a herd of waterbuck often grazed across the glade. No one had ever lived there, no soil had been broken, everything had achieved a perfect harmony and balance without the intervention of man.

At night, the air pulsed with the screech of hyraxes. The forest must have been alive with these arboreal cousins of the coney, although we never saw a trace of one; by day they slept deep in hollow trunks, by night their voices were tireless. At first, you thought sleep would be impossible, but you quickly got so used to them that you were disturbed only if they fell silent. Now and then they did, for no clear reason; then, in the distance, one of them would let out a screech and this would start them off again. The full moon was their challenge. Then the whole range of hills above us seemed to quiver with sound. All those little furry throats vibrated with a serenade that grated on and yet excited the ear, and seemed to be the very voice of the forest.

When Robin and Tilly did at last acquire the farm they called it Gikammeh, the Kikuyu word for hyrax, and when we returned to Thika it was the hyraxes that I most sharply remembered, and the clean smell of cedars, and the evening light on thorn-trees, and the aromatic warmth of Trevor's cedar-log fire that we sat round in the evening, after baths, eating salted nuts and talking of a splendid future in this high, secret country, in a land where history had only just been born.

Chapter 22

THE trip had been exciting but I was thankful to get back to Thika and to find everything the same. The road up to the farm was not beautiful but I knew every step of it; one of the planks in the bridge over the second stream had broken, the branches of the erythrinas were bare, a film of dust lay, as usual, over the sodom-apples with their yellow gooseberry fruits, the fine, feathery grass with pink panicles bent and rippled in the wind. Doves were calling from every tree – two full, high quavers and then four semi-quavers in a lower key – puffing their breasts and pumping out their melody. The hard *vleis* sounded hollow under M'zee's feet. He was as thankful as I to recognize familiar landmarks, and quickened his pace into his favourite triple as we neared the house.

The dogs rushed out with their usual tremendous welcome, writhing and leaping in frenzies of delight, and Kigorro greeted us as if we had returned in triumph from an exploration of untold danger lasting two years. Mugu, too, was there shaking hands, grinning with apparent rapture and reporting all well on the farm; on all sides were smiles, waving hands, warmth and pleasure. Even Mustard stared at the commotion with tolerant eyes and wagged his beard as if in greeting.

How could anyone possibly wish to leave all this? The passion-fruit that had spread itself over a low wall in front of the house was in cream and purple flower, the orange tree beyond starred with sweet-smelling white petals. The coffee bushes, too, were out in bloom, every branch loaded with tight creamy clusters and the air drenched with the sweetness of orange blossom. This I found heady, bewitching, almost intoxicating, but Cousin Hilary had complained that the odour of nuptials nauseated him, and brought the dreaded sound of

Mendelssohn to his ears. Mwangi the gardener was pushing our blunt mower, and his small assistant walked ahead as usual with a string attached to the machine. No one ever mowed a lawn singlehanded; a small boy had to go ahead leading the mower on a string, just as a lad always walked ahead of a team of oxen. Unlike the rest of the staff, who dropped whatever they were doing to welcome us, he began his task on our arrival so as to demonstrate his devotion to his duties.

When the excitement had died down, less auspicious news was related. Something mysterious had happened to one of the coffee pulping drums, which refused to rotate. Pruning knives had been stolen from the store, an unknown animal had killed half the pullets, *siafu*, the dreaded warrior ants, had devoured a precious brood of Muscovy chicks, the oxen had strayed into a plantation of young eucalyptus trees, and a grass-fire had scorched a whole line of coffee bushes. All these things, Mugu suggested, were acts of God to be deplored but not avoided. A considerable sick parade awaited Tilly. Several babies had fallen into fires, the usual deep, raw, suppurating lesions caused by yaws needed treatment, people attacked by aches in head and belly came for quinine or aspirin, others complained of coughs, bad chests, tapeworms ('a snake in the belly' was their own diagnosis) or just plain cuts and bruises.

Most of Tilly's remedies were standardized, but sometimes she would grow experimental and bring about unexpected cures. Robin had been given a bottle of port for Christmas which proved to be corked, and this, combined with ipeca-cuanha, arrested several cases of dysentery. Eye troubles, common among children, were normally bathed in a solution of boracic; one day, when this ran out, Tilly mixed face lotion with baking powder and immediately relieved the inflam-mation. You had to provide something. The patients reposed a touching, absolute faith in European medicines, and perhaps eighty per cent of their recoveries took place in the mind.

Kigorro kept until last his surprise. Then he led me to a shed near the kitchen and produced a box made of neatly woven twigs with a lid secured by a strip of bark. Something furry was inside. He opened it very carefully, sliding his hand inside to grasp a sharp-eyed little creature that spat and struggled despite its size, not more than six inches long. It was a kitten of some kind, browny-grey in colour, short-legged, with a long blotchy tail. A bush-cat, Kigorro said, fierce when grown and fond of eating chickens. Someone had brought it from the bush and wanted a shilling.

Tilly, when summoned, said resignedly that Rupert was bad enough, this would become an even worse pest and kill all the poultry, but she gave Kirorro fifty cents. The bush-cat was installed in a box in my room. He did not take to milk, but devoured with a kind of swearing little scraps of raw meat. He had the brightest of eyes and a pointed nose and was long and thin, almost like a mongoose. No one quite knew what he was, but after reference to a pocket encyclopaedia Robin plumped for a genet, and this proved correct. In time he grew to have a long, heavy tail ringed with dark brown, brown spots on his body and big, rounded ears. Confinement in a box distressed him, and he soon had the freedom of my bedroom and then of the house; the dogs grew used to him quickly, and he ceased to contort himself into a furious ball and spit and curse whenever they approached. He house-trained himself from an early age, preferring to do his business in some bushy spot out of sight.

In a remarkably short time he learnt to know each of us individually and seldom scratched a friend, but with visitors he was unpredictable and, like a domestic kitten, would play for hours with an old tennis ball and tear slippers to bits. He also demolished the veranda cushions, Tilly's knitting and several sweaters; he seemed to have a hate against wool. But to balance this he would rub his slender head against my hand or ankle and then spring with a bound of joy on to a table or pelmet, landing with a magical accuracy. The problem was what to do with him at night. Being a nocturnal animal, he slept a good deal during the day, and after nightfall became alert and anxious to be up and doing; but freedom for him would clearly finish off the chickens and ducks. The only solution was to barricade the poultry, who were bolted into houses with corrugated iron walls sunk a foot into the ground.

After that Genet – we could think of no better name – went free. Sometimes, in the moonlight, I caught a glimpse of a silvery, banded tail vanishing like a snake into a bush; and sometimes he would glide across the lawn to squirm against my legs and jump into my arms. Once, at the full moon, I found him tearing at a hare he must have killed among the vegetables by the river. He never went very far, or at any rate he was always to be found curled up in his box in my room in the morning; he jumped so softly through the window that he never woke me. I was afraid that one day he would disappear, and my first conscious act was to look at his box; but (unlike most pets) he could fend for himself, and even if he had vanished I need not have thought him trapped or poisoned. I have never seen a wild genet about, but perhaps some inhabited the bush-clad valleys and I supposed that one day, when he was fully grown, he would go in search of a mate.

I thought often of Rupert, and missed him, and kept asking Tilly when we could go to fetch him back from the Beatties. To my great disappointment I had heard nothing from Alan, but a letter came from Barbara saying that Rupert had run down several gazelle in the plain, disgraced himself by killing a goat, and that one of Alan's clients, an Arabian prince, had offered by buy him for a hundred pounds. So great a sum – if this tale was true – might have tempted some people but Rupert was not for sale, not for a hundred pounds, not for a thousand. But what about ten thousand? Or even more? Could one, for instance, refuse a million for a cheetah? This was a disturbing thought. For if there was any sum in the world that would buy Rupert, then after all he was for sale, it was only a question of degree; like Judas, I was willing to exchange something that was priceless for gold. I told myself firmly that even a million pounds would not pry Rupert from me, but all the same I could not wholly suppress a little canker of doubt.

One thing I was quite sure about: I would never, even for ten million, let him go to a zoo. How people could condemn animals who had done no harm, and who trusted them, to the slow agonies of life imprisonment I had never been able to understand. A grim enough fate for men who had deserved punishment, it was far worse for animals who had not, and whose freedom was their element, as cardinal to them as the sea to porpoises. Rupert cost more to feed than we could afford, and I suspected that zoos had been discussed behind my back, but I had resolved to shoot him myself rather than let him go. In fact a suicide pact between us at times appeared to be the best solution.

At last Tilly found the time to retrieve him, and as we drove along the corkscrew road my inside grew hollow with excitement. I imagined Rupert's tremendous greeting, yet with all that strength he controlled his actions and never knocked me down. Once more we arrived in darkness; Rupert would no doubt be in his polo cage. The Colonel had gone to a meeting and Mrs Beattie fussed over us, insisting on drinks by the fire and trying to subdue the wolf-hounds.

'I hope the road wasn't too foul,' she said. 'Water or soda?'

'Water, please. The dust –'

'Shut up, will you! Come and warm yourselves. The rains are late and scrappy here, what about you?'

'We're getting a bit anxious. But up Njoro way –'

'Be quiet, damn you! We've got some neighbours coming to dinner, new people, with money I should think, they've got sheep on the way from New Zealand and she reeks of scent. Alan's gone off with a party of Rothschilds, or it may be Rockefellers, extraordinary how many there are; if he'd only smarten himself up he might bag a daughter, better than a heavy tusker any day. But of course he – down, Vishnu. Quiet, will you, Siva!'

'I hope that cheetah hasn't –'

'For God's sake shut up!'

Barbara, when she came in, was so affable that I wondered whether one of her smart suitors might exist after all. I asked her at once for news of Rupert, but she went off at a tangent about a dance at the White Rhino where a Hungarian Count who owned herds of wild horses had invited her to stay on his hundred-thousand-acre estate.

'Can I go and see him?' I asked. 'Rupert, I mean.'

'He said I was the only girl he'd met who could stay on a wild horse when it was tamed. Or semi-tamed.'

'We needn't let him out of the cage.'

'And I could help round them up and break them in.'

Her elusiveness aroused suspicion, and I thought there was
an undercurrent of anxiety in the room.

'Is he all right?'

There was an uneasy silence. The dogs had at last settled
down and even Barbara held her tongue.

'Has he ...'

'I'm afraid we've got bad news,' Mrs Beattie said, smiling
at me and then looking away. 'It's a horrid thing to happen,
but I don't see how we could have prevented it. Of course,
he –'

'Is he dead?'

'I'm afraid so.'

'But ... who killed him?'

'We don't know exactly what happened, but we think it was
poison.'

'We've given him a proper burial,' Barbara said. 'I can
show you his grave.'

But I did not want to see his grave, although next day I
picked a few flowers and put them on a mound of stones behind
the stables which was all that remained to commemorate
Rupert. That I had not been there to comfort him was the
worst part. He had trusted me, I had abandoned him and he
had died painfully, with no friend at hand. And he had never
harmed anyone. But Njombo recalled that he had harmed
goats.

'Their owners put down the poison,' he said.

'But they were paid for the goats.'

'Perhaps: but the goats were theirs. The men of these parts
have black hearts. Their hearts threw out Rupert.'

'If we had come sooner ...'

'*Shauri ya Mungu:* the affair of God.'

Tilly felt guilty because, if we had come a few days earlier,
Rupert would have been safe.

'But he would have become a problem,' she pointed out.

'No, he wouldn't. I'd have earned the money to pay for his
food.'

'He'd have got bigger and hungrier, and he'd have missed
the company of other cheetahs. It's a tragedy, but no amount of
grieving will bring him back. You've got Genet.'

'Genet isn't the same. Besides, how do I know he isn't poisoned or something awful too? I never ought to have left him behind.'

'It's no good getting hysterical. We'll see him soon.'

Now Rupert's only memorial lay in my memory, and that was fallible: already I could not recall as sharply as I wished the flowing action of his haunches, the silky texture of his skin, his confident, affectionate purr. And when that had faded, what would become of Rupert? Nothing would remain of so much love and beauty. No one would know that he had ever been, had leapt and played open-heartedly and rubbed his chin against my knee. His life was pointless and would have vanished like a bead of dew. I had killed his mother, I had failed him in his life and now I would fail him also in his death by denying him the least spark of immortality. My grief was wordless, like a surge of sorrow summoned up by music, or by a sunset at sea, and I was thankful when we left the Beatties and drove home to find Genet safely asleep in his box in my room.

Talk of emigrating to Njoro had died down for the moment, but there was a feeling of change in the air. Betty Clewes came over and told us, among other items of gossip, of a rumour about Alec. He was said to be courting a rich widow whom he had met at the Nairobi races.

'But Alec never goes to the races,' Robin said. 'Even if he never had a bet, it would cost him five shillings to get in.'

'He went this time, because a man owed him some money, and the only place Alec felt sure of catching him was on the race-course. So it was worth five bob. There he met this widow, and he's been laying siege ever since.'

'Is she really rich, or just pretending?'

'It's all hearsay, but I believe her husband was a coal merchant in Newcastle, and the only possible way of surviving that would be to be immensely rich. Although I suppose, if she's a widow, he *didn't* survive, but anyway there she is, I'm told she dyes her hair and has lace-edged hankies and isn't related to *anyone*, but Alec won't mind that, and needn't go to Newcastle, so I daresay it's all very suitable.'

'Do you think she'd like to buy a coffee farm?' Robin asked.

'She'll have one, I suppose, if she marries Alec,' Betty pointed out.

'This is larger, and next door. What's her name?'

'I can't remember, but I expect Alec does.'

Too many changes were impending. I hated to think of a strange woman at Alec's, probably a large and domineering one altering all the furniture about and no doubt getting rid of the Kikuyu girl with ringlets I had seen sunning herself on the veranda steps. And now there was talk of the twins being sent to England to school, because Harry did not want them to grow up with a colonial accent. Betty, we gathered, wanted them to stay.

'You'll miss them, certainly,' Tilly agreed.

'Yes, it will be dreadful. There's a perfectly good school in Nairobi but Harry's suddenly got this idea that only England is good enough, and who *is* Harry, I ask you? Anyone would suppose his family came over with the Conquest but I believe his father was an ironmonger or something. He's getting *folie de grandeur*. Of course, it's all that woman's doing; fancy taking up with Germans when you've spent four years trying to kill as many as possible; anyway I should think he's put his head into a viper's nest. I suppose it'll serve him right when he gets bitten, he's got it coming to him, but I can't help worrying about the twins, and it all seems so unnecessary.'

Betty was on the verge of tears and causing embarrassment to Tilly, who looked rather pink in the face.

'I shouldn't worry too much if I were you. That women is a bloodsucker; he'll soon get tired of her, or she of him. She's got that awful Germanic male-worship.'

'He'll never get tired of *that*.'

'He might get alarmed. Harry's too fond of his own reputation to make a fool of himself.'

'More than he has already, you mean. You're very consoling, Tilly, but then you're lucky with Robin, I don't think he looks at anyone else.'

'One should never be sure of that. But I think at the moment he's more interested in machinery and minerals. They can be just as fickle as women are said to be, and even more expensive.'

'At least he doesn't sleep with them,' Betty said.

Chapter 23

ALEC'S widow was not interested in our farm, but Robin kept up his search for a buyer and one day a small, dapper young man appeared at Thika. He was a new-comer to the country, and had been in the Brigade of Guards. A few weeks later he came back with his wife, who created a great stir. She was beautiful and Russian and smoked long, black cigarettes embellished with a monogram, and stayed in bed until lunch-time, when she emerged in a Turkish sort of attire made of black velvet, with jade ear-rings and the most delectable scent.

Nothing like this had ever come our way before. I had, it was true, seen members of the Happy Valley set and once, when on a visit to the dentist in Nairobi, someone had pointed out a drug fiend: a slim, attractive, healthy-looking young woman with a gay, fresh laugh who looked half her age. But her thighs were said to be like pincushions from being punctured several times a day, a supposition which put drug fiendishness more into the class of diabetes than of debauchery. Alec, learning of our brief encounter, asked Tilly what she was like. 'I hear she's very clever with her needle,' Tilly replied. Although our visitor was certainly innocent of any such dashing vices, I could scarcely take my eyes off her, and watched the door of the spare room as if I expected to see it unfold like a cinnamon-throated orchid, to release a flight of jewelled birds.

Alec's widow had returned to Newcastle to collect what she called her bits and pieces, which everyone hoped meant securities, and Alec came over on some pretext or other about twice a day. Harry Clewes cancelled an up-country visit, the Judds came to call and the house hummed with masculine life. At the centre of it all our visitor remained unmoved, slim and elegant as a lily, smoking her black cigarettes with gold monograms and, when she was not holding court on the veranda, reading French novels. It was only with difficulty that Robin detached her husband for long enough to explain about the seedling beds, the windbreak versus no windbreak controversy, the life cycle of the mealie-bug and other cognate matters. If it came to that, Robin himself was perfectly happy to remain on the veranda talking French and lighting her cigarettes, until Tilly looked in to say something pointed about the need for a potential buyer to inspect every detail of the farm.

The sophisticated elegance of our visitors put to shame what Tilly called our rough colonial ways, and she decided that we must all be smartened up. She made new curtains for the spare room, borrowed a rug from the Clewes and washed the dogs, while Robin fetched cigars and hock from Nairobi. The silver was polished, a litter of puppies removed from the sitting-room and the chair covers mended. Kigorro and the houseboy were given new *kanzus* with a red sash made by Tilly from an old evening dress sent out by her sister, and never worn. I had to put on a dress instead of shorts, and this I resented, especially as I never liked my frocks, which were cast-offs of English cousins who seemed to favour a lot of fringes, bows and dangling things like beads and bugles, as I think the long-shaped beads were called. Our efforts were rewarded, and the farm sold : although I daresay the accounts, neatly kept by Tilly in several coloured inks and different kinds of ledger, and the state of the coffee bushes, had more to do with this than our unaccustomed tidiness, whose effect was impaired by Genet demolishing a handsome pair of embroidered leather slippers, Kigorro going sick with stomach-ache and a dead frog blocking the water supply.

Everyone was pleased about the sale but me. I was heart-broken, and went round saying good-bye to everything almost every day, although we were not to leave for six months and all the animals would come with us, as well as several of the Kikuyu, most of the furniture and all our personal belongings. But not the twisted erythrina on the edge of the *vlei* where doves always cooed, not the *vlei* itself with its flighting wild-fowl, not the pool below the waterfall where pythons lived, not the bluff across the river where reedbuck lay concealed, not the grenadilla creeper over the lizard-sheltering wall, not bright flame-tree avenue, nor the old grass house whose walls the hillside shambas where guinea-fowl cried after tea, not the rustled with white ants, nor the house itself with its veranda looking towards the snow-topped early-morning mountain, and its comfortable, untidy sitting-room with Tilly's hand loom in one corner where she struggled with fluffy angora wool, and a worn lion skin by the fireplace, the walls hung with water-colours of scenes in India painted by my grand-mother which had come out by mistake in a crate labelled Kitchen Utensils. Perhaps some of these things would come with us, the movable ones, but they would not look the same, and I could remember the house before it existed, when it was merely some pegs and lengths of string. And many of the Kikuyu I knew would not come with us either; Mugu the headman, for instance, and, of course, Kupanya the chief whom we often visited, now the possessor of twenty wives.

Njombo, however, was coming to Njoro, and did not share my regrets.

'The land there is fat,' he said. 'Fatter than at Thika. There is more rain, and grass for cattle, and as far as you can see no shambas, only forest, and room to cultivate, and grazing for goats. I shall go to Njoro and ask bwana for a shamba, and there will be plenty to eat.'

Kigorro was also coming but, as he had not seen Njoro, he was more dubious.

'Elephants and buffaloes,' he said to Njombo, 'are they good things?'

'No, but bwana will shoot them.'

'Is there not forest there?'

'Yes, there is forest.'

'Who can shoot all the animals in a forest?'

'They will be shot when they come out.'

'It is cold there.'

'Yes, it is cold, but there is plenty of firewood. No one has to search for firewood, it is all around.'

'When I was a boy, I lived at Thika. Now I am a man, I must go far away. Why is this?'

'Very well: stay here, and your wife's granary will be empty. Go to Njoro, and it will be full as a calabash of beer. It is your affair.'

'If bwana goes, I must go too. But it is a long way.'

Perhaps he was thinking that not only the climate, the countryside and the crops would be different, but the spirits also, because for the Kikuyu there was not a tree, a rock or a spring without some supernatural inhabitant or meaning. When the time came to go to Njoro all concerned would, I knew, get charms from a witch-doctor to guard them on the journey and protect them from the perils of a strange place.

All this, I supposed, was superstitious nonsense, yet I looked with a mixture of curiosity and awe at the arm-bands and little leather pouches full of medicine that Njombo and the others wore. These had magic powers to influence events, and missionaries disliked them, but they had nothing to do with God. The God of the Kikuyu was more aloof than ours, and not presumed to take an interest in each individual, much less in sparrows and the like. He had no son, no wife or children, and had never made an effort to redeem or even to instruct mankind. I do not think any living man's behaviour was thought to influence his attitude; he did not punish offenders or reward the just hereafter. Rewards and punishments were the business of chiefs and elders and society in general; God was not concerned with such trivial details, but with more important matters like sending or withholding rain or epidemics, and such cosmic affairs as flood, lightning and earthquakes.

So the Kikuyu would not have put the blame on God for the disaster that befell Miss Cooper before we left Thika. Whether Captain Dorsett had actually proposed to her or not was a matter for speculation, but there was clearly an understanding. When his next leave fell due he would have completed his spell on the Northern Frontier and be posted to some more clement spot where Miss Cooper would in due course, everyone felt, come into her own as a Major's wife, dispensing gracious hospitality to wives of officers of junior rank. Meanwhile she was to take the twins to England, where the Captain would follow for his long leave. The twins had a birthday shortly before they were due to depart, and Tilly and I were asked to tea. Miss Cooper had made and iced a cake, and invited us to make a wish with our first mouthfuls.

'You only wish with mince pies,' Tilly protested. 'And of course new moons.'

'I always did so with a birthday cake when I was a girl,' Miss Cooper replied, 'and I'm sure we were careful to preserve the traditions. Perhaps they are foolish, but I always think that in the colonies it is most important to observe them, they help to keep up one's standards, and there is nothing easier than to let one's standards go in the tropics. That is a thing I am always very strict about. I pride myself that any child *I* bring up out here will not be a colonial, but just the same as any well-brought-up English child.'

'All right, we'll wish,' Tilly said. I thought it was just as well that this was only superstition, otherwise Tilly's wish might have brought little joy to Miss Cooper. Whenever I was obliged to wish, at least a dozen possibilities swept into my head and I never knew which to select. I wanted to attend the next polo tournament, to own a vest-pocket-Kodak, to visit the Mountains of the Moon, to concentrate better and argue less, to learn Portuguese and typewriting, to have a tame parrot, to hear from Alan Beattie and to find a tidier way of doing my hair. By the time I had made my choice of wishes I had eaten my slice of cake, so it did not count anyway.

'We are sailing on the *Malda*,' Miss Cooper continued. 'It's sad for the children to go without their mother, but she knows that I shall look after them night and day regardless of my own convenience. Children are a great responsibility on board ship and need to be watched every moment of the day. I shall be delighted to see England again, of course, but I have grown very fond of this country, and I don't think I'm betraying any secrets when I say that I have every expectation of returning, before so very long, in quite another capacity. I don't expect to look after children *all* my life, I can assure you. Although I would never have chosen any other profession. It gives me great satisfaction to feel that I'm living for others, and in my case I've seen something of the world as well. Vicky, what are you giggling at? You must eat your tea.'

Vicky was giggling at an object called a wiffle-waffle Tilly had made out of sheet of paper. It was possessed of an enormous mouth with which it gobbled up pellets or crumbs and then spewed them out again, much to the enjoyment of the twins. Miss Cooper looked disapproving, but gave a half-hearted smile to demonstrate her sense of the ridiculous.

I do not remember how we first heard of the wreckage of Miss Cooper's plans. News generally reached us on the bush-telegraph and was often exaggerated, but seldom false. At any rate we heard one day that Captain Dorsett had returned from the Northern Frontier, but not as he had hoped. He had returned as far as Nyeri on a stretcher carried across several hundred miles of lava desert and shadeless scrub, with scarcely any food or water and no medical supplies. Captain Dorsett had been wounded by Havash raiders and only a miracle of endurance on his part, and devotion on his men's, had got him as far as Nairobi hospital, where he was on the danger list.

On the next monthly visit to Nairobi to draw money from the bank, Tilly left fresh eggs and fruit at the hospital and was told he was still too ill to see visitors. He had been wounded in the leg and his only fellow officer killed, so it had been left to an African sergeant to extricate the detachment. There was no transport, and nothing for it but to carry Captain Dorsett on a stretcher to the nearest hospital at Nyeri, about three hundred miles away. Four askaris set off, and carried him for eighteen days. Wells were far apart, they could carry no more water than the content of their service bottles and once they all went without any liquid for two days. And, of course, the heat was appalling. So far as they could, they travelled at night and in the early mornings and the evenings, but towards the end they had to march by day as well with the sun beating down on the delirious man.

His leg, naturally, festered, and gangrene set in. They ran out of dressings, and a little rationed aspirin was all he had against the pain. Had the four men abandoned their stinking, raving burden to the death he could scarcely avoid, no one would have questioned their story that he had died on the way. At night, if they halted, lions and hyenas, probably attracted by the smell of gangrene, grunted and howled within a few yards and sometimes the askaris fired at eyes they saw glinting in the dark. The nomadic tribesmen of those parts might at any hour have overwhelmed them and stolen their rifles, always a rich prize. But the men continued on their way with the jolting stretcher until they reached the hospital at Nyeri, and then they turned and walked back again to report to their headquarters at Wajir. We never heard what reward they got, or indeed if they got one at all.

Captain Dorsett was moved to Nairobi where both legs were amputated above the knee. His life lay in the balance for some time and then, being young and strong, he gradually began to recover. What sort of future his recovery could lead to, no one could surmise. He was presumed to qualify for a very small pension, not enough to live on by himself, let alone to support a wife, even supposing marriage to have been a possibility in the circumstances. His case caused a good deal of comment about the niggardly treatment of officers disabled in the course of their duties, but did not lead to any revision of the terms.

So, in a cowardly fashion, we avoided Miss Cooper, and when we next saw Harry Clewes he told us that he had taken her to the hospital to see what remained of Captain Dorsett, but that it had been a wasted journey.

'He sent a message out to say he couldn't see her,' Harry explained. 'I daresay it was the best thing he could have done. She snivelled all the way home. I'm sorry for her, of course, but I don't believe it would have come to anything. I think poor old Raymond had more sense, even if he did make an ass of himself. At least he's well out of that.'

'At a price,' Tilly remarked.

'Yes, poor devil. Let's hope he has a mother or sister or someone at home who'll look after him.'

That was the last we heard of Captain Dorsett, and not long afterwards Miss Cooper and the twins departed for England. Then Tilly left us too. Robin had to stay on at Thika to see to the handing over of the farm to its new owner, and Tilly was impatient to start clearing forest at Njoro in preparation for a crop. The sale had put Mr Playfair in the best of humours, and it was arranged that I should attend a course of studies in Nairobi at the Government school.

The idea appalled me, but there was nothing to be done. Fortunately it turned out that the dormitories were full, so lodgings were found for me with a warm-hearted, hospitable and English-speaking family of Afrikaners from the Cape. By a great stroke of luck, their house was on the edge of the polo ground; I could almost have reported the matches by looking out of my bedroom window, and was therefore able to continue my connection with the *Standard*. At week-ends I took the train to Thika and found M'zee waiting for me at the station to ride up to the farm, or to Makuyu if a polo tournament was being held there, so things did not turn out so badly as I had feared.

Chapter 24

TILLY left Thika with three dachshunds – Bluebell, Foxglove and Hollyhock – two Siamese cats, Genet, an assortment of goods ranging from cooking pots and camp chairs to pickaxes, chains and skeys and yokes for oxen, and Kigorro for an escort, with two of his wives. Njombo was to conduct M'zee and Fair Play over the Kinangop, and for the time being he and Kigorro were the only two Kikuyu she intended to take. Everyone told her to avoid Kikuyu, they would only make trouble, and were not so strong and willing as men from the Kavirondo Gulf, who were larger, blacker, and heftier, and did what they were told.

The Kikuyu, however, had other views. When Tilly disembarked at the little station at Njoro she was amazed to see a number of familiar figures already grouped on the platform, greeting her with delighted smiles.

'But how did you get here?' she inquired.

'In the train, with you,' they said, roaring with laughter. 'We are coming to Njoro to help you with your shamba.'

'But I did not ask you to,' Tilly pointed out.

'How can you start to dig a shamba without people? We shall help you, memsabu.'

They wanted shambas for their wives, of course, and grazing for their livestock. The reserve near Thika was overcrowded because many families had moved there in order to be near the European farms, and the employment these offered. Cattle and goats had been boarded out with relatives who lived farther away. This had led to disputes and lawsuits, or at the least to suspicion and ill-feeling; for who was to say whether the brindled cow's calf really had been stillborn, as her caretaker reported? And how was it that she-goats farmed out in this way never had twins? The Kikuyu had heard about the ample grazing at Njoro, and the fat soil, and were not going to let this opportunity slip.

A concourse of men, women and children escorted Tilly up the hill. A half-brother of Njombo's called Gitende carried a basket with the cats, someone else had charge of Genet, one of the women slung Tilly's suitcase on her back and the three dachshunds walked behind their owner. It was a five-mile climb up a stiff hill. The women trudged uncomplainingly under heavy bags of millet, sweet potatoes and beans, their cooking-pots slung around them and babies bobbing about on top of the loads. The twin thorn-trees made an arch for the little procession to walk under as they approached the doorless bungalow, whose rooms were filled with maize. Tilly spent her first night in the open: damp, cold, serenaded by hyraxes and terrified of leopards, who preferred dogs to any other food. Bluebell, Foxglove and Hollyhock shared her sleeping-bag. They survived this night and many others, but none died peacefully. Foxglove disappeared in Tanganyika some years later, Hollyhock was speared by Africans hunting wild pig, and Bluebell's fate remains to be told.

Next day, Trevor Sheen lent Tilly a cart and four oxen to fetch her gear from the station. The cart slipped over a log bridge and capsized, spewing pickaxes, *debes* of paraffin, stores and personal belongings into the river. The next arrivals were about fifty black, bewildered men from a remote part of the Lake Victoria basin. In theory, they were volunteers, and each one had affixed his thumb-mark to a legal document, but how or why they had arrived at Njoro must have seemed to them a profound mystery. They spoke no word of any language either Europeans or Kikuyu could understand, and the Kikuyu were unsympathetic.

'They are uncircumcised, and wild like animals,' Kigorro said with distaste. 'Why do you not return them to their country and send for some proper men from Thika?'

Trevor Sheen lent Tilly a headman who knew a few words of some common tongue, and he distributed pickaxes and pangas and set them to work on the bush. They worked hard the first day, and a number of trees were laid low, but during the night they took the pickaxes and pangas and vanished in a body. Kigorro and Njombo were delighted, and said 'I told you so' in several ways. Their wives were at work already, digging shambas without bothering to clear anything but undergrowth. Europeans, intending to plough, had to remove all the tree stumps, whereas it cost a Kikuyu much less effort to get a crop into the ground. His wife did it all, working hard from sunrise until about five o'clock.

Far from complaining, the women were delighted to find this fat soil, for each wife reaped the crop she had planted and fed her own family. And this was virgin ground. No tribe claimed it, no one had cultivated here before, the only occupants had been a few, a very few, dwarfish and wandering Dorobo who inhabited the forest like leopards, sleeping in lairs and living on beasts they trapped or shot. They made their own bows and arrows from branches and sinews, and wore the skins of beasts they had killed. Meat was their delight, necessity and sometimes obsession. Often they ate it raw, but they could make fire by means of a stick twirled in the fingers against a hard piece of wood. They had a weakness for tobacco; the more adventurous among them would, from time to time, go down into Masai country to trade honey and skins for the dried leaf. Their language was a debased kind of Masai.

The Dorobo who lived in the forests of the Aberdares and Mount Kenya were the same in looks, habits and origins – the only survivors, it was supposed, of an indigenous people – but spoke a kind of Kikuyu. It was strange that their own Dorobo tongue had faded, and taken on the complexion of whatever stronger people they encountered. But no one had studied the

Dorobo closely and it may have been that their ancient language did secretly survive among them, in their forest fastness.

The Kikuyu had bought from the Aberdare and Mount Kenya Dorobo the right to hunt on cultivated land and to take honey in those regions of the forest that abutted on cultivated land, and had then moved in and cut down trees and planted shambas, and called the land their own. This was going on all the time, and in this way the Kikuyu were spreading into the forest, eating it away and pushing the Dorobo farther back into the mountains. What the Dorobo thought of this no one knew, and perhaps they did not think any more than buffaloes and elephants when their domain was diminished in the same way, for this happened patchily, to individuals, and no one could see it as a whole. Much smaller than the Kikuyu, the Dorobo smelt musty and strong like an animal, they wore the chestnut pelts of bushbuck, carried bows and arrows and a sword in a roughly made leather sheath dyed red, and their eyes were bright as black diamonds. They had the same wary, poised look as a buck has when it pauses for an instant before its flight, and you felt that if you made a sudden movement, they would vanish in a single bound. As with all wild creatures, there was a gentleness about them seldom found among the civilized, and yet they were predators, and in pursuit of meat could display relentless ferocity. But like most bestial, as distinct from human, predators, they killed only when they were hungry; full-bellied, they would let the beasts go about their business without interference. As they became, very gradually, acquainted with civilization, they learnt to kill for profit: a leopard skin would buy a great deal of tobacco. But when we knew them at Njoro they were still ignorant and did not offer us skins, only the dark forest honey, full of grubs and tinged with smokiness from the fires with which they drove the bees from their hives.

The fifty Kavirondo who had absconded were legally bound by the contract to which they had affixed their thumb-prints, and in course of time found themselves in Nakuru under a police escort. Here they were fined a month's pay for breach of contract and theft of tools, and told they must earn it by working on the farm from which they had absconded. So back they came, chastened but not downhearted, for they were assured of food and shelter and were able to trap the buck which then abounded. This taste for game the Kikuyu regarded with immense contempt.

'They are *shenzies*, savages,' Kigorro said. 'What decent man would eat the flesh of wild animals? These are not men, but hyenas.' No doubt the Kavirondo held similar views about the Kikuyu.

The Kavirondo worked hard but progressed slowly, for the tree roots went deep and an enormous number had to be dug out and hauled away by half-trained oxen with chains that often broke. The Kikuyu seized upon the timber and turned it into charcoal. All day long blue smoke curled into a bluer sky from smouldering fires, banked down with earth, that reduced felled trees to black skeletons.

Robin and I set out to join Tilly at Njoro in the rains. As our old box-body car slithered round corkscrew bends and down the long, steep escarpment, clouds of smoke poured from its brake drums and (since we were in bottom gear) even denser clouds from its radiator, and the floorboards grew so hot I had to dangle my feet out of the side. On our left an almost sheer precipice dropped about two thousand feet, and nothing but skill and luck kept the wheels from sliding over; a number of wrecks, smashed to smithereens, were said to lie at the bottom. The real trouble arose when you met a car coming up, jinking from side to side like a demented hare and not daring to slow down. Model-T Fords were common, and exhausting to drive up the escarpment, because, to stay in bottom gear, you had to keep your foot stamped down on the clutch pedal; if your aching leg could stand it no longer, the car slid backwards. The lights ran directly off the dynamo and grew dimmer as the engine revved up, so when, at night, you ground your way uphill, peering ahead into the darkness to locate the precipice, your headlamps threw no light on the scene.

Another peculiarity of the Model-T was that you could reach its carburettor only by crawling underneath and lying flat on your back. As the clouds of dust through which you travelled in dry weather often blocked the jet, this was a serious inconvenience to all except the most athletic and mechanically minded. An alternative method was accidentally discovered by a caller who one day arrived at our house propelled by a squad of Kavirondo stump-clearers. This was Lord Francis Scott, a man neither mechanically minded nor athletic, since a war wound had permanently damaged one foot. His wife travelled always with a high sense of adventure and a great assortment of cushions, rugs, veils, scarves, handkerchiefs, books and bottles of smelling-salts, and managed to create an impression, even in the oldest Model-T, that she was taking carriage-exercise in the Park, or on the race-course of Delhi, where her father lived as Viceroy of India.

Lord Francis was so convinced that the carburettor would clear itself on the homeward, downhill run that he refused all offers of help and set off for home with a coughing, spluttering engine. Tilly went with them, I forget why, and about half-way down Lord Francis, whose impetuous enthusiasm for whatever topic of conversation he was pursuing was such that he often ignored side issues, failed to see a curve in time, ran the car on to a bank and overturned it, spilling out his passengers in a shower of cushions, rugs, scarves, veils, hand-bags and books. No one was damaged, but the Model-T lay on its back like a turtle, its heels in the air.

'But this is perfect!' Tilly exclaimed. 'Now we can get at the carburettor.' And, indeed, there was this contrivance, to be reached with ease by anyone who merely stood beside the upturned car. In no time spanners had been found, the carburettor dismantled and Tilly and Lord Francis blew happily through the jet, charmingly admired and praised by Eileen Scott sitting on a pile of cushions with her smelling-salts. Nor did it take long for a crowd of curious Africans to gather, summoned from the seemingly deserted bush like djinns from the air. They righted the car, everyone climbed in and the engine purred as smoothly as on the day of its first run.

Our elderly Chevrolet was less compliant. Robin called it the goat-in-milk: a bad pun, but a fair description of its gait. At frequent intervals on our descent of the escarpment we had to stop, lift the bonnet and cautiously ease off the radiator cap, while noises like angry bees came from beneath it and jets of boiling water leapt into the face of anyone rash enough to remove the cap prematurely. While Robin kept the engine running, Simon cautiously added water drop by drop. Simon was a cheerful, lighthearted Kikuyu extrovert, endowed either with a skin so thick nothing could pierce it, or with patience so infinite that no trial could break it; for Robin, although kind by nature, must have been a trying employer. He often lost things, and accused others of hiding or destroying them, I suppose on the ground that if he got in first, he would shift the blame. His poor Swahili needed a mind reader to interpret, and led to frequent misunderstandings. Simon took all this in good part and was fond of Robin, who never counted his money but created a rumpus if he missed a pair of socks, a box of matches or (and this often happened) his silver cigar case, engraved with his initials and with the legend *Siempre simpatica*. This, Robin said, was incorrect Spanish, but the valued relic of his friendship with the charming wife of a foreign diplomat in Madrid. I hoped she had been a spy, but he said not. For some time he had a photograph of her in a little silver frame; she had a cheerful, if rather cow-like, face, a lot of hair and bare shoulders; but the photograph grew yellow and one day Genet jumped on to the dressing-table and demolished it, and now nothing remained of this romantic interlude but the silver case.

Every motorist stopped at a little stream near the foot of the escarpment to fill up with water, and this had become a well-known meeting-place, like the wells and oases of the desert where travellers exchanged news. We halted to cool the engine and eat sandwiches in the shade, amid an aromatic scent from the sage-grey *leleshwa* shrub all around us. The air had become much hotter, red-and-royal-blue glossy starlings had appeared, the soil became powdery grey instead of a thick chocolate red. At the foot of the escarpment the wagon road, which had been banished to a different course, rejoined the highway and ran alongside it across the valley, and in dry weather each wagon creaked along in a great cloud of dust which choked and stung you and sometimes blinded you like a gritty fog. We had two punctures, and beyond Nakuru slid off the road into a morass of mud from which only oxen could extricate the car, so we spent the night with the Dawsons, a hospitable Scots family nearby.

Like Trevor Sheen, W. J. Dawson had ploughed a thousand acres of veld, but instead of wheat he had planted geraniums, and erected a still. When it came to essential oils, most people thought in terms of single acres; a thousand could be expected to yield a fabulous fortune, and Mr Dawson laid his plans accordingly. But one morning he noticed a few wilting plants; within a month, every single geranium was dead. Now he was gathering himself together to plant wheat.

Tilly had not aspired towards the fashionable figure of a thousand acres, but had hoped for a modest hundred. In fact, she and the Kavirondo had cleared about ten. Still, there they were – a beginning. And we found other improvements. A floor had been laid in the house, and the sitting-room was crowded, indeed too crowded, with furniture from Thika. One afternoon, when Tilly had been down on her hands and knees measuring the floor, she had been seized by an acute pain in the back, and her legs had become paralysed. Kigorro had lifted her into a camp chair and there she had spent a cold and painful night.

Tilly regarded any kind of illness in herself as vaguely shameful, and would not talk about it; we heard all this from Kigorro, who next morning had hoisted her into Fair Play's saddle, using the veranda as a mounting block. Somehow she had managed to sit there and proceed to the shamba, and when she got back was just able to stand. Although this cannot have been an orthodox treatment, gradually Tilly had recovered and by the time we arrived she was mobile. But her hands were wrapped in bandages to protect the veld sores with which they were covered. Veld sores, in the end, healed themselves, but they were raw, deep and painful while they lasted, and sooner or later everyone had them, Africans and Europeans. Like the eclipse of leprosy in Europe, their subsequent disappearance from the list of natural hazards was a mystery.

Chapter 25

PERHAPS my greatest pleasure in returning to Njoro was to be reunited with Genet. He knew me at once, and rubbed himself against my legs with a lot of chittering and leapt into my arms to sit on my shoulder and tug at my hair. At Njoro he found many smaller creatures to hunt and the freedom of the forest was his. I often wondered how he got on with the hyraxes, but no doubt, in the manner of wild animals, he ignored them, and each kind went its own way.

Now and again there was an exception to this rule. Genet had never overcome his taste for poultry, but at Njoro he was only one of many hazards ranged against the birds: ratels, mongooses, civet cats from the forest, even hawks were after them. Most of the Kikuyu kept a few hens in neatly made miniature round huts on stilts, into which the birds clambered at night up a little ladder, then removed; this defeated rats, but not mongooses or, alas, Genet. When there was a killing the Kikuyu always blamed him and tried to claim compensation, but they could never prove Genet's guilt and a mongoose or a ratel was just as likely to be responsible.

Every evening, Genet vanished to a secret life of his own, returning in the early morning to curl up at the foot of my bed, or on an arm-chair in the sitting-room, moving so softly that I never heard him come. But one night, soon after our instalment at Njoro, I was awakened by an odd sound and a damp, soft touch on my face. I came to with a jerk, sat up in alarm and reached for my torch. Something was moving on my bed and I felt a weight on my middle. The torch-beam shone on to a pair of glittering eyes. It was Genet, but his fur was wet and he emitted curious half-whimpering, half-clucking sounds. I groped for the matches and lit the safari lamp while he sat there, staining the blankets, as I soon found, with blood.

He had been involved in a terrible battle. One ear was almost torn off, lumps of fur had been pulled out and deep scratches ripped through his flesh to display the raw sinews.

He must have lost a great deal of blood. I woke up Tilly, who dissolved some permanate of potash crystals, and together we bathed his cuts and tried to make him comfortable. The wounds were gaping, and I wanted to take him to the vet in Nakuru as soon as it was light, but Tilly said the vet was away for a few days and his partner on leave, and there was no one nearer than Nairobi. She looked again at the worst slashes, pinched the flesh together and said:

'They'll have to be stitched, all the same. Fetch my nail scissors, and a needle and cotton.'

'But we can't ...'

'We can try, if you hold him.'

'It'll hurt him dreadfully.'

'I'm afraid we can't help that, but he may bite and scratch. Have you still got that chloroform?'

I had a butterfly collecting outfit with a small bottle of chloroform, and there was some left. We soaked a wad of cotton wool and I held it over Genet's nose. For the first time he resisted and started to struggle and writhe, but he was very weak and we were able to hold him. Neither of us had the least idea how much was needed to anaesthetize a wild cat.

'Go on till he stops kicking,' Tilly said. The kicks grew feebler and finally he lay inert and, so far as I could see, no longer breathing.

'I think he's dead,' I said.

'Not he. Now give me the scissors and hold the lamp up and keep it steady. And if he starts to wriggle, give him another whiff.'

I was convinced that his limp body was lifeless, but Tilly cut away the fur and got to work with her needle and cotton while I held the lamp up, sickened by the unpleasant smell of chloroform, the blood and disorder, and by grief for Genet.

'It's no good if he's dead,' I pointed out.

'It can't do harm and it may do good,' Tilly replied, digging boldly away at the rubbery flesh with her needle.

She made a neat job of the stitching and I laid Genet in a dog-basket and watched for signs of life. After a while I thought I could detect a very slight movement under fur stiff and matted with dried blood. It was always very cold before dawn and I covered him with a blanket, and must have dozed off. I was awakened by a movement on my bed. Genet had indeed come to life, been sick in the basket and managed to scramble up and lie down beside me. He slept all the next day.

Njombo came to the house after breakfast, said he had something to show me and led me up the hill to a group of huts where he had installed his family, surrounded by a palisade of stakes. At night a hurdle blocked the entrance, and while this kept out strangers, prowling beasts and probably spirits, it was no barrier against animals that could jump over, or burrow under, the palisade. Njombo took me round to the back to point out a small hole made by something digging under the fence, and a place in the bush that had been trampled and disturbed.

'Here was a big fight,' he said. 'You see how the bush is damaged.'

I picked a tuft of greyish fur off a spike of thorn. 'This is Genet's.'

'Yes, and look . . .'

A large, chestnut body with a short tail lay in the undergrowth where Njombo had thrown it down. He had found it, he said, a little way off in the bush, covered with wounds and with its throat torn out: a creature much bigger than Genet, and more savage-looking. Its pointed ears with black tufts on each tip showed it to be a sort of lynx. Such beasts were rare and fierce, and I could scarcely believe that Genet could have killed it, but perhaps he had been lucky in securing a grip on its throat. To fight such a creature, so clearly his superior in size and power, was most unusual. Njombo thought that the lynx had disturbed Genet when he was trying to get at the poultry, and that Genet so firmly regarded all local poultry as his own property that he had refused to obey the lynx, and sprung at the surprised animal.

'It is because Genet belongs to the house,' Njombo said. 'He thinks this farm is his, and all the hens and frogs and hares, he will not let any other cat come near it. Genet is like the Governor, or a man with a young wife and a new shamba. Pride makes him fierce.'

Njombo evidently wished the fight had gone the other way, but I was proud of Genet's courage and pugnacity. Thanks, I daresay, to Tilly's needlework, and to his own willpower, Genet survived. For some time he had a strange appearance, owing to the hastily chopped off bits of fur, but gradually a spruce new coat grew over the scars and Genet was as good as new, and no less fond of poultry.

There was only one bedroom in the house, so I occupied a tent in a clearing among the long grass, olive trees and thorns. One of these thorns was a weaver-tree where the yellow finches brawled and chirped and built nests, most of them useless, all day long, save in the afternoons when they had a siesta. Birds of all kinds abounded at Njoro. Below the house was a gully made by natural erosion in whose walls the green bee-eaters nested. They flashed by like animated emeralds, with bands of rose on their wings and a creamy white front. Little seed-eaters that we wrongly called humming-birds grew so tame they hopped about round the door; some were blue as turquoises, others a dark-red plum-colour; and sunbirds with their long, curved beaks and quivering wings were always busy among the creepers and the wild scarlet and orange *gloriosa* blooms. Early in the morning anvil-birds (a kind of cuckoo shrike) kept up their bell-like double call and response, high-low, high-low, like a blow on an anvil followed by a lighter sound as the hammer bounced. This was made by two birds, not one: a cock calling and a hen answering, as regular as the tick of a clock. The rain-bird (a kind of bulbul) rolled his soft notes from his throat, like water from a bottle, in a sad falling cadence that quickened as it fell; doves cooed as they had at Thika; flights of green parrots whirred by, coming from the forest.

Every day a cup of tea arrived before sunrise, and through an open tent-flap I could see long streaks of rose and lemon rimming the black mountains, and then a gradual paling of the stars in a sky of royal blue, and the valley with its slumbering lake slowly drawing light from the sky. Although the ground sheet was icy to the feet and I groped quickly for a sweater, it was no effort to dress and go out into the gathering daybreak with a rifle. For I still looked upon the graceful and abundant animals as game to be shot. To know a thing is beautiful and yet take pleasure in destroying it seems, in retrospect, an odd frame of mind, but the best hunters were the best naturalists; they loved the lives they extinguished, and enjoyed nothing more than to watch a buck at play, a herd of impala leaping, a lion on the kill, an elephant searching the wind with his trunk – unless it was to bring them down with a well-placed bullet.

There was, of course, a code to make this blood lust respectable. You must not kill females or youngsters; you must shoot only when you felt reasonably sure of killing cleanly; and if you hit an animal you must follow and despatch it. The worst crime was to fire 'into the brown', merely in the hopes of hitting something. By killing only males, hunters argued – and with truth – they did not reduce the total quantity of game, but merely culled older males – the best heads were normally to be found on fully mature animals – and so kept up the vigour of the breeding stock. If everyone had stuck to the code this would have been so, but they did not. The Boers, especially, massacred animals in vast numbers either to sell their hides, or to protect their crops. Africans had no code at all about wild animals and no wish to preserve any. Wild beasts ate crops or else menaced people, and the sooner they were exterminated the better.

Tilly was torn in two ways. She did not want to see the buck killed off, but they ate the young maize, the vegetables she grew beside the river, the roses she planted round the house. They leapt the highest fences, and smelt out the most hidden shoot. So she could not forbid Kikuyu to trap and hunt them, but nor did she encourage their destruction by offering a bounty on tails or heads. For my part I was obsessed with the importance of an eighth of an inch on the end of a horn. I had an old copy of Rowland Ward's compendium and knew the record length of horn of every species I was likely to encounter. Hunters like Jock Cameron, whose name appeared in this book, were invested with the kind of glamour that children of a later age, and in other countries, found in singers, actors and racing drivers. It was not beyond the bounds of possibility that, on one of my early morning walks, I should myself encounter a bushbuck or reedbuck with a record head – perhaps even a buffalo.

The forest boundary provided my favourite walk. This trace ran straight from the river to an iron beacon-post under a big cedar, and then turned at right angles to plunge in and out of several deep gullies. I never reached its farther end; it followed the forest margin for sixty or seventy miles along the range. I never went along this trace in early morning without seeing bushbuck whose lovely chestnut coats, dappled with white spots, glowed in the sunshine. Their short, sharp bark of alarm was as familiar as the night-time screech of hyraxes, or the plantain-eaters' cry. They could vanish more completely and abruptly than any other animal: apparently without motion, they just ceased to be. Duikers were smaller, fatter and looked bluish in a pale morning light. The sweetest were the dikdik, those miniature fawns, always to be seen in pairs, with match-stick legs and feet as delicate as the brush strokes of a Chinese calligrapher. I never in my life fired at a dikdik; they were too appealing, too firmly paired, and luckily too small to make much of a meal, but, of course, they were caught sometimes in snares.

By the corner beacon-post and the giant cedar, a very faint path took off into the thick undergrowth. I followed it a little way but then lost it and had to retreat, torn by prickly creepers and covered with burrs. As a rule the cedar tree was my turning point, and I often stood and gazed at this little chink in the forest's armour, but I knew it was useless to go farther without a guide.

'It would be good to find a Dorobo,' I said to Njombo, 'who knows the forest paths.'

'Why do you wish to go into the forest? It is bad up there; no shambas, no men.'

'There are Dorobo.'

'Are Dorobo men? They are like monkeys.'

'They would show me the way to Masai.'

'Eeee! Masai is far, very far, very far indeed. It is no good going to Masai.'

265

'Well, find me a Dorobo if you can.'

Njombo laughed. 'Perhaps we shall catch one in a trap, instead of a bush-pig.'

I knew the Dorobo came down sometimes to barter honey and, sure enough, one day Njombo brought to the house two small men clad in skins. The dogs rushed out barking, as they always did. By now the Kikuyu knew the technique, which was to stand quite still and let the dogs seethe round their legs, like sea round a rock, amid a great deal of barking and shouting. The Dorobo had no such experience, and in a flash they had vanished, just like the bushbuck. At one moment they were standing by the door, at the next they had gone, evaporated. The dogs gave the game away by surrounding an olive tree and baying round it, as if at a cat. In the branches crouched what looked like two large, dark birds. Everyone howled with laughter and Njombo nearly rolled on the ground. Even when the dogs had been driven indoors, the Dorobo would not descend. At last, in what looked like a single motion, they slipped down and stood again at the spot from which they had vanished, clutching their bows in their hands.

'They say they will show you the path if you give them tobacco,' Njombo said.

Njombo spoke to them in Kikuyu and they replied in Masai.

'Very well. Can we go tomorrow?'

Neither side spoke the other's language, but in some mysterious way an understanding seemed to arise from the exchange.

'They cannot come tomorrow,' Njombo translated, 'but they will return when the moon is half dead.'

'Why not before?'

There was another exchange and Njombo said: 'I don't know. They ask whether they will have meat.'

'Yes; if I shoot a buck they can have a leg.'

More conversation resulted in the query: 'Which leg?'

'The hind leg. And the tobacco.'

'They will be back in three days.'

But they were not, and by then trouble had blown up between the Dorobo and the Kikuyu.

The little shambas dug in forest clearings were about to

266

bear their first crop. The season had been kind, and the Kikuyu went about with springy steps and open faces and beamed at Tilly or myself when they encountered us. All day long the women weeded with their skin-clad rumps in the air, the sun shining on their bald heads and winking on their bead ear-rings and coils of wire, and at night the owner, or one of his relatives, took his spear and occupied a platform built of sticks to scare away bush-pig, monkeys and porcupines.

Kigorro had one of the best shambas, for his wife was strong and energetic and had a daughter old enough to help. He should have looked as pleased and happy as the rest of the Kikuyu, but about the time of the Dorobos' arrival we noticed a change in his manner, which became rather surly and abrupt. His cooking continued to deteriorate and he lost his grip on the housekeeping, and ran out of several ingredients. Then one day he marched up to Tilly with a scowl and said in a belligerent fashion: 'There is a *shauri*, memsabu.' This was a recognized opening gambit, to which Tilly returned the stock inquiry: 'A *shauri* of what kind?'

'A *shauri* about my wife.'

'Your wife is not my affair.'

'She has run away. I am going to find her. I am going today.'

'Very well, Kigorro, go; but you will not find your work waiting when you return.'

'She has run away! Run away in the night, and not alone. Is my wife to be stolen? Are there not thieves on this farm? I shall go to find her and then I shall demand fifty goats, a hundred goats from the family of Njombo! The men of his family are wicked, and they must pay!'

Kigorro was getting worked up, and there was always a danger of a fight when eyes began to roll and limbs to tremble. This was the moment for a verbal splash of cold water in the face.

'Be quiet, Kigorro,' Tilly snapped. 'You have no right to talk like that about Njombo. If you have a complaint to make, then make it before a meeting of the *kiama*. Now go and pre-pare the lunch, and after that I will listen to you if you speak like an elder, but not if you shout like a child.'

It was always a surprise to see how an angry man like

Kigorro, truly an elder, strung up to a high pitch of tension and fury, would defer to Tilly, who was after all a woman, even if a white one, and meekly accept a rebuke. I suppose it was partly because the Kikuyu were conditioned to authority. They expected and needed a ruling, they desired order and decision, and when they got it they accepted it with inward relief: they had shifted the galling burden of decision on to other shoulders. Kigorro turned and walked towards the kitchen and, sure enough, he did prepare the lunch, a better meal than any he had produced for several days.

Meanwhile Tilly found Njombo, now the headman on the farm, and asked him sternly what was going on. He looked deeply offended.

'Eeeee! You do not think that I would take away a wife of Kigorro's, memsabu? A wife of your cook? Have I not got two of my own? His senses have left him, that is all.'

'And his wife?'

'It is true that she has gone. But have I gone with her? Am I not here?'

'You have a brother,' Tilly remarked. One of those to follow us from Thika had been a young man called Gitende, Njombo's half-brother. So far as Tilly knew, he was not married, but she did not know much about him, as he had worked not for us but for the Clewes, and never made any particular impression.

'I have many brothers,' Njombo rejoined.

'But only one here. What has happened to Gitende?'

'I do not know if anything has happened to him. Is Gitende one of my goats?'

'If he has strayed, you had better find him. I have told Kigorro to take his complaint to the *kiama*. He says he wants a hundred goats from you.'

Njombo gave a wail of incredulity and outraged innocence, but Tilly told him he must settle matters with Kigorro and not bother her, and walked away while still delivering her ultimatum, after the manner of the Kikuyu, who talked as well when they were walking as when they were standing still.

Part of the mechanism of Kikuyu life was the *kiama*, a

council of elders to which everyone brought his disputes. It was something like a bench of English magistrates except that everyone who reached a certain age-grade could belong, provided that he paid an entry fee in goats. Wherever the Kikuyu settled, as for instance in Njoro, they established a local *kiama*, and although the legal system of the country did not recognize it the people did, which perhaps mattered more. It could not send people to prison, but prisons, in any case, were an alien device. The *kiama* imposed fines, and these were the traditional sanction of Kikuyu society. Quite soon Tilly was approached for a permit to brew beer, an essential preliminary to any *kiama* meeting. She found out that Gitende had indeed gone away and if he had taken Kigorro's wife with him he would have to face a crushing penalty. Few crimes were considered worse than to steal from a man the most valuable of all his possessions.

In reply to my inquiries about the outcome of the *kiama* meeting, Njombo shook his head and said: 'One cannot decide so big a *shauri* as you can shoot a buck, with a single bullet. It is like a fierce elephant, many bullets are needed, spears, perhaps a trap.' He would not be more explicit, and when I asked what had become of the Dorobo, who had failed to turn up, he answered huffily that one might as well send messages to wild bees; anyway the Dorobo were undesirable characters, not wanted on a respectable farm.

Chapter 26

AN atmosphere of unease continued to prevail at Njoro. Kigorro was at the centre of it; he was still upset, and took no interest in Tilly's daily consultations about food. Robin had been summoned back to Thika and Tilly was out on the shamba when a police inspector arrived. He came in a car, an event for us because we lacked a road and ourselves moved about on ponies. He had come all the way from Nakuru in order to see Kigorro.

'But he's our cook,' I protested.

'Cook or not, it looks as if he's been a bad boy.'

We could not find out what Kigorro was supposed to have done. If Gitende had stolen his wife, it was Kigorro who was the aggrieved party; and as he had not left the farm, it was hard to see what crime he could have perpetrated. An askari was sent to fetch him and returned leading him by the arm. Kigorro looked as dark and outraged as a wounded buffalo and stood there glaring with his arms hanging at his sides. When the inspector asked him to confirm his name, he said nothing.

'Come on, answer, you,' barked the inspector. Kigorro admitted his identity with a furious mumble, and the inspector cautioned him in high-class Swahili he probably did not understand.

'What have you done with the body?' the inspector demanded.

'What body?'

'The body of the Dorobo you killed.'

'I have killed no Dorobo!' Kigorro exclaimed, stung now into animation, and with fright in his eyes.

'I have the news written here,' the inspector said, flapping some papers in his hand. 'You had better admit it, because the Government already knows. There was a Dorobo killed on this farm with an arrow and you have been accused of firing it. Now you must come to Nakuru and tell your story to a bwana who will write it down, and know at once if you are telling lies.'

Kigorro was being led away towards the car when Tilly arrived in a cloud of barking dogs, hot and flushed from hurrying up the hill. The young inspector saluted and explained the situation and she looked, as I had expected, more and more displeased.

'But no one has been murdered on this farm,' she said.

'Our information is that a Dorobo has been killed by an arrow.'

'Nonsense!' Tilly said firmly. 'If anyone had been killed, I should have known. And what's become of the body?'

The inspector shrugged his shoulders. 'We all know what

becomes of bodies in this country. I'm sorry, ma'am, I'm acting on information received and your cook must come to Nakuru. I'm not arresting him at the moment, only taking him to the station for questioning. I shall leave a corporal here to make inquiries and I hope you'll give him all the assistance you can.'

'This is ridiculous,' Tilly said. 'If a Dorobo had been killed, no one would have gone to the police about it. The Dorobo themselves would have run as fast as they could into the farthest bit of forest they could find.'

'It wasn't the Dorobo who lodged the information, so far as I know. At any rate it came from Nairobi.'

'You don't mean to suggest that any Dorobo went down there?'

'I think the information originated at Fort Hall.'

A light then dawned on Tilly and she understood half of it, if not the whole. She looked round for Njombo, who had appeared with several of the other Kikuyu and was standing just within earshot, a fascinated spectator.

'Njombo, what has happened to Gitende? Is his shamba near Fort Hall?'

'Memsabu, I do not know what has happened to Gitende. I have told you, he is not one of my goats.'

'But his home is near Fort Hall?'

Njombo said nothing, as he could not deny it.

'And now,' Tilly continued, 'he has gone to the police with this ridiculous story about Kigorro because he has stolen Kigorro's wife, and he wants Kigorro put in prison to prevent his getting her back. Is that the truth?'

'No, no, it is not,' Njombo protested, stung at last into a response to this attack upon his brother. 'Memsabu, you say that he has stolen Kigorro's wife, but that is a lie. The woman ran away because Kigorro beat her unjustly, she was going back to her father. If Gitende went away at the same time to return to his father's shamba, is that stealing Kigorro's wife? Can Gitende help it if she travels in the same train? Gitende has not stolen anything. It is Kigorro who has punished his wife.'

This outburst broke all the bonds that had constrained the

271

Kikuyu to silence for the past week or two, and that had made the atmosphere heavy with unspoken enmities. Even Kigorro was no longer mute.

'Who has told husbands that they may not punish wives who are lazy and stupid? And how will the elders drink beer if thieves have emptied the hives? Ten goats I have paid for my wife already, and a young bull and two heifers, and her father still demands more. Am I to pay goats to get a wife for Gitende? I will not pay another goat, even an old, he-goat with a broken leg; not a cock will I pay, not a handful of snuff, not a hen! Not a flea from the head of the Dorobo who come to steal our crops in the night and leave their faeces in the path like hyenas!'

At this, everyone lapsed into the Kikuyu tongue and harangued each other until the inspector quelled them by shouting and smacking several of them lightly on the legs with his cane. 'Silence, silence, all of you, and Kigorro must come with me to tell the truth which will be written down on paper. And if he has killed the Dorobo we shall find it out, so don't try any tricks with me.'

But Tilly was not satisfied, and told the inspector that there was more in this than met the eye. 'There always is,' he agreed.

'If you take Kigorro away they'll all lie and lie from sheer panic,' she said, 'but if you leave him here, I think we can get to the bottom of it. They've said too much now to go back. He won't run away.'

'That's just what he will do,' the policeman objected.

'I think I know him better than you do,' Tilly said stiffly. I could see she had decided to stand on her dignity. She seldom used this gambit, but when she did, it generally worked. And so it did now. The inspector finally agreed, with reluctance, to leave Kigorro for the moment and let Tilly make an attempt to get to the bottom of the whole affair, or at least as far down as she could.

'I shall get into trouble for this,' he said. 'Leaving a lady alone on a farm with a murder suspect.'

'If he wanted to murder me, he'd have done so long ago,' Tilly pointed out. 'I sometimes wonder he hasn't. Any English cook would have, with meals at the odd hours we have them. How about a glass of beer?'

So the policeman departed without Kigorro, and Tilly's prestige rose; to show herself stronger than the police demonstrated to the Kikuyu that they had been correct, wise and prescient in attaching themselves to her when she had moved to Njoro.

'Now everyone must go home and stop all this nonsense,' Tilly commanded, 'and tomorrow morning there will be a meeting and the truth must be told. If anyone lies, I shall call for the police to take away Kigorro, and very likely the Government will hang him, and they will take away Njombo as well. Now bring some tea, and don't bother me again until tomorrow morning.'

Next day the meeting was held, but Tilly did not attend. She believed in letting the Kikuyu manage such matters in their own way. Besides, the pace of all discussion was immeasurably slow. The gathering took place under a tree. The younger men squatted on their heels, but elders used the low, three-legged stools to which their age and dignity entitled them. The speaker grasped a bundle of twigs and threw one twig to the ground to mark each point in his argument. They spoke impressively, with dramatic pauses and many gestures, pursing of lips and changes of tone, in voices that were soft, varied and musical. From a European point of view such meetings wasted hours of time and were maddeningly long-winded, but to the Kikuyu they were a form of pleasure, like a game of chess, or watching a cricket match.

About tea-time, Njombo came to report to Tilly the findings of the *kiama*. He hitched his blanket on to his shoulder, spat, and said: 'On this shamba the land is fat, but there are troubles. For instance there are moles, porcupines and creatures of the forest – cats, badgers, buck and pigs, especially pigs. And also Dorobo. These Dorobo are thieves, every one of them. In the night they come to steal maize and potatoes from our shambas.'

'What has this to do with Kigorro?'

'Has not Kigorro a shamba? He saw the crop was poor, and told his wife that she was lazy. His wife said the maize-cobs

273

had been stolen by the Dorobo, because Kigorro had not sat up at night to drive away the pigs and the Dorobo. This angered Kigorro and he beat his wife several times.'

'That was very wrong of Kigorro.'

'It is against our custom for men to beat their wives without cause, but if a wife is lazy and does not look after the crops and the shamba, then he is right to beat her. But no wife is right to leave her husband unless he is impotent. So Kigorro's wife was wrong to run away from her husband.'

'Where is she now?'

Njombo shrugged his shoulders. 'How do I know where she has gone? Perhaps she has returned to her father. But the *kiama* has fined Gitende ten goats.'

'So she did go away with Gitende,' Tilly concluded.

'They went in the train, but who knows if they were together? Trains carry many people. And Gitende has no shamba, so how can he pay ten goats? But so it has been decided.'

'All this has nothing to do with the police. Why did Gitende tell the police at Fort Hall that Kigorro had killed a Dorobo?'

'Perhaps Gitende is afraid that Kigorro may follow him to Fort Hall and demand goats from him. If the police catch Kigorro, then he cannot go to Fort Hall.'

'I am not a half-wit, I can understand that,' Tilly said sharply. 'I don't think you have told me the whole story.'

'If a wild pig comes and destroys the crops in your shamba,' Njombo said with feeling, 'is it wrong to shoot the pig? Or is a man to say, let the pigs eat their fill, I am growing these crops for the pigs, not for my children? And if thieves come are they not the same as pigs?'

'Men are not the same as pigs, even when they are wicked.'

'Eeeee! They are pigs, but worse than pigs because they are more cunning. If a shamba is protected by a strong magic then no Kikuyu can steal anything, but Dorobo are like animals and magic does not keep them away.'

'Come on, Njombo, you must tell me the truth,' Tilly insisted. 'If you won't, then I shall have to send for the police.'

'I am telling you the truth, memsabu. Every night there are people sitting in the shambas to shoot arrows at the pigs and throw spears if they come close enough. In the darkness, who can tell a pig from a Dorobo? These little men, they come crouching like this.' Njombo gave a demonstration, shrinking himself to the size of a baboon and circling round with bent knees and humped shoulders. 'When they are crouching like monkeys, and it is dark, and a man sees only something that moves among the maize-stalks, how is he to know if it is a pig or a man? And if a thief comes at night to steal crops, is he not like a pig or a porcupine?'

'You are saying that Kigorro may have killed a Dorobo thief without meaning to,' Tilly said. 'If anyone was killed, you know very well there would be a body. Has any dead Dorobo been found? Or was this all a story of Gitende's to get Kigorro into trouble?'

'I have not seen any dead body,' Njombo said. His evasiveness convinced Tilly that he was still holding back the full truth, and that, after all, a Dorobo had been shot without her knowledge.

'Why was I not told about this?'

'About what, memsabu?'

'About a Dorobo having been killed.'

'Who says that a Dorobo was killed? If a Dorobo had been killed would not his family have asked for blood money? No one has come with such a claim.'

'This is a very bad affair indeed,' Tilly said. 'If anyone was hurt or killed you should have told me. What am I to say to the police when such things happen and I know nothing about them? You are all fools. Now go away and see that nothing like this happens again, do you understand? And if the police come back to take away Kigorro, it will be nothing to do with me.'

'You will not let them do that,' Njombo said confidently, and left to carry out his instructions.

Next day, Tilly rode into Nakuru to tell the story to the police. Although it was still vague and unsatisfactory, Njombo was right: she did succeed in protecting Kigorro. In any case the police could scarcely have proceeded without proof that anyone had been killed. The dead Dorobo, if indeed one had been killed, had been spirited away. I understood why the

275

Dorobo had not returned to act as guides, even with the lure of meat and tobacco. Tilly's reputation rose among all the Kikuyu. Clearly she possessed the power to repel enmity and danger, even when they came in an official guise, and those who enjoyed her protection could expect to share her immunity.

Chapter 27

TILLY reposed great faith in experts, and would travel miles to consult one on such a matter as the grafting of fruit trees, the sexing of chicks, the conduct of seed germination tests or the diseases of cucumbers. From the experts' point of view she was the ideal farmer, always ready to try any new method they recommended, or wished to investigate. This should have made her more successful than her less enterprising neighbours, but in practice it did not, because the experts were groping in the dark and their advice often turned out to be wrong.

'Wait till someone else proves anything new,' Trevor Sheen used to say. 'Never be the guinea-pig.' 'But if we all did that, nothing ever *would* be proved,' Tilly protested. 'There'll always be a sucker – don't let it be you.' 'That's a chicken-hearted outlook,' Tilly said. 'The great thing is to get in on the ground floor.'

Her anxiety to do this, even when experience showed the ground floor to be bare and draughty, led her to start many side lines, some of which later developed into economic industries when the experts had found out more about them. On one of her expeditions to the Government laboratories, she discovered a severe shortage of experimental mice. No one else had thought of breeding them, and she decided to build up a profitable side line by supplying the laboratories. In due course half a dozen pairs of white mice arrived from South Africa and were installed in cages, and fed on carefully balanced rations drawn up by the scientists.

The mice multiplied, and went off in batches to the labs. But after a while they began to develop a most distressing habit. They ate each other. When Tilly visited the cages she would come upon stomach-turning sights of carnage. An S O S to the labs resulted in a new diet sheet which only sharpened their depraved appetites. The knowledge that mice who had seemed so gay and friendly were constantly chewing each other to death oppressed her, and after some hesitation she had the cages loaded into the Scotch cart and taken to the forest, where the mice were liberated. She knew they would all perish, but lacked the heart to drown them, and thought they would at least have a run for their money. Meanwhile she warned Trevor not to ride in that direction, knowing that a glimpse of white mice in the undergrowth would be bad for his nerves.

On one of her periodic visits to the labs she met an expert on earthworms, and returned full of the great benefits worked by these nematodes in the soil, and their essential rôle in the cycle of fertility. Many types of African soil, this expert believed, were deficient in earthworms, and this accounted for their relative poverty. Tilly was a great reader of farm and garden journals, and in one of these found an advertisement by a breeder of pedigree earthworms, which he claimed were larger, more prolific and juicer than the ordinary kind. This breeder, not surprisingly, lived in California, and Tilly entered into a correspondence with him to discover whether earth-worms could be sent so far with any hope of survival. The difficulties were great, but about a year later a box of soil arrived said to contain earthworm capsules, a kind of rest-ing stage, which could be hatched out by warmth and moisture.

Tilly put the soil into a frame, mulched it and watered the capsules every day for a month. When she dug in with a trowel, there indeed were earthworms; she was delighted, scattered maize-meal for their nourishment and in due course transferred them to different parts of the farm. Robin was sceptical about these earthworms, believing them to be the ordinary, non-pedigree variety that had burrowed into the frame; but Tilly remained convinced that she had introduced a valuable new strain for the benefit of the soil's fertility.

One of the experts – I think a student of earthworms – told her that the inexhaustible fertility of virgin forest soil, an article of faith among farmers, was nothing but a myth. He said this forest soil was acid and quickly spent, and that all its goodness resided in the top few inches; deep-rooted plants would go hungry unless artificially fed. He was in favour of bone meal and dung.

One of Tilly's ambitions was to grow champion delphiniums, even better blooms than some she had admired in a show garden outside Nairobi. Delphiniums she knew to be hungry feeders, and after pondering the experts' theories she had a trench dug, five feet deep, in the garden, and a ramp made at one end. By now she had acquired two mules, who were more sure-footed than Fair Play and also drew the old buggy to and from the station. These mules were driven down the ramp and into the trench, which had been lined with straw, and there they stayed, copiously fed, treading their dung into the straw to make a deep, rich compost fit to sustain the finest delphiniums in Africa.

As the litter thickened, the mules began to rise. First you could see two pairs of ears sticking up out of the ground, then a head and neck, then their backs came to the surface. The expression on the faces of visitors who did not know about the delphinium-beds, and saw the tops of mules growing out of the lawn, caused everyone a great deal of entertainment. And in due course the delphiniums were, as Tilly had hoped, quite magnificent. It was a great blow when, just before a flower show in Nakuru, a vicious hailstorm stripped the heavy spikes and left a heap of broken stalks and battered petals on the ground.

To leave the interest and freshness of Njoro, where something was always afoot, for the stuffy classrooms of Nairobi was always a wrench. However, there was polo to be watched and reported, and I had at last made the acquaintance of my editor, Mr Rudolf Mayer, who had arrived from Germany some twenty years before with nothing but five pounds and an old hand-printing press. A smudgy weekly news-sheet published in Mombasa had grown into the flourishing daily news-paper I worked for, and into a number of subsidiary enter-prises.

The rains had started with unusual vigour and everything was deep in red mud. Raindrops hurled themselves so violently against the tin roofs of our decaying wood-and-iron classrooms that no one could hear anything, so the lessons did not make much headway, and thunder and lightning envel-oped the town. At week-ends I could not get to Thika because the railway line was washed away in several places and great swamps covered the road. I used to look across to the furrowed slopes of the Ngong hills, a brilliant vivid green against a deep violet sky, and wish that I could see the torrents of brown water racing down the gullies and, when the storms were over, herds of buffalo coming out of the forest to dry their black coats. When the moon was full and the night was fine I watched a herd of zebra on the polo ground. The absurd, long-legged foals capered in the moonlight, trying to get their mothers to play. From my bedroom I could hear lions plainly as they hunted on the Athi plains, and in the morning the bugles of the K.A.R. woke me with reveille. After tea I sometimes walked along the road towards Ngong to watch cars sticking in the mud and being pushed out again by ragged men who waited there to earn a few cents, and sang with a tremendous rhythm as they heaved, spattered all over with a stream of red mud from the spinning wheels.

The rains brought me an unexpected experience. Alan Beattie found himself stuck in Nairobi, unable to proceed with a safari, and I found a note to say that he would take me out to dinner. I was at once gripped by panic. To start with I hated my only wearable dress, a cast-off like the rest: it was pink, a colour I detested, and had a round neck and a fringe of beads. In fact I disliked everything about it, and it did not even fit well. I had no proper shoes to go with it and no time to wash my hair. The wives and daughters of Alan's clients must, I knew, be rich, elegant, sophisticated, witty and irresistibly attractive, trailing clouds of glory from Paris, London and

New York. Alan had invited me out of charity, to show his sympathy for Rupert's death, and could not fail to find my company as stimulating as blancmange and tepid water after caviare and champagne.

I climbed with cold hands and a dry throat into the pink dress, which looked more horrible than ever, combed hair which was mousy, badly cut and straight as a die, wishing with all my heart that I had refused the invitation. I had never seen Alan in anything but farm clothes, and scruffy ones at that, and the sight of his tidy suit took my last remaining shreds of confidence away. His dark moustache was neatly clipped, his nails were clean and he appeared to be a wholly different man, and so good-looking that I felt more than ever like a moulting sparrow confronted by a lilac-breasted roller in his full breeding plumage.

'It's good of you to come at such short notice,' Alan said, as if I had a dozen social engagements every day. Before, I had always thought him condescending, but now, when condescension was to be expected, he was much nicer, and behaved to me as if I was an individual and not a tiresome child. And then he had become more talkative, and told me all about the Beelers from Kansas City, who had for him a special significance, since they were the first clients he was taking out on his own. Up till now he had always been a second hunter. After the Beelers we went on to Alan's family and mine, and it was not as difficult as I had feared to find things to talk about. But then I noticed that all I was doing was to ask questions: I could think of no witty or original remarks, nor anything to raise a smile, let alone a laugh. The dining-room was clean and efficient but not inspiring, and had bottles of Worcester sauce on every table, and little vases with two or three Barberton daisies in each. So many waiters were in attendance that they whisked away our plates the very moment we had finished, and the meal seemed to gallop by. We had coffee in the lounge, and when Alan leant back with a small cheroot and asked: 'Well, what are you doing with yourself these days?', every idea fled precipitately from my mind. I could not say learning quadratic equations and the Navigation Acts, or writing a play about Elizabeth and Burleigh, or saving up to buy a Somali pony, or reading *If Winter Comes* and *Gosta Berling*, or making a collection of butterflies – none of these things would interest him.

'I'm supposed to be working. I'm to go home when I'm eighteen.'

'To be finished?'

'Well, I haven't really been begun.'

'I suppose being quite a good shot isn't much use as an accomplishment when you come out.'

'No, but I shall stay in. I don't want to go home, anyway. I don't see why I shouldn't stay here, like Barbara.'

'It isn't doing Barbara much good,' Alan said. 'So far she's merely invented all these extraordinary characters, so it hasn't mattered, but now she's got hold of a real one, a frightful stiff who plays the trombone in a dance band in Durban.'

'She seems to have a passion for South Africa.'

'It's her passion for the trombone player the family's worried about. It's amazing to be able to find anyone like that in a place like Nyeri. Mother's afraid she'll elope. Dad keeps saying she must be locked in, but you can't lock anyone into a rondavel. Apart from anything else, the trombonist's almost certainly got at least one wife already.'

'Perhaps we could change places,' I suggested. 'Barbara wants to go away and can't, unless it's with a trombone player, and I don't want to, and must.'

'That's life,' Alan said. 'Anyway, I'm staying, though Dad was dead against it at first. I think he's coming round now I'm starting to make a bit of money. If you come to think of it, it's a funny sort of life. Wet nurse to a lot of bloated meat-packers and their dreadful wives, or pouter pigeon Italian counts, and Indian rajahs looking for a new thrill. Leading them up to animals that have never done them any harm and doing everything but press the trigger for them – that too, sometimes, only they mustn't know it. A lot of male harlots, that's what Jock Cameron says we are. Gigolos. Lickspittles. Sometimes you wonder whether it wouldn't be fairer for the lions and buffaloes to hunt the clients, rather than the other way round. And yet there's something about it that gets hold of you and, speaking for myself, I never want to do anything

281

else. Except of course, safaris without clients,' he added. 'They're the only snag. But they're a big one.'

All this cheered me up tremendously. 'Are their wives really dreadful?' I inquired. 'Fat and silly? Spoilt? Puff like a grampus if they walk five yards?'

'Some of them do,' Alan said guardedly. 'Of course, some have beautiful daughters.'

'Yes, I suppose they do.'

'They think hunters are romantic, and lay it on with a trowel. Mother thinks I ought to grab on to one, and then the old man could pay off the overdraft.'

'Yes, I suppose . . .'

'Well, I don't. I'm not going to spend the rest of my life running round after a poor little rich girl, that's one thing I *am* sure of. One might be able to make a living catching animals for zoos.'

'It's cruel to put them in zoos.'

'You're thinking of Rupert. Yes, I suppose it is, though zoos are improving. But if I don't do it, someone else will.'

I felt there was a flaw in this logic, but his views on his female clients had made me feel too cheerful, confident and admiring to argue. Few men, I felt, but Alan would have the good sense to see through the harpies who pursued him, the strength of mind to resist them, and the independence to reject the least notion of being bought for gold. He probably would change his mind about zoos, and anyway it was only a passing notion. Without thinking, I remarked: 'I'd love to go on a real safari.'

'Would you?' Alan said. 'I'll take you one day.'

'I didn't mean that!'

'No, but it wouldn't be difficult. I often run down to the Tana when I've got a week or so to spare. It's stiff with game, and you can get there in a couple of days.'

'I couldn't afford it.'

'It doesn't cost much if you travel light. Just the wages of a dozen porters, and the stores. I have to pay my tracker and gun-bearer anyway. We'll fix it up one of these days.'

My head swam: here was my most cherished wish no longer hopeless and impossible but suddenly almost within reach.

The prospect of a genuine safari was exciting enough: a safari with Alan, perfection. Obviously this was too wonderful a thing ever to happen, and I must dismiss it from my mind. My thanks sounded gruff and perfunctory, and when I had uttered them I thought with dismay that even if he had meant what he said, my response would make him change his mind. Why did people think one thing and say another? What went wrong between mind and tongue? Robin sometimes quoted a saying: speech was given to man to conceal his thoughts. Evidently it was given to women to confuse theirs, which was worse.

Alan suggested a run in his car, but the roads looked too slithery and we went to the Norfolk hotel to sit on the veranda and watch the people come and go. To reach the Norfolk bar you had to climb a short flight of steps and, during race weeks, some of the more dashing spirits used to ride their ponies up these steps and into the bar. In the unpaved street outside, illuminating a line of waiting rickshaws, stood the most shot-at street lamp in Africa. Convivial and sometimes drunken parties would debouch from the bar, draw their revolvers, place their bets and see who could score the first bull. Once or twice Lord Delamere had hired a rickshaw and proceeded up Government Road shooting at the street lights as he passed them, with an indifferent aim.

After a while we walked along the muddy road under the eucalyptus trees to Ainsworth bridge, and stood looking into the darkness that pressed in all round, faintly tinged by the heavy smell of frangipani. Traffic had ceased and everything was silent save for the perpetual croaking of frogs. Then a hyena gave its curious hooping call from down-river, blood-chilling only, I suppose, because of its association in our minds with death and the disposal of corpses. A fish jumped below us, a glowworm flashed for a moment in the thick velvet dark, through the still air there came a distant, plaintive sound of song and drumming.

'Twenty years ago there was nothing here but a few tents,' Alan reflected, 'and ten years before that nothing at all, just a very minor river, a drinking-pool for game I expect, and a few wandering Masai. Nairobi's about as old as I am. I suppose, if I ever get to be fifty, it will be a huge great town with proper streets and big buildings and cinemas and goodness knows what. Civilization. Even the natives will perhaps be civilized, on the surface anyway. And what will happen to the lions then? If I'm still alive I suppose I'll be a staid old farmer, but I think I'll miss them. I think I'll still sneak off to find them now and then.'

A rickshaw went by with a man and a woman in it arguing in raised voices, heatedly; they sounded as if they had been drinking. The rickshaw boys were panting, their bare feet padded on the drying mud and a waft of their sweaty smell drifted towards us.

'Civilization,' Alan repeated, looking after them. 'One wonders sometimes. But there it is. Perhaps if I took more saints and fewer sinners on safari I should keep more of my illusions. You must try to hang on to yours.'

'I know I must have some,' I said, 'because everyone who's young has, but I can never quite make out what they are.'

'Let sleeping dogs lie,' Alan advised.

As we turned to leave the bridge he took my arm and we walked in silence beneath the eucalyptus trees whose tall, straight trunks were always peeling, like a man with skin disease. For this reason I never liked them, despite the freshness of their leaves when you crushed them, leaves that were always faintly moving even without a wind, and that now dappled a sky overflowing with stars. I sometimes imagined that I could smell the stars, a dry, crisp smell like ice on a sedge-fringed pond at dawn. I felt elated and lightheaded, as if my blood had bubbles in it like sparkling wine, and yet at the same time near to tears – why, I could not tell; perhaps because some phrase of Alan's had put into my mind the sombre sentence that the wings of a man's life are barbed with the feathers of death. But now an endless life seemed to stretch before us both, and I wondered whether we should be fated to spend any part of it together.

I had to halt before we reached the Norfolk to take a stone out of my shoe. Alan ran me home in his car, cut short my thanks with: 'Glad you could come. I've enjoyed it, and I won't forget that safari,' waved good night and chugged away into the dark.

Chapter 28

I REMEMBER Cousin Hilary saying that the point about Cain and Abel was not that Cain killed his brother, but that one was a ploughman and the other a shepherd. All humanity sprang from one or the other, and you could still tell their issue apart. When they started on a journey the descendants of Cain fussed about tickets, the descendants of Abel lifted their eyes to the cab of the locomotive or the bridge of the ship; and although Cain must always murder Abel in the end, in the meanwhile Abel had a better run for his money.

Robin and Tilly belonged to Abel's brood. To start on a journey, any kind of journey, was an adventure that never lost its tang. Even a trip to Nairobi created a small bustle, a feeling of being up and doing. But the start of a safari united and magnified all these little springs of interest into a swelling wave of excitement. The great point about a safari was that you had no idea where you would spend the night, or the next night, or the one after that: you simply went towards the sunrise, or to the north or south-west, and stopped when you came to a likely camping spot, or when the porters were tired, and stayed a day or a week as you thought fit. You needed no clock but the sun, no roof but a tent; you travelled away from cities and swarms of people into a world whose wild creatures lived their sweet and graceful lives, untouched by humans, as they had done a thousand or ten thousand years ago, and indeed long before that, when men were merely extra-cunning apes who had learnt to kill with arrows, but not yet discovered how to spoil the natural world. In short, you tasted freedom.

We were going to the junction of the Tana and the Thika rivers, to the hot plains stretching below the heights of Kenya mountain and inhabited by tsetse flies and red pepper-ticks and animals innumerable. The quantity of gear we needed, even for a fortnight, was surprising: such, for instance, as a tin bath full of lamps, the paraffin to fill the lamps, several kinds of ammunition, saltpetre for curing skins, *debes* for drawing water, cooking-pots and kettles, groceries for us and salt and maize-meal for the porters. A safari could be ruined by little things, such as running out of sugar or leaving a mosquito net behind. The Tana valley had a bad name for malaria, and for three weeks in advance we took quinine every day.

Almost at the last moment, Robin fell out. For some time he had been suffering from an itch for Tanganyika, caused by rumours of a railway to link the southern highlands with the central line. These cool, green highlands were reputed to enjoy a splendid climate and to support few inhabitants; land, people said, was to be had for next to nothing, as had been the case in Kenya twenty years before. To Robin this was a clear invitation to get in on the ground floor. Besides, there was talk of minerals and their exploitation, and these attracted him more than farming; they offered speedier fortunes and drew the shady, genial, free-spending characters with whom he liked to mix. To pay for his drinks with a bag of gold dust would have seemed to him the most splendid thing in the world. So Robin had been feeling restless, like a yarded beast who smells fresh young grass in spring.

Shortly before we were due to start on our safari, Walter arrived at Njoro talking of a great opportunity. A friend of his was setting forth on behalf of a small, secret syndicate, to stake out mining claims in Tanganyika in the path of a prospective railway. Inside information had reached the syndicate as to the route likely to be chosen for this new line. Here was something that simply could not go wrong, provided that everyone concerned took an oath of secrecy, and it was more than Robin could resist. He tried to look sceptical, but the attempt failed. A week later he left for an unknown destination and an indefinite length of time.

'What about an address?' Tilly inquired.

'The club at Iringa might find me. After that I've no idea.'

'Please don't buy a ruby mine from a syphilitic Arab in a beer-shop on the Portuguese border,' Tilly implored.

'No one's said anything about rubies,' Robin said huffily.

'I expect they will.'

'You don't seem to take seriously my efforts to restore the family fortunes.'

'Never mind, Robin, have a good time. And do send a telegram from Iringa.'

'It would hardly get delivered in the Tana valley,' Robin pointed out.

Tilly and I were to meet Alan and the porters at the house of a couple called McKay who occupied the last farm, beyond Makuyu, on the borders of the settled area, where this abutted on the tsetse bush. The first part of our safari would be the hardest because we had to climb the Ithanga hills. Although these were not very high they were steep in places, and broken by ravines. No clear tracks crossed them, but hunters of game and honey had made little paths, barely perceptible through the long grass. Neither mules nor ponies could be taken because of tsetse fly.

When we arrived at the McKays', late and brown with dust, Alan was there to meet us with a white fox-terrier called Samson and with John, his hefty gun-bearer, once a K.A.R. askari, and the only member of the safari, apart from ourselves, to wear shoes. Alan's successful expedition with the Beelers had started a satisfactory flow of clients, and he was booked for a year ahead. Our promised fortnight filled a gap between the leading mortician of Cincinnati and a canner of seafood from Baltimore.

At home, he said, things were in confusion. Barbara had indeed gone off to Durban with her trombone player, the Colonel had followed on the next ship with a hunting-crop but had belaboured the drummer instead, and in the lounge of the best hotel, so he was under prosecution for about half a dozen offences. Meanwhile the trombone player had fled and Barbara had taken up with a Portuguese wine salesman who wore diamond rings, and both had disappeared, leaving the Colonel at bay among the Durban police.

Next morning all our loads were laid out on the lawn and the usual arguments broke out among the porters as to who should carry what, and the usual re-packing took place. Once on the go, safaris always struck camp very early, in the dark, marched until ten or eleven o'clock and then rested in the heat of the day, but the first morning was an exception; no one expected to cover many miles, the great thing was to get away and to settle each porter with his load.

Ours were all Wakamba, thin but tough and wiry men whose teeth had been filed to points, giving them a wolfish look. They had volunteered less for the extra pay than because they could indulge their passion for meat. The Kikuyu seldom, if ever, volunteered as porters, partly because of their deep-rooted custom that only women carried loads, but also because they would not touch venison, even if they were starving. We had cut our number down to eighteen, very few for those days, and of these nine had to carry loads of maize-meal for the porters to eat. There was no food to be bought down the Tana valley, which was uninhabited. Besides the porters we had the gun-bearer John, Alan's tracker, Kigorro, and a headman.

By about ten o'clock our safari had straggled off, in good spirits if one could judge by the shouts, laughter and taunts flung to lesser men who stayed behind and did not venture into the haunts of lions. Safari porters, even when attached to humble expeditions like ours, enjoyed some prestige, as well as opportunities, seldom neglected, for subsequent boasting of strength and prowess. We stayed behind to eat a large breakfast with the McKays, and then walked off along a narrow path into the bush, festooned with water-bottles, binoculars and cameras. Alan carried a shotgun in case we put up edible birds, Samson trotted at his heels, John followed immediately behind with a light rifle, next came Tilly, then myself, and Kigorro brought up the rear.

We climbed pretty steeply up the shoulder of the hills and soon could see the plains towards Makuyu stretched out behind us, green and gold like fields of corn ripening unevenly, for rain had flushed the burnt-over reaches with young growth, while those parts that had escaped burning were dry and tawny. We saw little life apart from lizards scuttling among the boulders, their heads held high above blue and orange bodies, and a pair of klipspringers who melted into the rocks.

The Wakamba had cleaned the game out of this side of the hills.

This Ithanga range was deceptive: it rolled ahead in fold after fold, studded with rocks and thorns and the bunched, cactus-like candelabra euphorbia trees, whose milky sap could trap birds and poison humans. Shreds of cloud hung about the shoulders and now and then you found yourself walking through a white mist with sunlight all around it, and then emerging into clarity shaking with heat. No springs rose here, and the water-courses were dry. Once they must have run with clear streams and once the ravines must have held deep, damp forest instead of the twisted, spiky bush and stunted trees we saw now. These hills appeared to be dying, you could not say why, but in them you sensed a listless indifference, the peace of the grave. Of men the only sign was a hollow beehive log here and there, hanging from a branch or wedged into the fork of a tree.

We crossed the top without knowing it, and on the morning of our second day caught a glimpse ahead through rocks and bush of a great view opening up before us and receding into a far haze. Down below rolled plains seemingly endless, speckled with bush, patterned with shadows, shimmering with heat, barren of landmarks, indifferent to man. Down there a whole safari column would be swallowed up as entirely as a shoal of fishes in the deepest ocean of the seas. Alan pointed out, through glasses, a distant, dark line that marked the river's course.

That night we camped at the foot of a ravine where water could be found by scooping out a muddy pool used by buffalo. The tracker reported that a herd had drunk there two days ago. Alan shot a brace of spur-fowl and we ate them by a fire which discharged a stream of sparks into the night when it was kicked, and played a flickering amber light over table and tent flap, over our faces and slippered feet and on the glossy, plum-like skins of the Wakamba. No food ever tasted so good as that eaten in the open beside a wood fire, no company seemed ever so warm as that of one's companions relaxed after the fatigue of the march, no wear so soothing as slippers on blistered feet, no couch so comfortable as a camp bed

when limbs are at rest that have been stung by thorns and
burnt by sun, no sleep so perfect as that stirred but not broken
by the thrilling vibrance of a lion's roar.

To depart on a safari is not only a physical act, it is also a
gesture. You leave behind the worries, the strains, the irrita-
tions of life among people under pressure, and enter the
world of creatures who are pressed into no moulds, but have
only to be themselves; bonds loosen, anxiety fades, the mind
closes against the world you left behind like a folding sea
anemone. Enjoyment of the moment, the true delight in living,
in life as it is and not as others in the past have made it, all
this returns. Each breath you draw gives pleasure, you wake
with a new sense of wonder at the pure light shining on
golden grasses and the web on the thorn, and at the cooing
of the dove. And the reason for praising the Lord all the days
of your life, a reason certainly withheld from men in cities,
comes to you: or, at least, you understand that this is not a
matter of reason, which destroys all need for praise, but a
buried instinct that you are one with all creation and that
creation is positive, delightful and good. Only when the chains
of civilization were loosened, when you escaped for an instant
from the mould, could you understand the meaning of spontaneous happiness. To live this life forever seemed the only
desirable form of existence and Alan, an initiate, at once the
most fortunate, the wisest and, in a sense, the most sacred of
men.

On the third day we marched over twenty miles to reach
the Tana, the only source of water in this arid land. To look
from a muddy bank at this brown, gently flowing river, broken
by sand spits and clumps of papyrus reed, you could scarcely
imagine its birthplace in a glacier. Many crocodiles lay doggo
in muddy inlets, only their nostrils showing, coloured like
logs, and scrub grew almost to the water's edge. While our
men pitched camp, two or three hundred yards from the river
to avoid the worst of the mosquitoes, the tracker went off to
read in sand and mud the movements of animals, and I went
with John and Alan to look for meat. When a shot from Alan
slew a kongoni, several porters sprinted to the source of the
distant bang with the accuracy of bees locating a flowering

lime-tree, and they bore back the limp antelope on a pole with a triumphant chant while its lolling mouth dripped blood on to grasses golden in the late evening light.

Alan took me back to camp a different way and, in a patch of sunlight, a wart-hog was standing motionless, his white tusks gleaming and his tail erect as a mast.

'There you are,' Alan said.

It had not occurred to me to shoot him; one could not mount a wart-hog's head; but, of course, he was edible.

'Shall I?'

'Yes, go on.'

I was nervous now, afraid of botching an easy shot and making a fool of myself. But I hit him in the brain.

'Nice shot,' Alan said, and I felt absurdly elated. 'Go on like that and we shall do well.' So our shooting had begun. But we did not want to kill many animals, and throughout our trip nothing that we shot was wasted, the men ate it all. They could eat meat in almost any quantity. An individual, single-mouthed, would polish off the leg of a buck the size of a sheep.

As we walked back to the camp by the river, dusk seemed to creep as silently from the ground as a serpent and to throttle the last of the light in its coils. In camp, the fire was already sending up its golden fountain of sparks. Our chairs were ready beside it, a tray of drinks, and the prospect of hot water, soft pyjamas, fresh food. My feet were blistered, my legs itched from tick-bites and many kinds of insect banged against the lamp glass, but this was the moment of peace and pleasure that crowned the day.

There was a difference in Alan hard to define, a greater quietness and relaxation, the authority of a man on his own ground. He did not speak much to John and yet they understood each other. The headman came with several small *shauris* which were settled in a few words, and went away satisfied. Samson came and lay at Alan's feet and the firelight reddened his white coat. The tracker, Alan said, had marked down a herd of buffalo across the river and we would make an early start to intercept them before they retreated into the bush for the day.

So Kigorro brought our morning tea in pitch darkness,

while the sky beyond the tent pole was still crusted over with stars. This was the coldest hour, and the most silent, but here the valley air never bit or stung. We dressed silently by lamplight. Tilly said that she had heard lions grunting close by in the night, but I had slept too well to hear anything. The sky was paling when we crossed the river, the tracker going ahead with a torch. It was tricky wading through black, waist-deep, torpid water where a hidden current tugged at your feet. The water swished as if breathing or faintly chuckling, and crocodiles were all about. You were supposed to be safer from crocodiles in the centre of a river than on the margins, for the reptile won his meals by knocking goats, buck or people into the shallows with his strong, scaly tail. But everyone is frightened of crocodiles and it was a relief to be over the river, squeezing out our trouser legs.

We prowled with caution up the river bank as the light strengthened and streaks of pinks and saffron-yellow appeared. The sky became like mother-of-pearl and a white mist rose from the ground. Through it every bush looked like a black, menacing buffalo poised for the charge. Perhaps it was the mist that cheated us. We came to trampled grass and hoof-marks, and the tracker and John with their heads down read the signs and clucked their tongues. The buffaloes had crossed the river less than half an hour ago to the side we had camped on, and the water was too deep here for us to follow. As we stood on the bank the sun came up and rolled the night back across the valley.

'We'll try to head them off,' Alan said. 'They'll be making for those hills.' We turned back, re-crossed the river and found the place where the herd had scrambled up the bank. The tracker cast round like a fox-hound, and led us off along the spoor. We followed it for two hours until it petered out in broken, rocky country at the lower end of a deep ravine.

'I'm afraid they've beaten us,' Alan said. We climbed to the top of a boulder and examined the hillside with great care through field-glasses. A long way up the hill there was a small bunch of eland, but no sign of so much as the flick of a buffalo's tail. They were deep in the ravine by now, dozing in the shade. The tramp home seemed much longer, and the heat intense. We arrived tired, deflated and not very hungry, although we had walked on empty stomachs, and soon after three o'clock started out again to shoot for the pot. Every animal in the wide valley was bound to come to the river to drink and, after five o'clock, the bush came alive with them. We brought back an impala buck for the porters and a little tommy for ourselves, but no further news of buffaloes, nor of the lions we had heard grunting in the night.

We spent two whole fruitless days looking for the buffalo. They were all about us, we kept coming upon their fresh spoor, we smelt them and once heard them crashing through the bush less than a hundred yards away, but not once did they reveal themselves. Alan was mortified and the porters disgusted, for they relished buffalo meat. Although Tilly did not say so, I think she was on the side of the animals and did not want them killed. And in a curious way I, too, was half-glad. I wanted desperately a long, hard, exciting stalk crowned with a perfect shot and a victim, but each evening I thought: they have won another day of life, they will see the sun rise tomorrow and enjoy their long drink in the river and their siesta at noon.

On the third day we followed the spoor of a small herd from their drinking-place across the river back towards the hills. It was always interesting to watch John and the tracker at work. They walked with heads down, peering at the ground and yet taking in, almost it seemed through their pores, all that was happening around them, and their pace was remarkable. Most of the marks they were following on the hard, dry ground were invisible to me. They went by little falls of dust, minute disturbances, by crushed grass stalks, a stone displaced here, a twig broken there, and sometimes, I am sure, simply by inspired guess-work: they thought themselves into a buffalo's mind and acted as he had done. In this way they leaped dead patches in the trail and hit it off again, perhaps several hundred yards later, without any apparent reason. Of course, sometimes they were wrong and had to cast round to pick it up.

At last, among rocks, the spoor petered out. We were used to this by now, but not comforted. Our little stock of days was fast running out and we had nothing to show for them. To Alan this spelt failure, and he was too new to his profession to take such a matter lightly.

'We'll go on for half an hour,' he said. 'There's an outside chance they've stopped short of the hills.' We had gone on for twenty minutes when the tracker's low whistle brought us up. Our rifles' safety catches clicked into their fully cocked position. The tracker was on one knee gazing intently to his left through thorn-trees: and there, just beyond them, we could make out black shapes motionless in a thicket, half obscured. Alan gestured with his head and very cautiously, putting down each foot as if it had been made of porcelain, I followed him.

You can remember little of a stalk afterwards, so great is your concentration on moving tortoise-like without any jerks, as near to gliding as you can, slowly, scarcely breathing, avoiding every twig and stone. And the whole ground becomes immediately littered with the most brittle of twigs and with slippery, tinkling stones. I did not have to worry about the wind, that was Alan's job. I did not even have to look at the quarry, only at the ground and at Alan's back. The buffaloes were crowded together so closely that no one could pick out the bulls. At a distance, the only way to distinguish between cows and bulls was by the weight and sweep of the horns.

We halted for several long pauses; Alan was hoping that one of the bulls would disengage himself from the herd and offer a shot. Our last advance brought us to within sixty or seventy yards, an easy shot if one of them would display more of itself than a bit of flank, a tip of horn, a deeper shadow. At last Alan breathed an instruction. One of the buffaloes had moved a little way apart from the others and was standing with its back to us. It had only to turn its head to offer a shot. The neck shot was the best if you trusted your aim, it was nearly always instantaneous, but the target was small.

We waited for a long time, sweating, our rifles raised. This made my arms ache, but I was able to rest my left elbow against the branch of a tree. All the same the sights waved about and the dark patch of the shadowed target came and went within the little v. This was not the right way to shoot a buffalo, and by now I was hoping they would move off. Then the beast did raise its head, slowly, and I held it in the sights and heard Alan breathe 'Now!' There was a crash and then a series of black explosions in the bush ahead. The whole place suddenly erupted with buffaloes. I squeezed myself against the tree as a large black object came straight at me like an enormous rocket, with a great pair of horns stretched forward like a battering-ram. All my instincts were to run for it, but there was no time to run, even to think; an explosion went off in my ear and the buffalo pitched forward and skidded to a halt ten or fifteen yards away. The earth was quivering and drumming and I knew what the thunder of hooves, that well-tried phrase, really meant. Then it was over, the drumming faded and ceased, the earth steadied under our feet. Alan put another shot into the buffalo but it lay still, its neck stretched out. Alan's face was flushed and happy and his eyes shone; the snapping of the tension made us laugh, releasing inside us delight, pride and pleasure to warm our blood; and this we shared. People would spend weeks of discomfort, boredom and even sickness just for a moment like this which passed as quickly as a bird's call and could not be recaptured, but lured you on like a drug to seek it again. Perhaps, I thought, like drugs, this was a vice, to exult over the death of a buffalo that was only trying to escape and probably had not even realized we were behind the tree. Alan was on his heels beside the carcase remarking: 'Not a bad head at all.'

'I missed mine,' I said, feeling suddenly tearful.

'No, you didn't, he went down: but wait here, they play tricks.'

He advanced with caution towards the bush I had fired into, halted, and waved me on. By that time the others had appeared. Tilly was rather cross, having been frightened for my safety rather than her own. John was grinning with satisfaction. My buffalo was lying dead, shot in the neck, and Alan's approval was a more lasting pleasure than the mixed sensation of being in the middle of stampeding buffaloes. But, after all his care, it turned out to be a cow, and so had a worthless head. Alan offered to exchange it for his own, as the hunt had been a joint affair and who shot which beast was mere luck. But I felt puritanical, and refused.

'In any case I don't know what you'd do with a pair of buffalo horns,' Tilly said. 'You could hardly take them to England next year and there really isn't any room in the house.'

Despite its sex, I was full of pride that I had shot a buffalo, although when I came to think it over later, I could not understand why. You required no more skill to shoot a buffalo than to hit a tin can at the same distance. I had not run away, but to do so would have been lunacy, there had not been time and in any case I had been in no real danger with an experienced shot like Alan, prepared for this very contingency, at my side. So I could see no reason for pride in the death of the buffalo and several reasons for regret, since it had not intended to harm me. Yet I continued to feel pride instead of remorse, and the hunt was like the taste of a new, delicious and intoxicating flavour that you crave to enjoy again.

Chapter 29

EVERY night we heard lions, sometimes close by, sometimes farther off across the river. The sound had an arrogant authority unique among animals, and I lay under a blanket thankful I was not a buck or zebra standing by the water's edge with that ominous, compacted grunt stirring the fine hairs in its pricked ears, and with nostrils wide to trap a hint of warning from the eddies of the air. The grunts shifted their direction, coming now from here, now from there, as the lions hunted. Alan said they were instructions, for lions hunted as a team; one would stampede the animals at a watering-place and drive them literally into the jaws of companions lying in wait, and then all would share the meat. To shoot lions, I thought, was fair enough, they preyed on others, and could not complain of being hunted in their turn.

Sometimes the lions would roar in the darkness, not grunt, making the whole air vibrate with their chilly challenge. This was a sound of such majesty, threat and power that it clutched at the very roots of your heart, recalling a primordial terror; the world seemed limitless and all hostile, with nothing better than a skin of canvas stretched between your soft body and a savage universe. Always, for a few moments, this full roar silenced every other sound, even the pinging, gossiping and papery scuffles of the insect world; frogs desisted, no zebra barked, nothing stirred. The whole of nature listened to the lion's assertion of authority. You could imagine shadowy herds frozen in the darkness, fear stopping up their marrows. Then a jackal yelped, an owl hooted, sound flowed back. Perhaps the roar had announced a kill and summoned others to the feast.

Unless, guided by vultures, you were lucky enough to find a fresh kill, there was no way to locate the lions, all you could do was to select a likely spot and put down a kill of your own to attract them. Zebras were their favourite food. Alan shot one about a mile from the river and the porters dragged it into a convenient position in the open, cut some thorn-scrub, and constructed a small stockade, just large enough to hold four people, fifteen or twenty yards away. Any lion, of course, could jump these thorns with ease; the object was not protection but concealment. On expensive, professional safaris the hunters rigged up searchlights that could be switched on to the kill, providing for the clients a moment to aim with certainty. This was considered unsporting, and there was talk of making it illegal. Plain moonlight was notoriously tricky, and this gave the lions the chance inherent in sportsmanship.

We took up our positions just before dark, and knew that we could not stretch our legs again for the best part of twelve hours. Each of us had a loophole in the thorns through which to watch the kill and, if a lion came, cautiously and noiselessly to thrust his rifle. Alan had rubbed boot polish on the barrels to prevent them glinting in the moonlight.

Under the light of a half-moon the kill was clearly visible, its stomach taut and distended with gas, the stripes grey and not black. Soon the bushes assumed their moonlit look of crouching animals. If you took your eyes off them, a few moments later you looked back expecting them to have closed in. Everything was black and grey except the moon itself, and the powdery brilliance of the great fleet of stars that so teased the mind with their numbers, their remoteness, their mystery and their power to stretch the imagination to its breaking point and beyond. Trying to understand the stars could send you mad, I imagined, make your brain burst with groping. I wondered what John thought about them, and envied his capacity to accept their existence without asking why. To ask why, people said, was the basis of civilization; we floated precariously on answers that could never satisfy, and because John and his kind did not ask these questions, they were not our equals. Yet at times I wondered if they were not more sensible merely to accept and enjoy. Certainly in this *boma* John was my superior in patience, in self-control, in strength and probably in courage if it came to be tested. But then his people had not invented the rifle over his knees, whose feel must at least reinforce his fortitude.

My eyes grew tired staring into the bushes and it began to hurt to keep them open. Noises that had at first been separate, sharp and significant blended into a lulling symphony. Innumerable frogs; tree-crickets; the squawk of a bird; a splash from the river; a coughing from the hills; and then a grunt. We stirred at this. Down-river, but some way off. For a few minutes I felt alert again, and then the dulling inertia of a craving for sleep returned.

Mosquitoes pinged in my ears, wholly personal in their animosity. However much you grabbed and slapped at them, they went on and on until sooner or later they pierced your skin with their horrid sharp prick and took a drop of your blood. They liked best of all to get inside your eardrum and ping there like a demented motor-horn, at the topmost limit of the audible scale. Even if twenty lions had been converging on the kill I could not have helped flapping at the mosquitoes. I heard a low protest from Tilly and pulled my sweater over my head. Now I could not see the kill, but at least I could not hear the mosquitoes. Evidently I was not very good at sitting up for the lions, and grew afraid that I would disappoint Alan. He had taken so much trouble, and was so anxious to secure a trophy for us, that I felt immensely grateful, and humble that he should bother about someone so insignificant and fidgety, and so incapable of rewarding his endeavours even by keeping awake.

And, in the event, I dozed through most of the night. At intervals I came to and saw that the moon had changed its position, the bushes had not advanced, the twisted boughs of an acacia were still black against the stars. Once I heard a whisper, felt a nudge from Tilly and was instantly alert, my hand on the rifle, my eyes trying to pierce the greyness of the atmosphere. There was the dead zebra, a great hump with moonlight shining on one of its extended hooves. Its head was stretched towards us and I could see its teeth under bared lips, white as pearls.

The least motion instantly drew your eyes. Something now moved, and a shape advanced round a bush beyond the zebra. Then a hideous cry close at hand made us all twitch, and our hearts jump. A hyena was giving notice of its find. Another shape slid through the darkness to join it and soon we could hear the crunching of jaws and a sort of ugly snuffling. I thought I caught their foetid smell, but this must have been imagination, for the wind had died away. If lions came, they would drive off the hyenas with a few contemptuous snarls and eat their fill while lesser fry waited in the shadows, snapping and complaining but never daring to approach. A little later, a lion shook the night with his roar; close enough, but across the river. Probably they had a hunt on themselves.

A pair of jackals arrived, and for several hours a lot of snappings and snarlings and crunchings came from the kill. I was cramped, stiff and cold but still hopeful, the lions might come at any time, even after dawn. And then it was dawn: the sky turned apricot and smoke-grey beyond the river, light was flooding back into the world. Everything was wet with dew. The hyenas perhaps caught some movement from our *boma*, or perhaps they were just satisfied; they slouched off, turning their heads in a cringing movement. No one loved hyenas, said (wrongly) by Africans to be hermaphrodites, and this pair looked shabby with their ugly high shoulders and spotted coats.

I had heard no kill, and Tilly said that I had slept soundly all night. We drank tea from a thermos and took our separate walks into the bush. Next time, I resolved, I would stay awake at all costs. Next time there would be lions. During the day, the zebra would rot quickly in the heat, and its stink would be sure to attract them. The hyenas had eaten all its insides and most of one flank and side, but there was still plenty left. John and Alan hacked down more branches to cover it against the vultures, and we walked back to camp. Coffee, bacon and eggs tasted even better than usual, and we warmed our stiff limbs in the sunshine and made plans for the day.

Alan sent scouts to look for traces of the lion's own kill. If we could sit up over that, instead of the zebra, we should be almost certain to see them. Through glasses, he picked out an eddy of vultures far away, black specks dropping behind some trees. The tracker went off to investigate and our hopes rose high. But he came back to say that the kill, a grantii, had been all but demolished, and what little was left would be picked clean by vultures during the day. So we fell back on our zebra. By now its flesh was crawling with tiny, writhing maggots, derived from eggs that must have been laid and hatched within twenty-four hours. Such fecundity was alarming. Things were born, lived, bred and died within a few hours. The dry soil seethed with termites, every thorn-bush was alive with ants, each speck of dust held a universe of creatures. Our whole complex, living, galloping, and beautiful zebra would have ceased utterly to be within a day and a night. Its carcase would be absorbed into the bodies of hyenas and jackals, vultures and beetles, and countless millions of maggots that would turn into flies.

This, indeed, was immortality; the body never died, it became part of a cycle that would go on until the end of time, and time itself was endless. In fact the body was more immortal than the soul, which must perish when the maggots ate you, for how could it be broken up? A soul was a personality, and a personality must be a whole. Its only chance of immortality, so far as I could see, was to find its way into a newborn baby as the Kikuyu believed, and, with a sensible economy, to start again. Then we should all have borrowed souls and not be able to create our own, which did not seem to make sense either. I wondered what Alan thought about it all, but did not ask him for fear he would make fun of me. He did not take life, or me, at all seriously. I knew nothing of his real likes and dislikes and ambitions, the things about him no maggots could eat. He talked more to Tilly than to me. They had discussed mutual friends and the future of the country, the breeding of horses, the Indian question, Ramsay MacDonald and Alexander the Great, evidently a hero to Alan. Tilly said he was nothing but a power-hungry tyrant who had killed tens of thousands of people and destroyed fertile civilizations for no purpose but his own vanity, but Alan defended him. The civilizations were rotten and had to be toppled over to make way for sturdier growths, and such was his genius that, two thousand years later, his name was respected in every country in the world. Perhaps in the core of his heart Alan wanted to be like Alexander, and tread the world underfoot. But, at the moment, money seemed to be his need. He wanted to save five hundred pounds and then go round the world, seeing remote places of which I had never even heard. Clearly he was one of the children of Abel.

'I shall do it one day,' he said. 'The Beelers were a start. Now others are coming.' He pulled out a sheet torn from an American magazine bearing pictures of his safari, one with a big lion skin in the centre, a Beeler on each side and Alan standing beside Mrs Beeler looking dark, manly and rather self-satisfied.

The people he most envied were the elephant hunters of a generation ago who had come upon regions as big as whole countries where no shot had ever been fired. So innocent were the beasts that a hunter could empty his rifle's magazine two or three times over into a herd, killing with each shot. before they took alarm. These hunters had made fortunes out of ivory, they had lived for and by themselves, with no one to defer to, no laws to obey. Now, he said, even on safari, there were game laws to be observed, regulations about porters, closed areas, protected species, District Commissioners.

The world was shrinking, soon there would be safaris with lorries and cars, one day even aeroplanes. The best of Africa was already gone.

When the time came to take up our positions in the *boma* again we dowsed our handkerchiefs with eau de Cologne, supplied by Tilly, to counteract the stink of rotting flesh.

'I suppose to the hyenas the kill smells like a delicious cut of roast beef and Yorkshire pudding,' Alan observed, 'whereas eau de Cologne is nauseating. It all depends on your point of view.'

At first I thought I should be sick, and certainly unable to sit through a whole night with the foetid stench turning my stomach. But gradually we got used to it, at least to the extent of overcoming nausea. Surely every lion within miles must smell this zebra? But if they smelt it, they did not come. We had another wasted night, full of discomfort. Tilly was more patient and philosophical than I. She had come not to shoot a lion, but just in case she missed anything.

We had only two days left. Hyenas finished off the zebra and Alan decided not to try another kill. Sometimes, he said, you had to go on like this for six or seven nights. You nearly always got your chance in the end, but we lacked time. The tracker said that a pride of five lions was lying up in a dry watercourse running from some nearby hills into the Tana. The gully was too thick to beat, and he had not been able precisely to locate the lions' resting-place, so it was an off-chance, but worth trying.

The tracker found fresh traces of a lion in the gully and we felt them to be near, perhaps even to be watching us from a hidden rock as we watched giraffe and eland browsing among thorn-trees, until a tick-bird squawked a warning and the eland vanished with their dewlaps swaying. We returned to camp weary and defeated, and that night were subdued. Only one more day remained. Once, Alan said, he had spotted five separate lions in the open in a single morning, all close to our present camp. It was just luck.

Tilly's feet were sore and she wanted to spend a day in camp for a change, and I was glad to be on my own with Alan.

302

I could not talk to him while Tilly was there. She had the knack of tapping every conversational nail on the head deftly, without effort; even before she had spoken, people often smiled and made up their minds to be amused. But now Alan was preoccupied with the search for game, and had more to say to John than to me. Not that he was unfriendly, just rather silent. Silence in some people meant that they had nothing to say, in others that their minds ran to thoughts before words. The first lot were dull, the second all the more interesting, and Tilly knew infallibly which was which before she had been five minutes in their company. I could never make up my mind, and when I did was often wrong, and Tilly said I lacked discrimination.

'As it's our last chance we might as well make a day of it,' Alan said. 'Can you foot-slog a long way?'

'I think so. My blisters have healed.'

'I don't want your mother to tick me off for wearing you out.'

'She'd be more likely to tick *me* off for being worn.'

'At any rate you can walk, which is more than can be said for some of my clients.'

'Oh, well ... it doesn't seem a very exciting accomplishment.'

'You mustn't get carried away by a passion for excitement,' Alan warned me. 'That's what my sister did, and look at her.'

'She may be having a wonderful time.'

'With a Portuguese wine salesman who's probably tight half the time?'

'Well, if she's in love with him ...'

'Love, my foot. She just wanted to get away from home. Not that I blame her for that, but she chose an idiotic way.'

'She couldn't go off and be a hunter or run a farm or something, like you. It's unfair.'

'So are most things, I suppose.'

Alan lost interest in the subject and strode forward with his eyes alert for the flick of a tail, the tip of a pricked ear. We scrambled across gullies and round clumps of waitabit thorn, we searched through glasses and even climbed trees to get a better view, we came upon a recent kill, but we never saw a lion. We returned dispirited, and yet it had been an exciting day.

On the last part of our journey, in the evening near the river, everything was coming to life. Reedbuck whistled and bounded away, we surprised a herd of leaping red impala, grey wildebeeste were filing down to the water and, as we rounded a bend, we saw across the wide stream a herd of elephants drinking. Some were knee-deep in the river, spraying themselves with their trunks. A cow edged her baby down to the brink with her tusks and pushed it in; it gave a little squeal, and then splashed about half in alarm, half in pleasure. A big bull stood on the bank surveying his wives like some benign and portly pasha taking his harem to an outing, and watching with kindly condescension their foolish but endearing female sport. In slanting sunlight the greenery of trees reflected in placid water contrasted with the pinkish colour of the great beasts – they must have enjoyed a dust-bath earlier in the day – and the scene was one of peace and tranquillity.

His eyes on the bull's tusks, Alan softly commented: 'At least ninety pounds, I'd say.' We had no elephant licence, and I was suddenly thankful. Otherwise that kingly, unsuspecting bull would have fallen trumpeting in agony; all would have been confusion, noise, fear and pain, and the baby elephants now splashing in the shallows would have huddled in panic under the bellies of their frantic mothers. It did not seem like sport – the shot would have been easy and without danger. And then those polished tusks would have been chopped out, carried away and turned into images of elephants crossing a humped bridge, or into billiard balls. Better the live, peaceful elephants disporting themselves in the river, than all the ivory imitations in the world.

We watched them until the sun withdrew and the blue dusk began to fall and Alan gave a sign to John, who led us quietly on a detour towards our camp.

'I'm glad you couldn't shoot them,' I said.

'Good tusks going begging,' Alan replied; but then, to my surprise, added: 'All the same, I never like it when I have to break up a herd. They're so intelligent. If one gets wounded, the others will often help him get away, using their tusks, and stay with him till he dies. They know what's happened – they use reason.'

'Then why kill them?'

'Ivory's sixteen shillings a pound. And if I don't someone else will.'

Our detour brought us back to the river as the light was fading and there, standing with his head raised and his fringed ears erect, a big waterbuck faced us, his curving, powerful horns black against a sky of deepening lavender. He looked larger than life, monumental, his nose thrust forward like a ship's figurehead, and I could just make out the creamy marking of his muzzle and the curious white rims round his eyes. He stood alone in the open, defenceless and beautiful, proud and male. In the whisper of the river rippling over sandbanks, in the evening call of francolins and in the quietness of the air he could read a message denied to me; one shot would have destroyed forever all the magic and the mystery, and left a kicking carcase in the bloodstained grass.

Alan breathed in my ear. 'Good head. Aim low.' But I did not raise the rifle. There was the waterbuck and there was I: each of us the temporary possessor of a little seed of life that, so instantly and easily crushed, would leave us equal in a mess of blood and bone. Who was I, a sharer in this mystery, to annihilate a seed that no one, nothing, could ever restore? To destroy a splendour I could never create, a mystery I could never fathom? Hadn't the waterbuck as much right as I to live out his life in his native country, cropping the grasses under the stars, drinking at morning and evening in the river, mating with his does at the call of the seasons, fearing the lion, dreading the bitter smell of men, savouring the sweet new growth after rain, dozing in thickets in the heat of the day? I was standing suddenly, it seemed, upon the brink of a whole new concept of the world where everything was upside down and rearranged, as if I was looking for the first time at a familiar scene with the eye of a bird or a cricket. Things I had taken for granted looked false and stupid, things that I had never seen at all obvious and certain.

'Quick,' Alan murmured in my ear. I shook my head slightly and felt a movement; he was raising his rifle to his shoulder.

'No, don't,' I said aloud, my voice sharp as a rifle shot. The waterbuck threw back his splendid horns and in a single motion turned and sprang; I saw him leap twice more, a flash of white under his tail and then his dark shape had dissolved into the shadows.

'What's the idea?' Alan asked.

'I just thought ... one can't eat waterbuck, anyway.'

'No, but you might have got a record head.'

Yesterday this chance would have excited me, now I had no regrets, but it was impossible to explain what had happened. Yet without my trying to do so, I think Alan understood.

'Well, let him go,' he said, slinging his rifle on to his shoulder.

'I don't think I want any more trophies.'

'If we ran into a lion, though, you would.' I was not sure. 'Jock Cameron told me of a place he stumbled on just before the war,' Alan added. 'At the back of beyond, tsetse country, even native poachers hadn't been there, or ivory hunters. So the animals had never seen a man at all, even smelt one. He said a kongoni came right up to him, within a few yards, to see what he was. It must have been a queer experience, the tommy and impala and oribi and even the eland, he said, walking up like dogs. A sort of Garden of Eden before the fall. And when he pointed his rifle at them, they did nothing, just stared.'

'But he didn't shoot them?'

'The porters had to eat.'

That was our last evening by the Tana, although we had three days' march to reach home. The porters carried our trophies in place of the maize-flour they had eaten. I took a photograph of them in a row, holding up heads and skins, and was no longer sure whether to feel proud or ashamed. The buffaloes, the eland and impala, the oryx and grantii and an earlier, unluckier waterbuck, what did they represent? Some effort in the stalking, a little steadiness when it came to the shot, and the pitting of wits, people said, against the creature's – a contest, surely, absurdly unfair. On our side, our boasted and evolved intelligence, a rifle that would kill from a quarter of a mile away, binoculars that would magnify by eight or ten the strength of the eye; on theirs, nothing but nose, ears, eyes and a profound sense of fear. The trophies now seemed mockeries, but I did not want to hurt Alan's feelings; they were the sum of his achievement, and so to me they had a value after all.

I asked him what he did with all his own heads.

'I only keep the ones I can sell.'

'But who buys them?'

'The safari firms. They use them to fill gaps in their clients' lists.'

'You mean the clients *buy* heads?'

'Not half. No sense in going back to Cincinnati without the buffalo you're entitled to, and have paid good dollars for, what's more. Or the kudu or eland. If you can shoot one, so much the better; if you're unlucky, the folks back home won't know, so long as you've got a pair of horns to show.'

'But that's not sport!'

'No; it's business.'

This shocked me deeply, but after I had thought it over I asked Alan whether any of my trophies would be saleable. I could not restore them to life, I needed money and had nowhere to put them, so they might as well be turned into cash.

'That waterbuck you gave a free pardon to would have done nicely. The impala might just qualify, the rest are too small.'

'I'm not going to kill any more animals,' I said.

'You're going to be a vegetarian?'

'I don't know. I hadn't thought about that.'

'If you eat beef, someone has to kill the bullock. There's no real difference whether you do it, or whether someone else does it for you.'

'There *is* a difference. I don't know what it is, but I'm sure there is one.'

'Well, you think about it,' Alan said, 'and tell me.'

My last memory of our safari was one of song. We climbed back across the Ithanga hills and dropped down to the McKays' at evening with the westering sun in our faces and long, narrow shadows prancing over the rocks and scrub behind. For a few minutes, just before the sun sank, a curious red-gold light, almost claret-coloured, immersed the hillside and ourselves. The porters were singing, as all porters did when they approached their journey's end and knew their wives, their beds, their pay and their familiar food awaited them. It was less a song than a chant recording the fierce beasts they had slain, the terrible distances they had conquered, the testing hardships, the strength of their limbs and the courage of their hearts. Nevertheless it was melancholy, its cadences rose and fell like waves lapping a deserted beach on the coast of Coromandel or some other faraway, forgotten shore. In part, perhaps, it was a dirge for the days that were gone, for death that had crept those few paces nearer, stealthy as a leopard, while they had been away. When I asked John to translate, however, there proved to be nothing sad about the words at all.

'They say that bwana is brave like a lion and cunning like a buffalo,' he reported, 'that the memsabus walk like girls going to a dance, and that they, the porters, are stronger than askaris, stronger than elephants, and have trodden on dangers like beetles. They are saying also,' he added with delicacy, 'that when they get home they will be like drums that play all night, or like gourds with beans in them used as rattles, and that when their wives shake these gourds, the beans will germinate.'

And so they sang their way through the golden light as it faded, a file of men striding down the hill, the sad cadences of their chant dying out among rocks within the dark ravine, until the journey ended and they flung their loads down on the McKays' lawn and crowded round to shake our hands and say good-bye.

Chapter 30

TILLY had left the forest farm for the time being and gone to live at Piggery Nook. This was on the plains below, where Lord Delamere had installed a pipeline to carry water from the hills to a stretch of country that, while potentially fertile, lacked rivers or springs. It had therefore been uninhabited, except intermittently by wild animals. After installing the pipeline, Delamere had chopped the plain into units of manageable size and sold their leaseholds, quite cheaply, to aspiring farmers.

Tilly had not bought a leasehold, but she had joined with two or three others to rent some of the land for three years. Clearing at Njoro was proving so expensive and slow that they had to find some other source of income to finance the development of their forest land. Their intention was to grow maize on the pipeline for three years, by which time they hoped to have prepared enough land of their own to make a living.

So Tilly and her partners had bought oxen and ploughed a thousand acres of plain, and were now planting the maize. In order to supervise operations, Tilly had moved down there to live in a couple of *bandas* built in as many days beside a clump of wattle trees. The only other building in sight was a long mud-and-wattle shed for the pigs she hoped to fatten on some of the maize. They lived, like her, on pipeline water, and were destined for a bacon factory that had been started near Nairobi.

Robin was still in Tanganyika where the mineral prospects, he wrote, were promising, and on top of that he had heard of an opportunity to acquire for next to nothing some wonderful land on which a fortune could be made, beyond the shadow of doubt, out of Turkish tobacco. It was two hundred miles from the nearest railway, but the new line would cut this distance by half, and whereas even a mere hundred miles would be too far for ordinary tobacco, the Turkish variety was so much more valuable that it would stand the cost of wagon transport on its head. The door of the ground floor, in fact, was opening, and Robin was staying in Tanganyika to make sure of getting through.

Meanwhile Tilly's life on the pipeline was strenuous. She was up by sunrise to muster the labour and get the ox-teams to work, and at night sat amid a cloud of insects entering the costs of everything in neatly ruled account books. In the dry season heat, dust and flies were oppressive, and scorching winds blew across the veld. Tilly got used to these, but never to the thunderstorms that, in the rains, burst with unrestrained ferocity. The lightning was forked and vicious; great crackling tongues lashed the earth, blasting any men or oxen in its path. While thunder seemed to crack the universe the dogs cowered beneath her camp bed and Tilly, huddled under a coat on top, knitted feverishly, to soothe her nerves. There must have been many thunderstorms, for she made me two sweaters and Robin several pairs of socks. Her thatched roof leaked so badly that she lived in a quagmire; this, she said, had the advantage of drowning the ticks. A woman visitor who came to lunch one day searched in vain for a mirror, and only then did Tilly realize that she had not got one in the place, except in the lid of her powder compact.

On Sunday mornings Tilly rode up to the forest farm, about ten miles away, to receive a report from Njombo, who greeted her always with enthusiasm, told her that everything was going magnificently in his competent hands and then revealed, item by item, a great many mishaps, troubles and *shauris*. The house was occupied by a family of strangers. One day, in Nakuru, Tilly heard of a couple called Baird whose house, with all their possessions, had been destroyed by fire. She wrote off immediately to offer them the use of hers, rent free, for as long as they liked. They arrived with three children, several dogs, a goat, two ponies, a parrot and all they had been able to save from the fire, namely a Chinese fire screen, some coffee spoons, a clockwork train, a collection of sea shells and a trouser press. Tilly fitted them out in her own clothes, as well as in mine and Robin's, and even lent them Kigorro to cook. The Bairds stayed about six months.

Tilly's sympathy did not entirely wither but it wore a little thin when the children, wishing perhaps to repeat a stimulating experience, set fire to the maize-store, when the goat ate the tops of her young trees and when Mrs Baird complained of boltless doors, lack of space and her fear of finding a snake in the privy. As Tilly said, it wasn't even as if she had lent them her second-best house; it was her best one.

Piggery Nook, when I returned for the holidays, was in a frenzy of planting. Tilly had acquired two ox-drawn contraptions which dibbled the seed into the ground, two rows at a time, and was planting maize for other farmers under contract, as well as for her own syndicate. The teams were inspanned by the light of safari lamps at five o'clock in the morning, so as to get the work done before the heat of the day. Thunderstorms came seldom now and a new anxiety had appeared, that the rains would peter out early and leave the young maize plants to wilt and yellow in a scorching sun.

Robin arrived unexpectedly one afternoon while a storm growled over the lake, a wind blew, but no rain actually fell. He looked brown and tattered, emerged stiffly from the old car and said: 'Oh, hallo, Tilly. Everything all right? I've got a beastly blister on my toe.'

'You haven't *walked* from Tanganyika, I hope?'

'That last pair of socks you knitted me was awfully nice, but seemed to have a lump in them somewhere.'

'I expect that was an extra loud crack of thunder. Have you had a good time?'

'I don't know about good; we had a lot of trouble with that friend of Walter's, and Walter himself's a queer fish to go on this sort of trip with. If he saw a girl he liked the look of, with heaps of beads and ornaments, he'd stop and ask if he could paint her, of course there's no word for that in Swahili and everyone jumped to the obvious conclusion; they either rushed forward asking for twelve heifers and a thousand shillings, or they looked sinister and fingered their guns – they nearly all have muzzle-loaders down there. I thought at any minute I should have to dig half a pound of rusty nails or a length of lead piping out of his guts.'

'You must need some tea,' Tilly suggested.

'Another thing, Walter's got second sight, or so he claims, and saw a lot of German officers walking about a tumbled-down old fort, holding themselves stiff as pokers he said – corsets I suppose – and the men shooting dice beside an old grave. It was rather uncanny.'

'It seems a long way to go for a good haunt, you could have stayed in Scotland and gone to Glamis. Is it raining hard in Tanganyika? The rains should come on here.'

'Most of it was pretty dry, but you must come and see that country south of Iringa; it's absolutely first-rate land, and rivers literally every mile or so, like veins on your hand. There's a Greek down there experimenting with every crop under the sun, and the best of all, he's found, is Turkish tobacco. It grows absolutely like a weed.'

'I always thought tobacco *was* one,' Tilly said.

'Another thing, it's top quality; this Greek fellow sent samples to London and I saw the reports with my own eyes. They were simply glowing. The finest flavoured leaf, they said ...'

Robin was well launched on his tobacco and did not ask about Tilly's maize, which I think hurt her feelings, she had been working at it so hard. But she gave him tea, and listened to the tobacco being praised, and to his opinion that it simply could not fail to make the fortune of anyone who got in on the ground floor. He had brought us both presents: for Tilly, a pretty native basket, skilfully woven and dyed, the skin of a giant lizard, and some seeds of a plant whose name he had forgotten given to him by the wife of a Lutheran missionary; for me, an ivory bangle and a stuffed baby crocodile.

'I'm afraid the crocodile won't be much use,' he said, 'but it's a real one, and as there are no shops, only a few little *dukas*, and hardly any people, it's rather a difficult place to do any shopping in.'

A few days later we rode up to the forest farm, now vacated by the Bairds, delighted to be going back to our own home. The hyraxes were out in force that night to welcome us and screeched wildly at the moon in a full-throated chorus that drowned the frogs in the *vlei*. Rain-birds were pouring forth their liquid notes at dawn next morning, green bee-eaters darting in and out of the red bank and the limpid double call of the anvil-bird seemed like the very voice of the sweet-smelling cedars and the dew-soaked grass.

Now that maize had been planted on the pipeline, some other crop was needed for the land cleared at so high a cost and so much effort on the forest boundary – something that would pay in small quantities, not a cereal calling for thousand-acre fields. Many ideas were collected, discussed, pondered over and set aside. At last Tilly hit upon an altogether new suggestion: almond trees. These flourished in South Africa, their fruit was in demand and its price high enough to enable a successful almond planter to make a living from a few acres.

Letters were at once despatched in all directions to research stations, Government departments, horticulturists and merchants and in due course – not very quickly, in the days before air mails – the sitting-room filled up with leaflets, books, memoranda and letters from places as far afield as Dalmatia, Australia, California and even Japan. The more we read about almonds, the more promising they appeared to be, and in our clearing in the bush we visualized an orchard covered with pink blossom, murmurous with bees, faintly Persian in its associations, wealth-producing and full of potentialities for interior decoration. Tilly said we should have to put a single twig in a plain vase on the writing-table and have no other flowers, or even pictures, in the room.

Almond trees proved to belong to several different varieties which, in a plantation, had to be mixed together in order to ensure cross-pollination. A large consignment of young trees of correctly balanced kinds arrived from South Africa. With high hopes these were carefully planted at the right distances apart, and enclosed in a wire fence to keep out buck. After that we had to wait three or four years before harvesting a sizeable crop. Beans and potatoes, meanwhile, could be grown between the rows, porkers and maize were to tide us over at Piggery Nook, and Tilly was starting to build up a small herd of future dairy cows. It was a matter of great regret to me that I should not be able to see the flowering of the almonds: although I hoped, my enforced education over, to return in time for the first crop.

The little trees survived the journey, and took root. Walking through their straight lines I envisaged a pink dust of bloom against a limpid sky, a tracery of arching branches, delicately-flavoured nuts cupped in their soft green shells, and dreamed of kimonos, tea gardens and flowered parasols. Alas, none of this was to be. The trouble was not that the almonds failed to thrive, it was that they throve too well. They found the soil so nourishing that they grew and grew, and would not go dormant once a year, as almonds should: or if they did, each tree decided for itself when to take its rest. This was fatal for the pollination, which required a simultaneous blossoming. The graceful pink flowers did indeed appear, and in profusion, but now on one tree and now on the next, with the result that the bloom, however beautiful, was barren. In three years, Tilly harvested seven pounds of nuts. To make matters worse, these were so favourably reported on in London that, had the trees flowered all at once, her rosiest hopes of reward would have been realized.

Tilly did not despair; there must be some way, she believed, to make the almond trees embark upon a simultaneous dormancy. After more consultation with experts, she pruned the whole orchard with extreme severity, just before the rains. And the trees responded: they burst into flower all at once. The difficulty seemed to be surmounted, and Tilly could at last expect a reward. At the height of their flowering, a vicious rainstorm stripped each branch and twig of every vestige of bloom. Not a single nut was harvested. It was too much; sadly, she had the almonds rooted out and destroyed.

Everything at Njoro was a matter of trial and error. Tilly planted peaches and plums, apples and raspberries, cherries and mountain pawpaws, to see what happened. Some thrived and some failed. All alike suffered from the depredations of birds, and especially mouse-birds: drab, mud-brown creatures with long trailing tails, guttersnipes of the avian world. Their claws could tear to shreds anything edible and even, it seemed, deal with wire netting, for they were always getting into the fruit cage. They avoided traps and succumbed only to poison, and this Tilly banned because of its indiscriminate cruelty. Hawks they respected, but managed to evade.

Nevertheless, Tilly reasoned, they must at least be afraid of hawks, and this gave her an idea. Robin shot a hawk, and Tilly had it stuffed and tied to the top of a pole beside the fruit cage. It had a most intimidating effect upon the mouse-birds, and enabled her to harvest a good crop of peaches and plums. But they were cunning birds; after a while they tumbled to the dodge, and no doubt derived an extra pleasure from squawking insults, as they fluttered by, at the impotent dummy, on their way to strip Tilly's orchard.

After our return to the forest farm, the drought hardened. At Piggery Nook the young maize plants were wilting, grain was getting scarce and expensive, the pigs leaner and hungrier. Grass in the Rift Valley was already brown and withered, and fires were consuming what little grazing remained. At night we could see these fires winking like cigar ends in the dark. They had a wicked, sinister look as they blinked away on distant hillsides, killing with the utmost cruelty innumerable creatures, from snakes and mongooses to beetles and mice, immolating helpless tortoises and newborn gazelles, in fact every living object too weak or slow to break through the flame barrier; and killing also, by delayed effect, thousands of sheep and cattle whose search for the least surviving leaf or thorn-branch must end in death from starvation.

In the wake of these fires, the countryside was blasted like a witch's heath and the gaunt, black arms of skeleton trees were raised as if in a bleak anger to the skies. By day, heavy plumes of smoke half obscured the valley, and in and out of them great flocks of cranes, storks, kites and other predators darted and lived on the panic-stricken creatures until the birds became too gorged for flight. Such fires were dangerous to men as well as to beasts. One evening, when we had been counting the red glows from a window, Tilly remarked: 'I hope your friend Walter cleared a firebreak round his house. That time we stayed with them, I thought it was very risky to let all that long grass grow right up to the door.'

Robin agreed, and said he supposed Walter would not have been such a fool as to leave it.

'I must go down and see him soon,' he added. 'I ought to hear any day now about that Tanganyika lease. Heaven only knows why they've taken so long. These Government departments ...' Robin was hoping that Walter would share his enterprise in Turkish tobacco, when he had negotiated a lease for the dirt-cheap land.

It was strange that Tilly should have spoken about Walter just then, because a day or two later Robin came back from Nakuru with a shocking tale. A grass fire had swept across Walter's land, jumped a firebreak, caught the thatch and totally consumed the homestead. And inside those gaily painted rondavels the flames had trapped Kate, her sister Freda and the daughter who was home from school.

Walter had gone to their rescue and managed to pull Freda out in time, but Kate and the daughter had perished. And Walter himself, dragged clear, unconscious, by Africans, had died of burns on his way to hospital. Only Freda had survived, and she was badly mutilated.

This fearful news, scarcely to be grasped immediately, silenced us all. At last Tilly said: 'There's the boy, I suppose, away at school. We could have him here, I should think; I don't suppose he's got any other relations.'

'I don't know of any,' Robin agreed.

'At any rate we could find out.'

Robin said that he would go to Nairobi to interview the headmaster. I could see that the pleasure he had been drawing from his plans for a new enterprise had been tarnished, for Walter and Tanganyika had been closely interwoven in his mind.

'There's something rather odd about it,' Tilly added. She sometimes brought a sixth sense to bear upon events and characters, and had a way of leaping over logic and appearances into the hidden heart of an affair. And so it proved now. Robin was away for three days, and on his return said to Tilly: 'It looks as if this dreadful business of Walter is even worse than it seemed at first.'

'I don't see how it can be,' Tilly replied.

'There's a theory that Kate deliberately committed suicide.'

'Surely not in that way!'

'Well, of course, it's a job to sort out rumours from facts, and it's being hushed up for the sake of the boy. But the story is that Walter got back one evening unexpectedly and found no Kate, only Freda in a panic. She told him that Kate was feeling seedy and had gone to bed with a poached egg. Walter found her in bed all right, but not with a poached egg.'

'Oh. You mean ... But Walter must have known what was going on.'

'He must have been the only man in the country who didn't. The story is he cut up rough, threw Harry out and beat Kate till she was practically senseless. A few days later she packed her bags and went to Harry, saying she'd done with Walter for good.'

But this had not suited Harry's book at all, according to the story. Dalliance on the shores of Lake Naivasha was one thing, responsibility for an hysterical Kate, and the end of his marriage, quite another. Harry had tried to send her back to Walter and had believed, as he put it, that she had seen reason. Indeed she had gone back, but not for long, because she had set fire to the place with herself and her daughter in it. People said that she had given her daughter sleeping-pills first and herself drunk half a bottle of whisky, but how they could have known was a mystery, and perhaps they had invented it to make the end of Kate and her daughter seem a little more bearable.

I found it impossible to realize that people we had known and stayed with, who had appeared so normal, friendly and fond of life, should have been impelled by the strength of such inscrutable emotions to perform so terrible an act, and that everything of theirs – the paintings, the absurd stuffed beasts and jokes, the heavy Teutonic furniture, the books and photographs – everything should have been wiped out as if they had never existed, leaving only Freda, who had seemed unimportant, and, of course, the unknown boy.

Tilly was distressed about the dogs, who had perished also. All humans, she thought, were guilty of something, even if they had not deserved so dreadful a fate, but why should animals who were innocent suffer for human stupidities and sins? Robin saw the headmaster, but the boy stayed on at school and Freda was expected to get well enough to take care of him. Or perhaps it would be for him to take care of her, so severe had been her injuries. In the end she did recover, returned to the farm and had a small house built there, and a stone cairn put up as a memorial. Years later I tried to find this cairn, but grass and bush had overcome it, or else rain, wind and sun had dispersed the stones.

Chapter 31

THE drought went on. At night the distant fires crept and writhed like caterpillars up the hills, consuming all living creatures save the fleetest of foot. Their cruelty was absolute, and yet they were beautiful. By day smoke billowed up from the valley and dust devils danced across it, forming and vanishing with the waywardness of dreams and sucking up blackened branches, withered grass, bones of dead birds, anything in their path. Even our forest river shrank to a muted trickle over the stones.

The disaster to Kate and Walter upset us all and started off a chain of lesser disasters. Some animal, a mongoose perhaps or a ratel – we hoped not Genet – got into the hen shed and bit the heads off all Tilly's cherished birds. On the pipeline, all the maize on which so much depended turned yellow and could not long survive. Njombo's second wife had a dead baby and would have died herself had not Tilly sat up all night applying rough and ready but effective treatment. A grade bull, bought to cross with our native cows, died mysteriously. The cause might have been a poisonous plant or it might have been a Kikuyu *fitina* involving the herdsman; to destroy someone else's property in order to get him into trouble would be a familiar gambit. *Fitinas* broke out like boils everywhere, tempers grew short, Robin's veld sores returned, the ponies went lame, many other trials arose as if a spirit sought malicious satisfaction in tormenting us all. The Kikuyu certainly put it all down to the umbrage of ancestral spirits, and this seemed as good an explanation as any.

318

The worst of drought was that you were so helpless. You had to watch crops perishing, animals growing thinner and weaker and eventually dying, unable to do anything to help them survive. One day when we were riding back from the station a pair of duikers walked ahead of us for about half a mile too weak even to jump off the track and hide. Tilly's mind, eager always to ameliorate rather than to repine, turned to thoughts of future irrigation, and one day we set off to visit a family said to grow vegetables and soft fruits in this way. They were delighted to show us asparagus and crisp-hearted lettuces, celery and broccoli, strawberries and figs whose quality was superb; their trouble was to sell them. A journey of forty miles over rough tracks, or roads that often degenerated into a chain of potholes, cost more than the produce ultimately fetched.

We drove back both inspired and baffled by the idea of irrigation, and stopped for dinner on our way home with a neighbour who was building himself a handsome stone house. He was a Bostonian called Billy Sewall who, during his travels, had acquired two Chinese servants. These silent men, wifeless and totally estranged from their compatriots, had brought with them only their kimonos and their coffins, in which their employer had promised to return them to Canton should they die in his service. We had a meal by our standards wonderfully luxurious and sophisticated, and wine from goblets tinted the colour of sunshine, and bumped our way home rather late, rotund with satisfaction. Kigorro came out, as usual, with a lamp, but said at once that something had happened.

'To do with the dogs?' Tilly asked quickly. She had left Bluebell in the office nursing a litter of month-old pups. With puppies, chicks or anything defenceless she was always nervous of the warrior ants who emerged from the ground just before and during the rains in great black, writhing, ruthless torrents, all the more terrifying because the countless creatures of which these were composed, equipped with vicious biting jaws, were not only sterile and sexless but quite blind, and flowed on towards their secret destination in response to instincts or directions no human being could sense or understand.

'No, not *siafu*,' Kigorro said. 'A bad thing, memsabu. I do not know how it was possible, I heard nothing, I saw no strangers, yet somehow there has been a thief . . .'

He led the way to the office where Bluebell and her puppies had been, but were no longer, at least in any recognizable shape. There was blood and disorder everywhere. The drawers of the desk had been emptied, papers were strewn about, everything had been flung out and trampled on not merely in search of money but in a desperate fight. Bluebell had defended her puppies as best she could. Kigorro had gathered up what was left of them, and of their mother, in a blood-soaked cardboard box.

'And there is something else,' Kigorro said. From the box he pulled a limp spotted body with a long, ringed, bushy tail. The head had been severed, but apart from that the body had not been mutilated. I took it stupidly, only half understanding. It was quite cold.

'He came from the forest after you had gone,' Kigorro said, 'and was with his friend, Bluebell. Perhaps he was asleep here, in the corner. And when the thief attacked his friend, he tried to help her. But he could not do so.'

Genet had often used the office as a sleeping-place when he returned from visits to the forest, which had lately become more frequent and prolonged. We thought he had a family there, and lived half wild and half free. He had strong, sharp claws, and I hoped that he had been able to mark his murderer before he died.

'It was a quick end,' Tilly said consolingly. Perhaps neither Genet nor Bluebell had suffered more than a few final moments of terror. Genet, I knew, had done his best, but I had failed him when he needed me and could not tell him of my sorrow and gratitude. He had never shown me anything but trust and love. He shared a grave with Bluebell and the pathetic remnants of her pups.

An inquiry was, of course, held next morning. Many theories were advanced, reports of strangers seen upon the farm delivered, and everyone united in blaming some unknown person of an evil tribe, not a Kikuyu. But Tilly was not convinced. Strangers did not wander about unnoticed, nothing had been taken from the office, nor had the rest of the house been searched.

The quarrel between Kigorro and the man who had stolen his wife had not ended, and never would end so long as either was alive. The fact that we had heard no more since Gitende's thwarted attempt to get Kigorro arrested for the murder of a Dorobo did not mean that nothing had taken place. If Gitende had failed once, he would certainly try again to undo Kigorro, and Tilly had been half expecting some such attempt to break through the crust that sealed off so much of the Kikuyu life from our own.

It was known that Kigorro was in charge of the dogs. What better way to get him into trouble than to attack him through his charges, and so present him to Tilly as one who had betrayed his trust? She might even suspect him of committing the offence himself. At the least she would convict him of failing to prevent it, and perhaps dismiss him from his post and send him out a wanderer, landless and shamed. That, at any rate, was how Kikuyu minds worked, and Tilly knew them well enough to follow, at least so far, their tortuous ramifications. They had put into her head thoughts she could not have avoided had she herself been a Kikuyu. Being a European, she did not blame Kigorro, but her trust in Njombo, Gitende's half-brother, was blemished. Not that there was a shred of evidence to link him to the disaster, but in Kikuyu matters evidence was the last thing that ever could be found, or probably would be relevant had it been forthcoming.

There was only one way to explore these labyrinths, however imperfectly, and that was by experiencing the subtlest possible responses to the slightest possible hints and nuances of attitude, of tone of voice; by finding a way into the thickets of calculating minds as a skilled tracker will find a way through forest by the faintest of half-imagined game paths. All this was something quite outside the scope of law as we understood it, and to attempt to apply the English legal system to the Kikuyu was to grope for the scent of spices with a dockyard crane. The mystery of poor Bluebell and her brood was never solved, and for a long time Tilly could not enter the office without blowing her nose, and I mourned for Genet, who had given his trust to human beings and been betrayed at the end.

The drought continued, every day the sick parade lengthened, there was a case of suspected anthrax, blight attacked the roses, people quarrelled, everything went wrong. At this disenchanted moment, Tilly received a letter that in better times she would perhaps have laughed at, but which now gave her and Robin cause to think. It was from Hilary, full of phrases that tinkled with his oblique wit, and after depicting for them both a lumpish future as a couple of dulled, brutish colonials conversing only about the qualities of muck and the faults of natives – merely one's own faults, he wrote, seen in a distorting mirror – he offered them a new life in an old land. 'By now, surely,' he wrote, 'you must be sickened of the narrowness, restrictions and conventions of a new country and anxious for the freedom, adventure and scope for initiative of the old. You spoke sometimes of making a fortune; how do you expect to do so among those who have nothing of their own? Fortunes are made among the rich, not among the penniless; and the rich are here, not among your naked savages and lions.' He had sold his place in Ireland, he added, and bought a small estate in Sussex; and he offered Robin the job of running it, and Tilly the opportunity to help him entertain and manage his household.

It was indeed a tempting offer. For Robin it would mean a congenial security, for Tilly a chance to shine in a finer society than Njoro's. Farming was in her blood and she would still be concerned with it, in a country where people did not slash to death defenceless puppies, where she would not have to deal with a constant succession of burnt babies and miscarriages in dark huts amid heathen spells, where a year's effort was not wiped out by an extremist climate, where ticks and *siafu* and veld sores were unknown.

They talked it over a great deal. Robin, I think, was less tempted than Tilly; he knew that the meticulous management of estate accounts was not his *métier*, Tanganyika was calling, and perhaps, too, an unspoken, indeed unrecognized, jealousy of Hilary had its influence. Hilary was rich, accomplished, intelligent, well-friended, amusing and attached to Tilly; their

322

minds set each other off, their wit played on the surface of their conversation like sunlight on ruffled water. But Robin did not argue against the proposal; on the whole he spoke for it, and mentioned courses in estate management.

'I think the life would suit you,' he said. 'There's something in what Hilary says about the rich, I daresay. Although I do think if I can get this lease in Tanganyika ...'

'We couldn't leave the dogs,' Tilly objected.

'We could take them.'

'They'd loathe the quarantine. And it's no good living among the rich if one's poor oneself. Sussex is full of rich business men.'

'As Hilary says, that might be better than poor business men.'

'We could never afford decent clothes.'

'We should get something if we sold up here, I suppose.'

At this, they were silent, and I appalled. To sell everything here, even M'zee – who was scarcely saleable, and might have to be destroyed – and Fair Play and White Lady, to sell Mustard and Cress and the old car, to say good-bye to Njombo and Kigorro and the other Kikuyu, to auction the furniture, all this to buy smart dresses for Tilly and smart suits, I supposed, for Robin – all this was intolerable.

'You'd have to wear spats!' I exclaimed, looking at Robin.

'Well, hardly in Sussex. And I think spats have gone out of fashion.'

'Still, something respectable ...'

'That's rather Hilary's point,' Tilly said.

'It would be awful.'

'It would probably be very good for us all.' When Tilly said that, my hopes rose. To do things merely because they were good for you was against her principles. I looked round at the small room crowded with too much furniture into which she had introduced some unsuitable but attractive red velvet curtains, at the sofa covered with dog-hairs, at the silver vases on the writing-table next to a bottle of cattle-drench, at the heavy sea-chest Robin had brought back from Zanzibar which was full of garden tools and dressmaking patterns, at the old sewing-machine in a corner and the Goya over the fire-

323

place and the patch from last year's rain on the ceiling, and felt that I would fight to the death for all these things, as Bluebell and Genet had done for the puppies. The Sussex house would be big and comfortable, the Sussex fields green and deep with buttercups, the Sussex children well-dressed and at ease; this was nothing by comparison, but ours.

But the country seemed in league with Hilary; even the hyraxes had almost ceased to screech at night, perhaps they had moved back to secret sources of water. The floor of the forest now seemed brittle and dry. But we still had some grass, and thin cattle staggered up the track from a farmer on the plains below whose grazing was totally exhausted.

'I hope you're making him pay through the nose,' Robin said.

'He's nothing coming in, poor devil. I don't see how I can.'

'Well, he can pay later.'

'I can't let the wretched cattle starve while we haggle over money.' In fact, Tilly kept the cattle for nothing, when any other farmer with spare grazing would have made the most of a profitable opportunity.

One day she said: 'I see there's an English mail out on Friday. I shall have to write to Hilary.'

'I'll fit in with whatever you say.' This was a remark that always annoyed Tilly; Robin passed the buck to her, while appearing anxious only to ignore his own inclinations. He did this whenever he could not make up his mind. They had the discussion all over again, and this time it seemed to be veering in the wrong direction. When it closed, I feared that Hilary's guile was going to ensnare Tilly. But at last, after a pause, and in the nature of an afterthought, she said: 'When all's said and done, we should simply be hangers-on. Parasites.'

'It was awfully decent of him,' Robin added, and I knew that after all we were safe.

Once the decision had been taken, the atmosphere underwent a change. Robin sang in the bath again and worked out a lot more figures, even better ones, about the Turkish tobacco, and also a scheme to open a hotel at the future railhead. A hopeful letter came from the land office in Dar es Salaam, his veld sores began to heal and the final payment for the coffee farm enabled him to start looking round for a new second-hand car. Tilly laid plans to import a pair of pedigree chinchilla rabbits and to irrigate a fruit and vegetable garden, once the money could be found to buy a pump.

Then the *siafu* appeared. Ashes were scattered round henhouses and stables and we walked carefully to step over the river of ants we encountered on almost every path. Sometimes you could not avoid them, and a stab like a red-hot iron smote you in a tender part. At any minute a conversation might be broken off by one of the participants clutching some part of his body and rushing for the nearest shelter to strip off his clothes and dislodge his attacker, whose tiny but immensely powerful jaws were clamped into his flesh.

The days grew sultry, and heavy clouds came up the valley in the afternoons to disappear with muttered curses over the Mau. Then, one afternoon, an indigo cloud came straight at us and opened itself out overhead. Rain drove down on to the tin roof like a continuous hail of bullets, deafening us, until it slackened and settled to a steady, satisfying downpour. We stood at the window watching it with thankful hearts. When it cleared we went out and the liberated scents of earth and grass and vegetation rose like steam into our nostrils, rich and delightful. It seemed as if the very drips off the trees came down singing, and the earth steamed with moisture. The dogs bounded about with a freshly generated energy, cattle mooed from the *vlei*, birds twittered and chirped in every thorn-tree and pounced on insects drawn from their earthy retreat by the moisture and effervescence of awakened life.

Rain fell every afternoon for a week – a good sign, for rains generally went on as they started, either falteringly or with a good heart. In a week an astonishing change transformed everything. Young growth welled up and over all the grass lay a film of delicate green, a precursor of the rich, vivid stain that soon would drench it so as almost to dazzle the eye. Tight buds formed on acacias and creepers, and the almond orchard came out in flower, a wonderful sheet of creamy pink whose scent had in it all the freshness and sweetness of spring. (This was after the pruning and before the hail.) Each morning burst upon the world like a new hope, a new creation, the sky was limpid and the sun mild, down below the dust devils were stilled and the valley turned from brown to green, and all the fires were put out.

And everything started to go right. Some of the maize at Piggery Nook had miraculously withstood the drought and Tilly reported that, although the crop would be a poor one, a crop there would be, if only enough to cover the expenses of planting it. The river rose and a couple of anglers came to stock it with trout. Cases of fingerlings were carried through the forest to a higher reach, and we went with them and picnicked in a glade I had never seen, dotted with purple *vernonia* blooms and a red creeper that made every bush seem on fire. At a show in Nakaru, Tilly secured nearly all the prizes for her vegetables and roses, and at a polo match she and Robin helped their side to win handsomely. The polo was followed by a gymkhana from which Tilly and I returned with several prizes, including a pair of clippers, a flower vase, a horse-blanket and a bottle of van der Hum. It was as if the gods or spirits, that had been so malicious were now rewarding Tilly and Robin for their decision not to look back when they had set their hands to the plough.

Chapter 32

BY the time they had waited for a mail-boat, letters to England took about six weeks each way, and it was three months before we heard again from Hilary. He was sad, but not surprised, by the rejection of his offer, and mentioned in a postscript that he had transferred to the bank a small present to compensate Tilly, if only very partially, for the loss she would suffer by not enjoying his company. Some time later, she had a notice to say that he had paid in five hundred pounds. She was over-whelmed by this, and wondered whether it ought to be returned.

'I don't see why,' Robin argued. 'You'd offend him bitterly. After all, he is a cousin.'

'Only a distant one.'

'Just as you like, of course. But it would come in handy.'

'Of course it would come in handy. Only would it be proper to accept?'

'I don't see that the proprieties enter into it. After all, he's not proposing to set you up in a flat in Maida Vale.'

'All the same, I think I ought to return it.'

'That's easier said than done,' Robin pointed out. 'I doubt if the bank would let it go. A boa constrictor that's just eaten a goat doesn't sick it up again.'

That settled the matter, and a great deal of discussion took place as to how to spend the money. Njoro offered all too many possibilities. Hilary's hope that Tilly would take a trip home fell by the wayside; she would not go without Robin, and neither wanted a holiday until they had plenty of money. 'No good doing it on the cheap,' Tilly remarked.

A permanent house was needed, but could barely be built for five hundred pounds. In the end it was decided to add two rooms to the existing house and install some revolutionary improvements, notably a system of plumbing. Except in the few major towns, most people preferred to let their houseboys go on filling the bath from *debes* and to use a garden privy than to spend on luxuries money more urgently needed for their farms; any pipes that were laid carried water to cattle, not to people.

Hilary had made only one condition. 'Spend it,' he had written, 'on something for YOURSELF, and of course Robin, not on cows, sheep, goats, dogs or other animals, or on ugly, savage farm machines. If you can bring yourself to devote it to something beautiful and quite useless, I shall be delighted; perhaps this is too much to ask, so if it is useful I shan't object; but do select something that affects your life in the direction of making it a trifle more civilized.'

This directive clearly did not rule out plumbing and a larger bedroom, even though Hilary might have preferred a set of early Sèvres teacups, or a painting by Fragonard.

'One would need somewhere to put them first,' Tilly said. 'Perhaps if I explain to Hilary that this is merely setting the scene, he'll give us his blessing.'

'He must think plumbing civilized,' Robin agreed, 'although I suppose Fragonard and the makers of the Sèvres china did without it. Without hot-water taps, anyway.'

'Still, it will be fun,' Tilly said. 'I wonder what the staff will think.'

I discovered one day, when talking to Kigorro, that they were deeply shocked, at least by the lavatories. To relieve the body indoors seemed to them a most indelicate, immodest habit, the privacy of the bush the only decent place for such activities.

In order to make Hilary's present go as far as possible, Robin undertook to install a plumbing system without the aid of expensive Indian artisans. He worked out levels, falls, circuits and such matters on the backs of old envelopes and seed catalogues, and recruited as operators some of the farm labour force. Robin's talents lay more in the direction of theory than of practice, and pipes were soon appearing in all sorts of odd places, propping up shaky walls made of mud stuffed between two layers of wire-netting.

It was a matter of great regret to me that I did not see the end of it all; the day of my departure came too early, when unconnected pipes were poking out everywhere. A letter from Tilly told me of the triumphal completion of the whole scheme. All the neighbours she could muster came to a ceremonial turning of the first hot-water tap and pulling of the first plug, and most of the farm staff, who had been swept into the enterprise, crowded round to see what would happen; they would not have been surprised had a magical snake come out of the tap, or the blood of the onlookers been sucked into it. What did come out was a live frog. Tilly then pressed the lever on one of the water-closets, there was a satisfactory gurgling and rushing of waters, and the room filled with clouds of steam as boiling water poured into the pan.

'Good heavens, Robin, what have you done!' Tilly exclaimed. Robin answered calmly: 'Summoned the Demon King.' In fact, he had inadvertently connected the cistern to a hot-water pipe.

The time, as I have said, had come for me to leave, and I could feel nothing but sadness. My sea passage had been booked and all the plans made. It seemed impossible to believe that, in little over a month, all that was now so real and living, people like Kigorro and Njombo, and the dogs and M'zee, the cattle and sleek snub-tailed goats, the green parakeets and yellow weavers and brilliant little bee-eaters, the Kikuyu chanting as oxen hauled at stumps, the smoke of fires, the fresh-turned earth, the smell of cedars and the moon riding high over the forest of the Mau – that all these would be nothing but memories flickering disjointedly, insubstantially, on the clouded screen of my mind. When I said good-bye to Njombo he exclaimed: 'Eeee, but you must come back and bring a husband who will help bwana and memsabu with the shamba, there is need of a strong man. What is it like in England? Are the shambas fat? The cattle many?'

'The cattle are big, two or three times bigger than cattle here, and there are many towns with shops, big towns.'

'As big as Nairobi?'

'Bigger than that.'

He shook his head. 'Then they must be big indeed, and many people. Are there black people?'

'No, everyone is white like us.'

'Then who does the work of the house and the shamba?'

'The white people themselves.'

'Eeee, that I do not believe,' Njombo said. 'You are joking. Why don't you take me with you to England, to look after you?'

'Because it is very far and costs many shillings, and when you got there you would be very cold.'

'Then you could buy me a thick blanket, and I should not be cold. But memsabu would not be able to manage if I went away. Don't worry, I will look after her well, and when you come back you will find her strong and fat, as fat as Moyale the white pony you had at Thika.' That, I was afraid, would not please Tilly, but Njombo was thinking of Robin's feelings.

There was a dance in the little club-house at Njoro the night before I left. I forget its occasion, or why we went in fancy dress, which seems an odd thing to have done without a special reason; perhaps it was because people had so few party clothes they tired of them, or that some of the men lacked dinner jackets. The rough floorboards had been chalked, and we had a gramophone that needed constant winding or it ran down in the middle of a record; it played two tunes called *Whispering* and *The Japanese Sandman* over and over again. Few of the men, who outnumbered the women by three or four to one, had much idea of dancing, and some of them got drunk in the bar. But we must have enjoyed it, for dawn was breaking when our car struggled up the hill.

It was too late to go to bed. I changed, and set out to walk for the last time along the forest boundary. I wanted to smell the fresh cedary daybreak air, to hear the plantain-eater and the rain-bird, to watch the chestnut bushbuck shake dew off their coats, to see the dikdik step across the path with the delicate precision of a ballet dancer, to watch the rough-ened bark of olive-trees stained with gold by the glory of the rising sun, so as to carry all these memories away with me as sharply and indelibly as the human mind allowed. All these things and many others I tried to trap with eyes, ears and nose: a pair of plump francolin slipping back from the shambas, the whiff of a sweet-scented creeper, the tinkle of a goat-bell, a freshly-opened ant bear's hole, a striped spider shaking in a film of web. Too many sights and scenes, too many wonders presented themselves, one might as well try to memorize a whole dictionary of words; yet to forget the least detail would be to break faith with places, things and creatures that withheld nothing from me. I should come back, I told myself, and things would be just the same; but in my heart I knew that while they would remain constant, I should change.

From a knoll near the highest beacon I looked across the forest, and it was like scanning an ocean, dappled with light, in a dozen shades of green: the grey-green of lichen, the pale green of bamboos, the bluish olive-green of cedars, the bear-black green of olives, all rippling away into the eye of the sun like waves frozen at a moment of time. And at my back, over an outstretched table-top of cobwebbed thorns which trapped the sunlight in a quivering silver net, long shadows leaned away from the great blue valley where wisps of cloud lay above the pink-fringed lake and the round breast of

330

Menegai, named by the Masai who had once herded their cattle there and hunted lions with their narrow-bladed spears.

The dew that bent the panicles of oat-grass also soaked me, but the strengthening sun had almost dried my clothes by the time I got home to breakfast, the last breakfast at Njoro for a long time to come. I had packed my photographs and conjuring tricks and books of poetry and said good-bye to M'zee, who would vainly look for me next morning, and many mornings after, and perhaps never again nuzzle a lump of sugar from my hand. Kigorro, Njombo and many others came to wish me God-speed and a safe return, and I waved to them and watched them waving back and shouting messages until we turned beyond the twin arched thorn-trees, and house and garden, dogs and people, dropped out of sight.

There was much to be done in Nairobi, and we encountered many friends. One was Alec Wilson, soon to marry his rich widow and hoping to add the Clewes' farm to his own, for Harry, he said, was going to try his luck in Tanganyika and Betty was following the twins to England. To everyone's surprise, and most of all their own, the Nimmos were having a baby, and had started to build a permanent house. I went to say good-bye to Mr Mayer and relinquish my polo correspondency. He said that he would not replace me, but would rely on his district correspondents to report the tournaments. I did not know whether to take this as a compliment, or whether he had been too kindhearted to get rid of me before.

We stayed one night in Nairobi and next afternoon, at four o'clock, I was to take the Mombasa train. That evening, Tilly was subdued. Some news, she said, had come her way that was not at all a good parting present: but I had better know.

'It's about Alan Beattie,' she said, 'and I'm afraid it's very sad.'

I had been thinking a lot of Alan in the last few days, and a snapshot I had taken of him sitting on a rock was in the wallet that held my passport, money and vaccination certificate, together with a note he had written about the cheetah skin. The skin itself was in my luggage, almost the only keepsake I was taking.

'He has died of blackwater,' Tilly said.

Her statement floated in the air without impact or meaning, a little puff of words. It was quite impossible for Alan not to exist in all his strength and reality, even though he was a long way off; it was a mistake, and not to be taken seriously. When at last I managed to speak, it was to say something ridiculous.

'What will happen to Samson?'

'I expect he came back with the safari. That Tana valley is a treacherous place. Poor Alan, it was very sudden, he was dead in three days.'

To my surprise I felt no distress, the news was like a blow that numbs the nerves. You know that they will come to life later, but at the time they give no pain. I seemed to be a second person standing aside to watch myself at a table with a plate of salted nuts, and thinking that I must be some kind of monster not to burst into tears. Had it been true I should have felt quite different, so it had to be a dream. After all the dangers Alan had mastered, he could not tamely have allowed his life to drain away in his bed. He would not even have lived as long as Alexander the Great, who had died at thirty-one. I should have no letters, ever, to look forward to; as for Colonel Beattie, there would be no one to inherit his farm, and Mrs Beattie would be alone with her wolf-hounds to face the coming of her old age.

None of this could possibly be true. Yet at the bottom of my mind a kind of epitaph was rising to the surface from half-remembered phrases flickering there. Courage was mine, and I had mystery; wisdom was mine, and I had mastery: to miss the march of this retreating world into vain citadels that are not walled ... I had never really understood these lines, and did not now, but in some way they seemed fitting.

'It won't do you any harm to have a glass of sherry,' Tilly suggested. 'Do remember not to leave your sponge in the bathroom again, and you'd better give me your wallet to put in the office safe.'

Tilly and Robin met several friends that evening and a spontaneous party developed. As it was to mark my departure, we had champagne; so Alan stayed in the shadows and did not interfere with our enjoyment, or at least not much; and this was as he would have wanted. He had been buried in an unknown spot marked by a few stones that would soon be overgrown with grass and bush; no one would know where he lay and his body would quickly dissolve into the ancient, indifferent soil of Africa. He would exist only as long as the memories of the living kept from oblivion the image of a man who would always be young, strong and amused, never withered up and crochety. At the time I believed my memory's grasp would never weaken, yet even then my reason told me I was wrong.

It was a cheerful evening that ended in song, as such evenings very often did, for the spirit of conviviality, bottled up for months on farms, bubbled forth when friends foregathered and the day's work was done. Tilly called me into her room on the way to bed and gave me a small parcel.

'I've got a little present for you,' she said. 'I thought we really ought to give you something besides a second-hand suitcase and a few undies, and I don't think you'd find an umbrella-stand made from an elephant's foot very useful, or even an ink-well made from rhino horn. Leopard coats I don't like; those hyrax skin karosses are nice, but I couldn't bear to think of so many little hyraxes being killed just to make a rug. So I've got this, which is something you'll at least be able to wear.'

It was a brooch in the form of a small golden lion mounted on a pin, and nothing could have pleased me more.

'The lion is a symbol of courage,' Tilly remarked; she seldom said anything with moral implications, and quickly added: 'You don't have to sit up all night for this one, so I should go to bed. And don't let the champagne give you ideas, it'll be barley-water from now on I expect.'

Robin gave me a locket that had been his grandmother's, with a wisp of hair in it said to have belonged to Bonnie Prince Charlie. 'It's much more likely to have come from one of her pugs,' he said. 'She kept a pack of dreadful, fat pugs everyone hated, and she had one stuffed in a glass case in the hall. Yes, a pug is much more in her line than Prince Charles Edward. I can't think what use the locket will be to you, but you'd better have it.' He also gave me five pounds.

'When will you go to Tanganyika?' I inquired.

'The lease should come through any time, and I hope to be down there before the long rains to get in some tobacco. As a matter of fact, I've been wondering whether it mightn't be an even better proposition to form a little syndicate to build a hotel ...'

It was raining when I left next afternoon, which was a good sign; we needed more rain. It was hard to realize that in a day or two I should not be knowing, and perhaps not caring either, whether it was fine or wet at Njoro, whether the dawn was overcast or clouds were piling up behind the Mau. To part is to die a little, and things that die are gone for good. But I would be coming back; and as the train steamed out and everybody waved and Tilly and Robin, standing side by side, grew small and vanished, I remembered the Swahili proverb: he who has tasted honey will return to the honey-pot.

MORE ABOUT PENGUINS, PELICANS, PEREGRINES AND PUFFINS

For further information about books available from Penguins please write to Dept EP, Penguin Books Ltd, Harmondsworth, Middlesex UB7 0DA.

In the U.S.A.: For a complete list of books available from Penguins in the United States write to Dept DG, Penguin Books, 299 Murray Hill Parkway, East Rutherford, New Jersey 07073.

In Canada: For a complete list of books available from Penguins in Canada write to Penguin Books Canada Ltd, 2801 John Street, Markham, Ontario L3R 1B4.

In Australia: For a complete list of books available from Penguins in Australia write to the Marketing Department, Penguin Books Australia Ltd, P.O. Box 257, Ringwood, Victoria 3134.

In New Zealand: For a complete list of books available from Penguins in New Zealand write to the Marketing Department, Penguin Books (N.Z.) Ltd, Private Bag, Takapuna, Auckland 9.

In India: For a complete list of books available from Penguins in India write to Penguin Overseas Ltd, 706 Eros Apartments, 56 Nehru Place, New Delhi 11019.